Schoolworlds '76

New Directions for Educational Policy

Edited by

Donald N. Bigelow

U.S. Office of Education,
Department of Health, Education, and Welfare

McCutchan Publishing Corporation
2526 Grove Street
Berkeley, California 94704

This work was developed under a grant from the U.S. Office of Education, Department of Health, Education, and Welfare. However, the opinions and other content do not necessarily reflect the position or policy of the Agency, and no official endorsement should be inferred.

To my fellow civil servants
Sam, Tony, Al, and Bruce

And to Gene

Preface

Looking back at the sequence of events surrounding federal legislation in the United States is often, at first, simply to see chaos. A great deal of legislation is, indeed, born of chaos. Crisis erupts— massive unemployment, drug abuse, dwindling oil supplies; experts promote conflicting "solutions" and the public makes concerned noises. At such moments the Congress responds, and eventually through legislation the federal government intervenes to "deal with the crisis at hand."

The initial legislation reflects what is known about the area in question; usually the information is scanty, the facts in dispute. No sooner has an act been signed into law than additional information becomes available, more often than not calling for amendments which, in turn, result in revised legislation modifying the original angle of intervention. Or the legislation is reshaped by competing bureaucratic interpretations which translate it into "programs." In

This book was edited, and its preface written, by Donald N. Bigelow in his private capacity. No official support or endorsement by the U.S. Office of Education is intended or should be inferred.

the process, the original legislation is altered, sometimes broadened, sometimes restricted, often without apparent logic or consistency— only with a kind of inevitability. No wonder, then, that trying to understand why legislation took the course it did is a difficult enterprise. Patterns are elusive; usually, however, they exist.

This preface describes a pattern that emerges as one reviews the educational legislation written between 1958 and 1968, legislation shaped in large part by a series of crises related to the "discovery" of poverty. Three major acts of Congress dominate the decade: the Civil Rights Act of 1964, the Economic Opportunity Act of 1964, and the Elementary and Secondary Education Act of 1965. But my interest here lies primarily in those laws that authorized the particular programs with which I have been intimately involved as program manager during the last fifteen years. The sequence of legislation begins with the National Defense Education Act (NDEA) of 1958, includes the 1964 amendment to NDEA known as Title XI, the Higher Education Act of 1965 (HEA), and ends with the Education Professions Development Act (EPDA) of 1967. Under EPDA, of the dozen or so programs that were established, I will focus on three, each one of which grew out of the experiences of the other. They are the TTT Program (Training of Teacher Trainers), the first program to be funded under EPDA, in 1968; Project Open, in 1972, based on the lessons learned from TTT; and the Southampton Summer Sequences held in 1974, the principal subject of this book.

Originally, the legislation to which I have referred (NDEA, HEA, and EPDA) had in common an attempt to introduce the academic disciplines into the training of teachers. (The irony that each effort resulted in taking a step farther away from the original intent is also part of the story.) But the most interesting elements of a pattern now discernible were: (1) a constantly broadening vision of interconnectedness, heightened awareness of previously unrecognized relationships among institutions and groups; (2) increased participation in the educational enterprise by social groups and "outsiders" heretofore written off as irrelevant; and (3) a realignment of levels of authority. During this period the movement of educational legislation was outward, the scope widening: more money, more programs, more people—guaranteeing, so the thinking went, a more truly participatory mix in the schools and thereby a more truly democratic society.

The pattern is most visible (and easiest to view optimistically) at about the mid-1960s, by which time the war on poverty and the fight for civil liberties were being fought on many fronts and the notion of participation was becoming widespread. By the time of the Southampton Summer Sequences, however, a sense of the limitations of "participatory democracy" was broadly shared. In the course of the 1960s many of us who were part of the programs initiated by the legislation in question learned not only the folly of the view that "separate" parts of the system could be dealt with separately—but also the folly of some assumptions held by the participants, those who asserted that "opening up the system of schooling" could change the larger society as well.

But the emergent pattern deserves more careful examination. Its effective beginnings date from 1958, when President Eisenhower signed into law the momentous and, by historians, relatively neglected, National Defense Education Act, designed "to strengthen the national defense and to encourage and assist in the expansion and improvement of educational programs to meet critical national needs." Partly a reaction to the uproar created by Sputnik, NDEA was also an effort by Congress to fight what it understood as "progressive education," a movement, as it was argued, responsible for the failure of "about one-half of the bright students of our nation" to go to college. The drop-out had been officially discovered. In addition to providing funds to help keep students in school, the Congress proposed "to beef up the opportunities for young men and women to study the hard subjects" by updating classroom teachers in summer institutes. At the same time, Congress proposed to take care of the shortage of teachers—another "discovery." The notion looked simple. A four-year, billion dollar program was proposed—it actually received about $115 million for the first year—to improve the teaching of science, mathematics, and modern foreign languages at all levels. Neither those who wrote the legislation nor its administrators knew that they were about to bring to the educational enterprise a new recognition of interconnectedness, but that was the consequence of their labor.

Initially, the nature of the bureaucracy in the Office of Education itself (originally NDEA was administered in a single "financial aid" branch) discouraged the notion that existing, separate parts of related educational activity must be dealt with each on its own terms.

The bureaucratic structure deriving from NDEA suggested that graduate schools, counseling programs, and student loans were all connected, if only by money. Some NDEA program managers seemed oblivious to the common self-containments and self-sufficiencies; they assumed that normally, if not ultimately, research, high school teaching, and state agencies all converge in focus, and that, sooner rather than later, this would be clear to everybody. Coordinating vast amounts of money and large numbers of people and institutions, a few NDEA administrators inevitably began to break down some barriers, challenging traditional power structures. Simply by entering the educational marketplace with their summer institutes, for instance, they were bringing together local with state educational agencies in new ways, this state with that state, even, to some degree, this discipline with that discipline.

People at nonfederal governmental levels heard the message—felt federal pressure and a threat of "federal control" (however subtle) and scrambled to arrange defenses, often decrying "soft" money as an unwanted "extra," harmful to an institution's financial future. But the modes of defense, the structures of resistance, further intensified the consciousness of interrelationships. New lines of communication *were* opened between the graduate schools and the federal government, in addition to the new lines established between graduate and undergraduate education. Everywhere patterns—even patterns of advancement—underwent change. (A "graduate" of an NDEA-sponsored summer institute for school teachers becomes a supervisor in a state educational agency; an economist learns to read Japanese; foreign language teachers begin to speak the languages they teach.) For a few, education did become a richer experience.

The development within NDEA having the greatest implication for later programs (especially, as it turned out, for TTT) was the establishment of new ties between academics in colleges and universities and those whom they had formerly disregarded or disdained. Groups unfamiliar with each other came together by virtue of a federal effort which—in its institute programs—aimed at something far more ambitious than "summer school as usual." A strange new "higher" authority entered the equation—not the professor, but the federal manager, probing, prowling, asking for "input," determining evaluation of "products." College professors had glimmerings of awareness of their responsibility to Somebody Else Out There, while at the same time the "lowly" school teachers shed some of their old and respectful docility. Brought into contact with secondary school French teachers, the university professor of Romance languages was forced to recognize that he simply had no idea of the problems of teaching French to children, or the needs of the teachers whom he, under federal contract, was supposed to be "helping." Authority therefore shifted a bit: the school teacher stepped forth as a figure of moment. The school teacher's need dominated and the professor was obliged to respond.

Title XI (the 1964 amendment to NDEA) increased funds and broadened the base of the original institute program by adding many new subject areas, including English, history, and geography. The effect was to make more explicit, even to help institutionalize, some of the developing interconnectedness that was occurring, almost, it seemed, by happenstance. The following year, with a major reorganization of the Office of Education, most of the training programs—in the disciplines, in special education, and in counseling and guidance—were brought together under the Division of Educational Personnel Training, which had the largest divisional staff in the Office of Education (and which I headed). This division was responsible for the administration of nine separate laws and had an annual appropriation of about $73 million. With this new alignment of staff and money it became possible (as it had not been before) to link programs previously seen as distinct. In fact, structurally, the division was able to combine programs from several different pieces of legislation in a manner expressing a new awareness of the wholeness of problems.*

---

*In testimony before then Congressman Hugh Carey's Ad Hoc Subcommittee on the Handicapped (June 8, 1966), I gave a full account of our growing awareness of "the wholeness of problems," and described in some detail how the division proposed to deal with them. Speaking of efforts "to blend the function of the specialist in education with that of the specialist in a particular discipline" (our initial operating assumption), I pointed out that "our goal is to place the education of the handicapped squarely into the mainstream of American education" rather than permitting it to continue to be considered "special"—with the result that too many students were, in effect, put on an "Indian reservation," instead of growing up with their peers. Professionals and others in and out of the Office of Education, however, disagreed and within a matter of weeks the handicapped program was removed from my jurisdiction and given bureau status. This same testimony also contains a rather full explanation of the Experienced Teacher Fellowship Program, describing how we tried to "integrate" some of the discrete parts, so that "education" could be "handled in a more unified fashion. . . ." See *Education and Training of the Handicapped, Part I* (Washington, D.C.: U.S. Government Printing Office, 1966), pp. 106-41.

A far more important forward step was the identification of a wholly new category called *the disadvantaged*. Suddenly, or so it seemed, a new amendment to the National Defense Education Act had provided funds not only to help teachers learn more about their subject matter but to change them in accordance with their students' needs. Indeed, Title XI contained a "sleeper" aimed directly at improving the qualifications of those individuals "who are engaged in or preparing to engage in the teaching of disadvantaged youth." Authority shifted once again. The Congress, under the impetus of having begun to write the Economic Opportunity Act, was shifting its focus from improving schools to improving society—an interest not visible in earlier legislation. The new law went on to say that only those individuals would be supported who

are, by virtue of their service or future service in elementary or secondary schools, enrolling substantial numbers of culturally, economically, socially, and educationally handicapped youth, in need of specialized training; except that no institute may be established under this title for teaching of disadvantaged youth unless such institute will offer a specialized program of instruction designed to assist such teachers in coping with the unique and peculiar problems involved in the teaching of such youth. . . .

In a word, students heretofore written off as drop-outs, emotionally disturbed, or "dumb," became overnight a new group of people invited into the mix, promised more space, more money, more programs, and more (if not "better") teachers. In no time there were not only institutes for history teachers but also for history teachers of the disadvantaged. (And the public was led closer to a conviction that education might be capable of "saving the country.") Section 1101(2) of Title XI made it plain that schooling was a function of and inseparable from society and its ills. Future legislation was henceforth constrained to do double duty by improving both schooling *and* society.

The expansion of programs meant, among other things, that even more educational personnel were exposed to this new world in which professionals, once isolated from each other, had begun to talk to one another. Over a five-year period (1965-1970), for instance, up to 20,000 school teachers joined some 2,000 college professors and other educational specialists each summer in several hundred institutes around the country. In addition, some institutes ran on an academic-year basis. Equally important, perhaps, was the effect achieved by bringing together annually in Washington the directors of all ongoing institutes. Here they talked across institutional lines, across those separating disciplines, specialties, and agencies. Literally, the directors represented a spectrum of American education. They came from graduate schools, liberal arts colleges, schools of education, community colleges, state educational agencies, and elementary and secondary schools. Nothing like it had occurred before. A national dialogue about American education had commenced. In such an atmosphere, the previously respected isolation of the disciplines themselves began to be perceived by some people as a convention of doubtful value.*

Soon thereafter the commitment to notions of a broad "federal role" in education and society reached a high point. The Higher Education Act of 1965 took as its center the belief that the time had come for the university "to face the problems of the city as it once faced problems of the farm," and that disadvantaged children were different and schooling must adapt to this circumstance. The Teacher Corps, established under this act, was a tangible and active assault on poverty—which was recognized, but not directly addressed, by Title XI. Similarly, the legislation's responsiveness to student needs was demonstrated by the manner in which the Experienced Teacher Fellowship Program was administered. Under Title V, hard-pressed teachers were given opportunities to learn more about disadvantaged children by working in inner city classrooms *together* with college professors (who left the temple of education for the city slums). The results were that a nation-wide learning experience occurred for both sets of teachers. At the same time, by bringing teachers to college campuses *en bloc* (in groups of fifteen or twenty) the Experienced Teacher Fellowship Program also helped to change some academic departments. Thus, on both counts, there was a further breakdown of enclaved professionalism.

The conviction was growing that education could do more. In asking the Congress for the 1965 legislation, President Johnson had

---

*See B. Othanel Smith, "The Liberal Arts and Teacher Education," in *The Liberal Arts and Teacher Education: A Confrontation*, edited by Donald N. Bigelow (Lincoln, Neb.: University of Nebraska Press, 1971), pp. 110-19.

spoken of "the potential of higher education to help deal with the perplexities of modern society." The universities, he said, must "have the skills and knowledge to match these mountainous problems." As the dream of match-ups between academic knowledge and complex social problems began to make some sense, diverse professional groups drew still closer. The professor-as-consultant became a regular feature (in and outside Washington) during the 1960s, particularly in some areas of social action, and, unwittingly, often became the "de-tribalized specialist" as he jumped old professional barriers in helping to solve new national problems. In the area of teacher training, for instance, where the educational research type reigned supreme, it was no mean trick to establish an Experienced Teacher Fellow-ship Program which advocated *training* as a better vehicle of change than educational research. This program tried to bridge the gap between the teacher trainer and the public school teacher on the firing line by bringing them closer together in the school itself (rather than meeting only on campus), and by working with the children in the schoolroom (rather than with rats in the laboratory).

Another thrust of this same legislation for higher education (that part which created the Teacher Corps) was for more cooperation among the major, still largely isolated parts of the educational system:

Recognizing that neither State or local educational agencies nor institutions of higher education acting independently can effectively prepare teachers for the disadvantaged, it is the intent of this bill to promote close cooperation between these institutions in carrying out the training aspects of the Teacher Corps.

Meanwhile, as the pressure mounted for education somehow to do "more," there was an emerging concern for community involvement (in large part fueled by community action programs and the "civil rights revolution") and for more direct participation by those who had always been excluded from the decision-making process. And here still another realignment of authority began to develop.

All of this helped to shape the administration of the Education Professions Development Act of 1967. Now, for the first time, a law authorized awarding funds directly to the schools—no longer making it necessary to support only institutions of higher education in connection with teacher training. Funds were no longer available just for the benefit of conventional teachers but also for "other educational personnel." These last words could be read as code words for every kind of paraprofessional—the street-wise, the self-taught scholar minus degrees. The aim, of course, was "to get something going" in the schools by reaching out to the community and, simultaneously, altering community feeling toward the school by remaking it as an agency for social change. By now *the school* was becoming the focus of attention and it, in turn, had begun to discover still other worlds— those of the "minorities" and of the "community."

Even before the passage of the Education Professions Development Act (EPDA)—especially since Title I of the Elementary and Secondary Education Act of 1965—the granting of more authority to the schools was a matter of consistent concern. When it established the National Advisory Council on Education Professions Development (a presidential committee to review the operation of all federal training programs), the Congress deplored the customary appointment procedures that prevailed, noting that they ensured too few advisory committee members who were state or local school board members or who were "actively engaged in teaching at the elementary level." And, by granting funds directly to local educational agencies under EPDA, the Congress underscored this point. Training programs more suited to the needs of local authority could now be designed. The bureaucrats were better able to place more emphasis on recruiting and training poor people, members of minority groups, and other individuals not previously part of the school establishment. As a consequence (following the lead of TTT and the Teacher Corps), the Career Opportunities Program eventually emerged as the primary effort to meet this demand of the new populism.*

Thus, even before 1967-68, both the range of participation in the schools and the scale of public expectations of schools rose to new heights, maintained by three successive programs funded under EPDA. First came TTT, in which the basic strategy in training the

---

*See Don Davies, "Reflections on EPDA," *Theory Into Practice* XIII, no. 3, pp. 210-17.

trainers of teachers was to encourage the several "parts" of the educational enterprise to rearrange themselves "out there," rather than to be arranged by fiat from the Office of Education. Its goal was to get at the "high church," to diminish, if possible, the power of the graduate schools over American education (the effort was unsuccessful). But the effort was responsive to the need for direct cooperation between liberal arts faculties, schools of education, existing public schools and the "served communities" in training the new teacher. Avoiding particular innovations, it was a grand attempt at reform by permitting alternative independent arrangements. Building on the then widespread assumption that the more "mix," the better, TTT initiated community participation on a "parity" basis. This meant that what teachers learned should no longer be left solely to graduate professors but, rather, should be determined by the professors' joint participation with the school teachers themselves, and with the "consumers," the parents of the children who were supposedly being educated.

At the very least, the principle of parity required that universities, schools, and communities should be equally involved in decision making, even in deciding what should be taught to school children. As one critic has written, the ensuing controversy over "parity" represented at best "a classic confrontation of radical and liberal ideology concerning the allocation of responsibility and power." At worst, the question of authority of lay citizens, particularly of the poor, "degenerated into skillful and artful evasions of the requirement [of parity] or into rather crude political maneuverings."*

With parity as a principle and a strategy of decentralized involvement that respected local conditions, several different kinds of TTT projects were developed throughout the country. Some stressed the college professors' involvement in the schools themselves; others imported lessons in ethnic pride into the conventional curriculum; and a few altered the way the disciplines were taught at the graduate

---

*David E. Purpel in the foreword to Malcolm M. Provus, *The Grand Experiment: The Life and Death of the TTT Program* (Berkeley, Calif.: McCutchan Publishing Corporation, 1975), pp. vi-vii.

level.* To a remarkable degree TTT administrators adopted a hands-off posture so far as central "control" of the individual projects was concerned—but by one means or another they always encouraged community involvement and worked for the reform of graduate education. In one sense, parity was a formal attempt to introduce "interrelatedness" into the educational system, the full results of which have yet to be determined.

During these years, 1958-68, the "message" behind the legislation was, first, outrage at the deficiencies of American schools; next, a discovery that to remedy the deficiencies would require schools of education and colleges and universities to join forces to produce better teachers; finally, guilt at the realization that efforts at "school reform" were so utterly remote from the needs and interests of the disadvantaged and—in different ways—from the realities of the middle American community as well. Each of these "discoveries" led to a re-examination of the schools in terms of "the larger society," and each challenged the power of professionalism. With Project Open, an extension of the TTT program, the endorsement of participation as a central democratic value was complete.

In a sense Project Open had no "programs," no "guidelines." There was simply a conviction that meaningful change in education was to be achieved "only through the interaction of specific people in specific circumstances, and through a developmental process unique to a particular place." Since it was clear that massive social problems were "insoluble in the schoolyard," Project Open expanded its focus and optimistically declared its goal to be that of promoting "awareness by each part of every other part, by each interest of every other impinging interest, toward the end of contributing to the creation of a new national climate of opinion." The ostensible subject was education; the real subject was the transformation of old concepts into new questions in order to help solve contemporary social problems.

---

*For a more detailed account of TTT, see Kirkpatrick Sale's essay in Appendix D of this volume.

Project Open operated through "networks," bringing together a wide range of citizens—school superintendents, administrators and teachers, city mayors and managers, college and university presidents, deans of education, and community leaders—to examine facts, attitudes, and problems. Getting and giving instant information were fundamental to a network's operation. A key word predictably was "interaction"; a key preoccupation was with "process." Inevitably that preoccupation led to the notion that a more basic understanding could yet be reached, both as to the need for a greater awareness of interconnectedness and the need to learn how to use that awareness as a resource for problem solving.*

It was at Southampton that the interest and possibility just mentioned received some sort of a test. And it was here that the program sketched above, ever-widening circles of involvement with educational reform, completed the pattern I've been describing. The Southampton Summer Sequences were an experiment in communication. They provided an opportunity to see how to deal with the interconnectedness that had been developed over the last decade or two, and to learn how it could best, most fairly and efficiently, be understood and used. These weeks of talk were, in fact, a more ambitiously conceived, and more concentrated, version of Project Open. And they helped to measure the distance from the early days of NDEA, when many still imagined that the task of "improving the schools" was one that need involve no one but school personnel.

Participants at Southampton included not only professional educators, but public officials, artists, authors, media people, lawyers, a few businessmen, and token representatives from industry. The brochure for the four meetings (see Appendix A of this volume) disavowed any intent to reform society by reforming the schools; the list of those invited hinted at least to some an intent to bypass the schools and, instead, start with society. The participants came together to explore the forces for unity and divisiveness, the currents

---

*A case study of one network, supported under EPDA, is in John Merrow, Richard Foster, and Nolan Estes, *The Urban School Superintendent of the Future* (Durant, Okla.: Southeastern Oklahoma State University, 1974); see chapter VI, especially pp. 59-61 which describe the role played by Malcolm Shaw, who was the first director of Project Open in 1971-72. See also p. 90 for some specific attributes of "networking."

of power between school and society, the effectiveness of past and present governmental initiatives in educational reform, and some directions for the future. They were also concerned with exploring the validity of the "participatory" premise itself: if enough intelligent, caring, creative people could come together to discuss issues such as these, would not something of value necessarily be accomplished?

This book stands as one answer to that question. It opens with The Charge addressed to the Southampton participants by three Congressional leaders in the area of educational legislation (all of whom were intimately involved in most of the legislation to which I have referred). Next comes a selection from the formal papers delivered during the Sequences by educational experts and others, and excerpts from the transcripts of the plenary sessions; then an essay in personal reportage describing the tone and ultimate meaning of the enterprise; at the end some proposals for the legislative future.

To speak of an "ultimate meaning" is to imply that what I began by describing as apparent chaos is in truth more than that —a direction, a pattern, providing some valuable lessons for the next administration. As an Office of Education program manager I could not reasonably be expected to perceive this page of history as meaningless. Neither, I suppose, is it surprising that while I am aware of the closing of a circle—the end of a particular aspect of federal intervention and ambition—I am more inclined to look for growing points, reasonable places for new beginnings, new ways to profit from the immediate past, than to lament old errors or persecute old error-makers. Still, I would argue that a pattern is discernible and that new initiatives drawing on recent lessons are both feasible and sensible. My hope for this book is that it contributes to the clarification of those initiatives.

Donald N. Bigelow

Walter Mill, New York
September 9, 1975

Contents

PART I

The Charge and the Keynote

1

Introduction

Marian Simpson

The Invitation

For most of the participants, the Southampton Summer Program began with a letter of invitation accompanied by a handsome gray and white brochure embossed with the keynote word, *paideia*. (The full text of the brochure is reprinted in Appendix A.) The Greek ideal of an entire society engaged in nurturing and transmitting its values through education suggested both the objectives and procedures of an ambitious meeting of minds and people. The brochure spoke of the desire of the administrators of a federal educational program "to engage a broad range of citizens—from inside and outside the formal education establishments of this country—in shaping recommendations for the development of educational policies for all societal agencies engaged in the teaching and learning process." This broad range was not merely to include those normally recognized as spokesmen on educational issues, but also representatives from all the institutions and groups that compose the social fabric, people who are or who ought to be concerned with the determination of what our education is and why it is that way. The participants were to include "public officials, community and media people, business, industry, labor union executives, plus teachers and administrators for secondary and higher education, foundation representatives and artists." They were to attend one of four three-day sessions on particular problem areas in American schools and society, and emerge with consensus proposals for appropriate action. The sessions were to take place at a small liberal arts college on the tip of Long Island, New York.

Here, then, were the makings of a true *omnium gatherum*. If we'd learned anything from a decade of social protest and revitalized interest in the commonweal, it was that decision making, the use of power, should be shared with those most affected by its exercise and results. The shape of our education for the future would affect everyone, and all sectors of American society should be represented at the creation.

The need for broad-based participation was further motivated by a view of the place of the educational institution amidst the forces of American society. Working on the schools alone, and those directly responsible for them, would not produce the needed reforms. As the "key assumption" of the brochure put it, "we believe that neither educators nor the schools they staff can reform society; we also believe that 'reforming the schools'—by whatever means—will not greatly improve the education of our people. The reason is that the schools are not the major educative influence in this society; they are only a reflection of the larger forces controlling all our institutions." Here was a lesson learned from recent history: that the social fabric is so woven that piecemeal reform is impossible. In particular, the schools—the instrument of our ideologies and systems as well as our needs—are bound to be shaped in the image of the society's stated or unstated pieties and goals and anxieties. You cannot reform the whole by the part, the substructure by the superstructure, and maybe you cannot even reform the part itself without reforming the whole. This view demonstrated a sophisticated awareness of the need to bring all possible vectors to bear in "reforming education"—and a note of possibly unintentional but nonetheless tempering pessimism.

But if there was a tinge of pessimism in the key assumption, the objectives of the Summer Program were optimistic and ambitious. They included clarification of the forces for unity and for divisiveness operating in American society; study of the role of the classroom in respect to roles in the "real world"; a blueprint for education in the good society; and use of public policy to bring us closer to realization of consensual goals. An idealistic banner was raised: "Public schools have a mandate of a sort to see that young people are humanistically oriented and prepared to function as effective citizens in a democratic society .... What kinds of intra- and inter-institutional arrangements, if any, could help to define (or even to develop) behavior appropriate to democratic society?" Whatever caveats might be issued concerning reform of and through the schools, the role of the schools was not going to be abandoned. On the contrary: the schools were as much as ever in our history seen as a key agency in the creation of a citizenry able to do justice to democratic ideals.

The statements announcing Southampton thus set the stage for confrontation of—and confrontation on—some important issues in grappling with a contemporary American meaning for *paideia*: (1) the question of how the schools participate in the larger society, and the society participates in the shaping of the schools; (2) the question of who does, and who should, participate in determining the content and form of schooling; and (3) the question of whether the schools have been too closed off from influences from society outside their walls—especially its denied and disadvantaged sectors—or whether, on the contrary, the schools have been caught between the cross-claims of social reformers and reactionaries, and possibly overextended by their use as a laboratory for working out all our social ills. In fact, a central issue at Southampton came to be: where do the strengths and failures of the schools lie? What should be considered their ideal and their real potential? What social agencies and institutions other than the schools should be playing a role in education? *Paideia* to the Greeks implied a society whose every segment was working toward the inculcation of the society's highest values, those values necessary to its harmonious existence and survival. When there is no working consensus on those values—the case in America, 1976—how is a participatory agreement possible about what the formal educational institution should be doing? What is to be done, how is it to be done, and who is to be empowered to say what needs to be done—and to do it?

The story of Southampton is thus in some large part a story about participation and power. Not so much "power politics"— though that had to come up—as the empowerment of people: how they could gain control over their own lives, how they could use

their institutions to overcome frustration, rage, and impotence. This
gain implied the empowerment of institutions themselves—particularly
the schools—so that they might be able to perform the tasks set to
them. Participation and empowerment led back to a classical question
seen in a new context: the problem of leadership. In a society that is
(no doubt with good reason) suspicious of its leaders and its old
elites, where is new, viable, and powerful leadership to come from?
Southampton was, then, about leadership and power. People met,
reasoned together, argued together, negotiated, got mad, and tried
to define goals and implements.

The Charge

The discussions were shaped in part by the initial statement of
goals and proposed activity (see Appendix A) and in part by the
perspective offered by the ranking members of Congressional education committees who attended one or another session: Senator
Claiborne Pell, Representatives John Brademas and Albert Quie.
Their words—both in the formal presentations and in the dialogues
and question periods—composed a charge to the participants, a
demand that particular jobs be done.

First, the legislators charged, *help us achieve a more rational
kind of planning.* They pointed to instance after instance of piecemeal, haphazard legislation for educational reform—the creation of
partial, ad hoc programs too often conceived and funded in response
to immediate social demands, without an informed view of the whole.
As Congressman Brademas put it, "we operate and legislate so much
by hip pocket in this country—I think that we don't do too badly . . .
using osmosis and experience and judgment and feel. On the other
hand, that is not good enough, just not good. . . ." Or Senator Pell:
"We seem to abhor any instance of planning . . . and avoid it, and
nowhere is this more apparent than in education, where federal
programs have grown and developed in fits and starts with no long-
term overall planning."

Pointing to the depressing implications of such a lack of direction,
the speakers called for a new purposefulness and coherence in policy
making for the future. "We can no longer manufacture social programs without relating them to each other and the whole spectrum
of current governmental activity," said Senator Pell, and Congressman

Brademas spoke of the urgency of "a more formidable but, in my view, more constructive task, that of developing . . . an analytical framework—an intellectual construct—within which, hopefully, all those who make decisions . . . can more soundly, more rationally, if you will, decide."

The legislators at times took an aggrieved tone ("we are legislating in the dark"), and they laid a large part of their grievance at the doors of the country's educational establishment. The substance of their second charge, then, was this: *help us get academe to help; we need to hear from those presumably most knowledgeable and most actively concerned about educational reform.* More than once frustration with the academic community's failure to produce informed analyses and clear priorities for action seemed to border on contempt. Here is Congressman Quie, for instance:

> We were asking questions about the direction we ought to go in higher education and could not find those answers from people in higher education. . . . If you want an economic study to support the AFL-CIO position, they will get it for you and they have hired a good researcher from a college or university to do it for them. You can ask the same thing on an economic study from the Chamber of Commerce. Either they have it available, or they can get it before very long.
>
> We asked the same questions of institutions of higher education or the American Council on Education, and we weren't able to secure any of that. They felt their role was to compromise the differences between the individuals and their members, and then to hand us the compromise. We were supposed to pick it up and run with it . . . .

There was general agreement, in short, that almost the last person to be concerned with national planning for education is the university professor, and that apathy, disinterest, and ineffectuality are the norm. Congressman Brademas described one experience of this lack of concern:

> You will all recall the several reports of recent years contending that many of our colleges and universities were in deep financial distress. But when our committee attempted to find an intellectually respectable definition of "financial distress," or even "financial need," our inquiries fell on stony ground.
>
> And as a consequence of this lack of systematic thought by the higher education community about higher education, four of us in Congress had to develop our own resources of information and analysis and, with some help from the Brookings Institution and the reports of the Carnegie Commission, wrote

the bill ourselves. On potentially the most important legislation to help colleges and universities since the Land Grant Act, the colleges and universities contributed almost nothing.

But along with this indictment the legislators expressed a genuine awareness of the complexity of the problem and a readiness to listen to positive proposals. They realized that the right mix is hard to get: as Congressman Brademas said, planning in the hands of professional educators alone can kill off innovation; in the hands of nonprofessionals alone it has little impact on the educational system. And all agreed that universities needed to participate more in creation of educational policy. Senator Pell probably described the task in broadest terms:

> Whoever is running the Executive Branch must be aware of the interrelationships between disciplines, between goals and certainly to recognize that the means to do so are at hand. This is where the academic world must become involved in the legislative and administrative processes. We must be able to take the style of the planner—both substantive and procedural—and bring it to the everyday world in English that is comprehensible.

But the responsibility for educational change lies not with politicians or educators alone, and the third charge was: *help us get information about schools or at least help us dramatize the need for good information.* That the body of received knowledge in this area is small and the means of analysis and evaluation uncertain or controversial cannot be denied, but the legislators called for help in pointing to the right questions, even if answers do not lie ready to hand. Those at Southampton were challenged to make participation a reality by helping the educational community and those in political power find out what they need to know about how to improve teaching and learning. If they are to establish goals and make decisions for the future, they must be able to proceed on the basis of clearer information than is now available.

Congressman Quie, for instance, referred to the lack of adequate, accessible data in such areas as education of disadvantaged children—the failure to examine critically such assumptions as "poverty means disadvantaged and disadvantaged means poverty." Such an assumption leaves too many unanswered questions, he pointed out, and there are just "not the kinds of studies available to the Congress that the Congress needs." In other words, until we have more accurate knowledge about what keeps certain children from learning, such a category as "disadvantaged" is not much help, at least not to those responsible for writing legislation.

Congressman Brademas (whose paper is reprinted in Appendix B) pointed to several similar instances of inadequate information or communication:

> You and I know that highly respected child development experts disagree deeply on the proper scope and purpose of early childhood intervention. And yet we also know that millions of American children do not eat well or receive adequate health care, let alone have effective intellectual stimulation. I hope that when Senator Mondale and I begin hearings on our bill next month, we shall learn of new knowledge about early childhood development, knowledge beyond what we heard in testimony a few years ago on the bill the President vetoed. For we want to legislate on more than our best intentions; we want the best evidence we can get for what is right for the lives of children.

And often it is not so much a failure of knowledge as a failure of concern. If no one—from the White House on down—cares enough to create a visible issue, then no one will bother to do the kind of studies requisite to solving a problem. Concern can expose a bad situation, dramatize it to the country, and perhaps ensure that it will never again be entirely disregarded. Congressman Brademas spoke of one memorable instance of effectively dramatized concern, the poverty program of the 1960s.

> In the real world, I think you have to hope that—well, there will not be perfection, but there will be the involvement of people. How you involve people in an honest, genuine way so that it is not simply a facade and not simply window dressing—all of us who had anything to do with the operation of the poverty program a couple of years ago know that it is enormously difficult. . . . Despite all of the criticism that one can level at the way in which that participation may have been carried out, I do think that the Poverty Act opened up a number of doors in this country which will never be shut again. The Mayor of my home town in South Bend, Indiana must now give some attention to poor people and black people and the Mexican-American community—in large part because we have raised the consciousness of the country to another level.

The speakers' consensus was that such accomplishments take place only when large numbers of people from diverse backgrounds and professions—Southampton many times over—care enough and know enough to keep citizens and legislators in touch with one another and with the way things are "out there."

This need for linkages between professionals and the rest of the community was implicit in the legislators' fourth charge: *help us define the proper tasks of schools—and the impossible ones.* That is to say, are schools taking on too much, trying to perform functions best left to other agencies in the community? And if they overextend themselves into these areas, are they failing to meet their primary responsibilities? Senator Pell, in particular, claimed that "the load to be placed on schools today is almost an intolerable one." As he saw it, we have forced our schools "to become the blunt edge of social reform." The result, said the Senator, is that "the schools are being forced to take on the responsibility of many of the nation's ills, and we have sometimes lost sight of the true objective of schools, which is an improvement in the quality of education." Congressmen Brademas and Quie, as might be expected from their consistent commitment to educational reform, were much in agreement, and like Senator Pell resented being distracted from their primary task. Such distraction—referred to more than once—is evident when Congress devotes most of its debate on education bills to questions of desegregation and busing; the problems that the larger society is unable or unwilling to work out devolve upon the schools, and the legitimate questions of education get lost.

Congressman Quie saw the school's burden as nothing less than the transmission of values from one generation to the next. With the traditional extended family diminishing in importance and influence, he saw no alternative but to turn to the school for lessons in morality and ethnic pride, and suggested that only by increased involvement with the community (decentralization is implied here) can the school accomplish this task. (The point is a perplexing one, and Congressman Brademas, basically in sympathy with strong local involvement in schools, saw some difficulties: what happens to minority rights when left primarily in the hands of local school officials?)

The legislators, then, were challenging those at Southampton to help rethink the function of the schools, and to make their knowledge felt. This in turn means rethinking the role of other community agencies that might take on some of the roles now illegitimately assigned to the schools, or might be given a more important supporting role, and here no speaker had easy solutions to propose.

The point of all this concern about sorting out tasks could be summed up in the fifth charge: *help us figure out what to do about "quality," not only in our schools but throughout society.* Each speaker in his own way made clear his commitment to excellence. For Congressman Brademas, quality was inextricably bound up with the urgent need to know, with distress "that there is so little first-class intellectual effort directed in this country to research and analysis of those institutions of our society that incarnate and advance intellectual effort." (And a man so concerned with the "first class" was, inevitably, self-critical, as well as critical of the community; he acknowledged often how far short of an ideal he and his colleagues fell.) Similarly, Congressman Quie's attention to the quality of life, both in school and outside it, was reflected in his interest in the construct of values which the child, from one source or another, receives.

But it was Senator Pell who was most explicit on this point, who referred again and again to "the serious problem of quality in our public schools." (The Senator proposed a "Quality in Education" Bill in 1965.) He admitted the dangers of elitism, but made it clear that he had in mind excellence in a vocation, good preparation for a place in society, as well as traditional academic distinction. Although acknowledging, even insisting, that schools cannot reform society, he saw the excellence of both as intertwined: if this country's enormous resources were directed toward the achievement of "quality," Senator Pell was sure that the result would be the "improvement of the education of our nation's citizenry, and ancillary to that an improvement of the social and economic conditions of the nation."

Requisite for quality in schools and in society, then, are intelligence, informed analysis, and participation. Congressman Brademas probably summed up these elements of the Congressional charge best in the last words of his paper:

We must, I believe, conclude that we need in the work of rethinking education for the coming decades men and women of both sorts, in both the worlds of thought and action. We have, indeed, men and women of both sorts from both worlds here at Southampton this weekend; persons who are not, in David Riesman's phrase "threatened by complexity" but challenged and stimulated by it: persons interested in rethinking policy as well as explaining it, interested not only in making present policies work but in asking whether they are right. . . . I like to think there is justification for what I have tried to say in the words of Woodrow Wilson in his address to the American Political Science Association in 1910: ". . . the man who has the time, the discrimination and the sagacity, to collect and comprehend the principal facts and the man who must act upon them must draw near to one another and feel that they are engaged in a common enterprise. . . ."

If such a charge as this were to be acted upon seriously and responsibly—both by those who heard it and those who composed it—American education would stand to gain considerably.

The Major Papers

Even before the legislators spoke and the process of exchange began, some positions for debate and negotiation had been mapped out in a number of papers commissioned for the conference. These were read by all the participants. They sometimes served as explicit focus for discussion. Sometimes their role was simply implicit; they became part of the mental baggage each person brought into the conference room. They by no means covered the entire field of education, nor did the paper-writers say all that could be said in their chosen areas. But they took some stands, engaged some issues, pointed some directions. They were supplemented at the Sequences themselves by a series of keynote addresses from a variety of educational and political leaders, all of whom issued important challenges to thought and to action.

The first keynote here—as at the Southampton Summer Sequences—came from historian Henry Steele Commager. Through his wide-ranging overview of the evolution of American education, Professor Commager introduced a theme that recurred in many of the addresses and papers and became central to the conference: the American penchant to confuse the whole of education with the work of formal schooling. He pointed out that traditionally, in European societies, education was held to involve the whole of society, and was expressed through a variety of formal and informal institutions; whereas America has put the entire burden on the schools. This led to an increasing disjunction between the society and the schools: the latter have been assigned the function of training the generations to come in the highest ideals of the society, while the society itself flouts these ideals. Schools simply cannot "provide" *paideia* in a society without school-culture continuity. It is not possible to reform the whole through the part. And nothing indicates that the whole—the society at large—wishes to reform itself along the lines suggested by the ideals taught in its schools.

Here then, set out in the largest terms, is the deep cultural bind. But Professor Commager's address was not wholly, perhaps not even mainly, pessimistic. He identified what the schools should not be asked to do—a certain unburdening of their function—and at the same time specified how the society as a whole might recommit itself to the continuities of education that would constitute a new *paideia*. And, in the process, he provided a clear framework within which more particularized questions—for legislators, for educators, and for laymen—could be formed.

2

The School as Surrogate

Henry Steele Commager

In his lecture on Education—a lecture which he did not publish in his lifetime—Emerson observed: "It is ominous, a presumption of crime, that this word *Education* has so cold, so hopeless, a sound. A treatise on education, a convention for education, a lecture . . . affects us with a slight paralysis, and a certain yawning of the jaws. . . ."

Awareness of this danger broods over every conference of this kind—perhaps, for that matter—over every conference. We cannot expect answers to the old and ever-importunate questions about the nature and function of education to emerge from this conference. After all, even the Greeks were not clear about *paideia* (not even as clear as Werner Jaeger (1944), who was himself not very clear about the matter, even in three stout volumes), and since Plato philosophers have raised questions about education without answering them. We must not expect to find answers: like Gertrude Stein we must be content to ask, "Very well, what is the question?"

My own task is perhaps the most difficult and the least reward-ing of all. I am expected to introduce a subject which has no bounds and no clear character, to raise questions for which there are no answers, to suggest explanations which have invariably proved unacceptable, and to clarify what is by its very nature obscure and perhaps incomprehensible. What is worse, I am—I gather from someone whose every whim is our command—expected to find unity in the diversity and disparity of the papers you are privileged to hear, papers which address themselves to the most elementary education, to adult education, and to new patterns of life for the old; which look at education as part of evolution and as part of structure and as quantitative and as qualitative; which come up with specific programs (266 of them in one paper alone); and which, by implication at least, reject the possibility of educational programs accomplishing anything. I am sure Dr. Bigelow had no systems in mind when he conceived this conference, but clearly it operates, certainly as far as you are concerned, on the elective system.

Yet I do have a thesis to submit to you, though not an argument, for I recall that *argumentum* originally meant to make clear. It is this: that education is not at all the same thing as schooling, for education involves the whole person throughout the whole of his life, while schooling affects only a small number of people for a very brief period in their lives. Yet in the United States, for reasons deeply rooted in our history, there is an almost irresistible temptation to equate the two: certainly most conferences on education turn out to be conferences on schools. In the Old World the informal and private enterprise of education has always been dominant—and perhaps still is; in the New World the formal or public enterprise has steadily gained ground over the private and now, numerically at least, dominates the field. Americans persist in the assumption that it is the public and formal education that is dominant; the Old World of Europe and of Asia knows better, and concerns itself constantly with the private and informal enterprise. Increasingly—in the United States as elsewhere—the formal or public sector of education trains for tasks and duties that are unreal; teaches conduct that is in conflict with the standards of conduct taken for granted by the public generally; and aims at objectives which have little meaning to the public or—we are tempted to conclude—to those who are exposed to them. The gap between the public and the private educational enterprise widens ominously.

This is our concern, and one of the justifications for this conference: the apparent failure of public education at the lower levels (perhaps even at the higher levels, but here the evidence is contradictory). Officially we seek to repair this failure by pouring ever more money into the public enterprise. In vain. For the failure will not yield to financial remedies. It is to be ascribed, rather, to the elementary fact that society does not practice what it wants the schools to preach and that as long as this goes on, the young—who are smarter than their elders—believe what they see in practice and not what they hear in the classroom.

Until all agencies of education, public and private, formal and informal, are prepared to teach, train, even to celebrate what we require the formal institutions to teach, education will continue to bewilder us, and to encourage schizophrenia.

History

Education has been a central preoccupation of the Western world for 2500 years, but only in the past two centuries has it been thought to be chiefly the responsibility of schools—that is of formal institutions of learning—and it is only in the past half century or so (a brief time in history) that the task has been handed over almost entirely to such formal institutions of learning.

Schools, in some form, and universities, are very old, but until almost our own day neither schools nor universities were for the whole population of a society or for the whole education of society. Both of these notions—that schools should educate everyone and that they should provide the whole of education—are so new that we are still working out their implications. Certainly there was no such thing in the Old World as universal or even widespread education until the twentieth century, although some German states, some Dutch, and Scotland provide partial exceptions. Nor, for all the rhetoric of the school laws of the 1640s, was there in the Bay Colony. It was not until well into the nineteenth century that Horace Mann and his followers called for what we would consider universal free education, and not until after the Civil War that public high schools outnumbered academies and private secondary schools. As late as 1900, while there were some 15 million children in public elementary schools, the public high school population was only 519,000, with an additional 1,351,000 in academies and parochial schools: proportionately fewer young people went to high schools and academies combined than now go to colleges and universities.

Doubtless throughout most of the eighteenth and nineteenth centuries the United States provided formal schooling for more children—certainly for more white children—than did any Old World country. That does not mean that it provided more education. For the new United States did not, after all, have the numerous and elaborate educational institutions of the Old World: ancient schools, academies, and universities; the Church, the Court, the guilds, the bar, the army and the navy, and—along with these and providing always a familiar background—a stable society on the farms and in the villages. Stable long after the disappearance of feudalism. Almost every child grew up in a society where things had been taken for granted for generations; they grew up knowing where and how they were to fit into a familiar pattern. Those who belonged to the ruling classes were provided with an elaborate education both in and out of schools—mostly out. The others—who were of course the vast majority—were not expected to have much if any formal education, but their informal education was amply provided for by existing institutions—the farm, the workshop, the great house where they worked as servants or gardeners, the Church, and above all the family where the father taught his sons and the mother her daughters what they needed to know to serve in the station to which God had consigned them.

In the New World everything was different. Coming to America was the greatest of changes—as it continued to be for millions of immigrants, for another 200 years. Nothing could be taken for granted, and almost everything had to be learned anew—climate, soil, flora, fauna, diseases and remedies, new forms of farming, new tools; within a short time almost everything was new socially and culturally too—a legal equality for the whites, slavery for the blacks, emancipation from a state church, the necessity of resourcefulness in order to stay alive; the almost limitless possibilities for the industrious and the clever; the opportunity to formulate your own theology, to run your own government, to form your own societies and organizations. Stephen Benet caught something of this in his *Western Star.*

> This is a world where a man starts clear
> Once he's paid the price of getting here,
> For though we be English true and staunch
> We'll judge no man by the size of his paunch,
> And my lord's lackey and my lord's station
> Have little to do with a man's plantation. . . .
> For we live under another sky
> From the men who never have crossed the seas.

But except for slavery, the new habits and practices were not institutionalized, as in the Old World, and could not be relied on for educational purposes in anything like the same way. Americans had no church which could impose its discipline on the whole people, no class system, no hierarchy, no guilds, no professions, even, with their rules and their titles; we scarcely had families, for families scattered with the wind. And what is more—in America and perhaps alone in America—it was taken for granted that authority in the family inhered in the young, who knew the ropes, and who were therefore better educated than their parents or their forebears, a situation which still holds true for the great majority of Americans.

In a very real sense the lack of discipline and of permanence provided a different kind of education: you were on your own, to make what you could out of life. You were not required to worship at your father's church; you did not have to follow your father's work or profession or to follow his footsteps along familiar furrows; you did not need to marry your neighbor's daughter but might marry whom you would.

Industrialization and urbanization marked an end to most of the informal education which American children had enjoyed from the early seventeenth century on. This was the first great revolution. Americans might, by that time, have created counter-revolutionary institutions or disciplines and, of course, to some extent they had. But by that time the bifurcation between formal and informal education was decisive; by that time education was being assigned chiefly to schools that were, for the most part, unable to provide more than formal schooling; and education—in the sense it had been known in the Old World for centuries, in the sense in which it had been provided even in America by the home and the farm—was going by default. It was to counter this desperate situation that John Dewey and Jane Addams raised the standard of what came to be called "progressive education" but what was really a throwback to Pestalozzi and Fellenberg and Froebel and, in America, to Maclure and Bronson Alcott; it was in part to counter this that school athletics came to occupy so prominent a place in the educational landscape (the perversion of that enterprise is one of the major tragedies of American education).

By the mid-twentieth century another revolution—or quasi-revolution—in the instruments of education was underway. In the

1940s and 1950s, as if to fill the vacuum left by the decline of the household and the church as major educational agencies, the film, radio, television, and popular journalism emerged as full-scale educational agencies. What we have here is a dramatic shift in the balance of educational authority. For the new instruments competed with the old both in attention and in effectiveness. They competed with schools, to be sure, but also with informal agencies. Schools continued to make their formal demands on the young, and after all an ever-larger proportion of the population spent ever more time in formal schools. Something had to give way, and it was—predictably— the remnants of an older informal education that gave way—education by work, by family, by church.

Concurrently there was another revolution—a shift in the center of educational gravity from the elementary to secondary and higher education. By mid-century it was taken for granted almost everywhere in the United States that all the young were to go to school until the age of 16 or even 18, and within the next quarter century post-high school schooling increased from roughly two and one-half to nine million: if taken at face value that statistic would be the most spectacular in the history of education! What this meant was that, where in the past the very young got their education largely at home and older children and young men and women at work, we now have the bifurcation of education extended by four or five years; the divorce between "education" and personal experience covers almost the whole youthful population.

We can see in some of the youth cults and the youth indulgences of our day a convulsive (albeit unsuccessful) revolt against this development: the rejection of traditional subjects of study, the fascination of life in a commune, the preference for the film over the printed word, and for rock music over traditional music—all of this is part of the effort to get back to reality—a reality simplistically equated with "nature" just as it was during the era of Sturm and Drang.

All this, I need scarcely remind you, is an expression of a neo-romanticism—a romanticism very much like that of the late eighteenth and early nineteenth centuries—of the sorrows of Werther and the new Heloise, Paul and Virginia and the Marquis de Sade, rather than like the more sophisticated and less robust romanticism of Wordsworth and Coleridge, of Emerson and Thoreau. The current romanticism has many of the stigmata of the earlier: an intense subjectivity, a preoccupation with the state of one's soul, admiration for uncontrolled individualism and acceptance of the notion that the artist (and is not every young person an artist?) is exempt from the ordinary regulations of society; a preference for the particular rather than the general, the isolated event or emotion rather than the social experience; a sentimental attitude towards nature and children and the primitive, especially the primitive; fascination with sex, especially in its more aberrant manifestations, and the pursuit of it, especially down labyrinthine ways; and hostility to all institutions, especially the state, law, the family, and education.

It is this latter which chiefly commands our attention. Romanticism is always excessive, but the excess usually confesses a reality. What is arresting here is that where in the decades of the 1830s and 1840s, one of the most striking manifestations of romanticism was the transcendental faith in education—a faith based on the conviction of the infinite perfectability of man—today one of its most striking manifestations is its disillusionment with education. There is still a rather touching faith, if not in the perfectability then at least in the goodness of man—especially if under 22—but none in the virtue of society or of the family, none in the validity of formal educational institutions.

One explanation of the growing alienation of education from what the young, at least, think is reality, is the professionalization of education (a professionalization for which this conference is designed to be something of a countervailing force). In the past most great educational statesmen were from outside the Academy. Comenius—perhaps the first of the moderns—was to be sure a teacher before he was a theologian; but John Locke was not an educator, nor for that matter was Joseph Priestley, although he did teach at the famous Warrenton Academy; nor, in the nineteenth century Cardinal Newman, nor Herbert Spencer. Rousseau had no interest in schools—his might be called an anti-education educational philosophy; Basedow was a clergyman who set up briefly his *Philanthropicum*, and so too Pestalozzi and Oberlin and the great Bishop Grundtvig, chiefly responsible for the Danish Folk High School. Nor is the story different in the United States. Jefferson—no doubt our greatest educational statesman—developed the ideas and policies that transformed American education out of his own philosophy, and so, too, did Dr. Rush. William Maclure was a businessman; Bronson Alcott a peddler, a philosopher, and a failed teacher; Horace Mann a lawyer and Henry Barnard trained in the law although he devoted his long life to the study of education. Calvin Stowe of Ohio was a clergyman, Thaddeus Stevens a politician, Margaret Fuller a journalist, Henry Tappan a philosopher even within the Academy. Eliot was trained as a chemist, William James as a medical man, Stanley Hall as a psychologist, and John Dewey was, in a sense, a philosopher manqué; Jane Addams, in many ways the greatest practitioner of education in our history, presided over the activities of Hull House and of almost everything else that came her way. Today the most fruitful contributions to education have come from a chemist turned university president, and the most incisive criticisms from a lawyer with the same experience.

The Contradiction

What is clear is that the function of every category of education, formal and informal, changed profoundly in less than a century and that we have not yet caught up with the changes. Old instruments and institutions have lost or forfeited their role; new instruments and institutions—so new that we do not yet understand how they work or how to work them—have invaded and conquered much of the traditional educational territory. Is it any wonder that we are bewildered? How could it be otherwise? And we should recognize that as change, in the United States, is more dramatic than elsewhere, so confusion is deeper, for we lack those ancient institutions, habits, traditions, and authorities which cushion the shock in most countries of the Old World.

The United States is now far more like the nations of Western Europe (and perhaps even the Soviet Union) in its social and economic organization, but we persist in that policy inherited from a very different day, namely in assuming that the school is not only the central instrument of education (which no doubt it is) but almost the only one, which quite clearly it is not. When the Coleman, the Moynihan, the Jencks studies argue that the home and social environment has more to do with the success or failure of education than the school itself, their observations are greeted as a kind of treason to education and to democracy. When investigators report to us that the average child spends more time in front of a television screen than in a schoolroom, their findings are greeted with the demand for more education on TV—more Sesame Street or Electric Company—rather than with a reconsideration of the interlocking roles of schools and the media. When sociologists—and I suppose public health experts—lament the disappearance of participatory sports in favor of voyeurism, we are treated—by our Vice President, no less—to homilies on the beauties of professional athletics or tributes to the lethal competition of the Little Leagues.

In the past we required our schools to do what in the Old World the family, the Church, apprenticeship, and the guilds did; now we ask them to do what their modern equivalents, plus a hundred voluntary organizations, fail or refuse to do. Our schools, like our children, are the victims of the failure of our society to fulfill its obligation to *paideia*.

Not only is there a bifurcation between formal and informal education, that is, between school and society, there is a latent hostility as well—a hostility which, in the realm of higher education, becomes overt. The divergence is more than mechanical or fortuitous; it is philosophical. Increasingly schools are required to take on the function of a moral safety valve: the more virtuous the sentiments and standards of conduct they inculcate, the more effectively they perform the function of a surrogate conscience, permitting society to follow its own bent while consoling itself with the assurance that the schools are training a generation that will do better.

What has emerged is something analogous to the juxtaposition of private and public sin that E. A. Ross described in his classic essay on "Sin and Society." Ross, as you will remember, pointed out that it was only the private sins that society punished with implacable severity—drunkenness, embezzlement, seduction, wife-beating (we would add drug addiction), and so forth. But society looked with amiable indifference on the far-flung "social" sins of "malefactors of great wealth"—those who corrupted the political processes by bribing legislators or judges, those who sold adulterated foods or bad meat or dangerous drugs, those who bribed fire inspectors or safety inspectors, those who employed child labor in violation of the law and of morality, those who somehow evaded corporate taxes. These, as Ross sardonically observed, sat on the boards of trustees, served as vestrymen for churches, and got all the honorary degrees. So with our disjunction between what is taught in the schools and what is practiced in society.

Thus society rejoices when schools teach that all men are created equal and entitled to life, liberty, and happiness, but has no intention of applying that noble principle to the ordinary affairs of business or government, or even to education itself. Thus society applauds the principle of racial equality, but does not itself provide the young an example of such equality—knowing instinctively that the example is more persuasive than the admonition. Thus society rewards pupils who can recite the Bill of Rights, but has no serious interest in the application of those rights to the tiresome minority groups who clamor for them. Thus society approves when schools celebrate—as they must in teaching the virtues of a Franklin, a Washington, a Jefferson—service to the commonwealth but rewards private, not public, enterprise. It requires schools to teach the primary value of things of the mind but itself prefers the rewards of more material things. It expects schools to teach that justice is the purpose and the end of government, but itself practices injustice in almost every area of public life—not least in education. It expects schools to teach respect for the law but elects to high office a President and a Vice President who display only contempt for the law. It encourages schools to teach the virtues of peace—indeed to make clear that the United States has always been a "peace-loving" nation—but exalts war, wages war, maintains the largest military enterprise in the world and spends more of its wealth on the military than any other nation.

We can put the disjunction even more pointedly. Can schools save the environment, when the most powerful business interests in the country are prepared to sacrifice it for immediate profit? Can education, even research, reverse the tide of pollution when the government is afraid to take firm action in this crucial arena—afraid to put an end to strip mining, afraid to arrest the insensate pollution of Lake Superior with poisonous chemicals, afraid to impose sensible limits and regulations on the automobile industry, afraid even to endorse plans for the sensible use of land? Can schools dissuade the young from senseless violence when the government itself engages in ceaseless violence on a scale heretofore unknown in our history and calls the result "honor"?

If our educational enterprise is in disarray it is in part because we have asked it to perform a miracle—to teach the young to understand the world they live in and the one they are to live in in the future, when we ourselves show little awareness of our fiduciary obligation to that future; to train them for the skills required to work an economy which will inevitably be public when we ourselves give priority to the private economy; to persuade them to respect all the values which we do not ourselves observe. Much of public education today is a massive demonstration in hypocrisy, and it is folly to suppose that the young do not know this.

The Reconciliation

Educators have of course long been aware of the dichotomy between what is taught in the schools and what is held up for approval and emulation by most other institutions of society. It was an awareness of this that led the Teachers College group—Dewey as inspiration, Kilpatrick, Counts, and Rugg as activists—to launch a crusade to reconstruct society, calling on the schools to

> face squarely and courageously every social issue,
> come to grips with life in all its stark realities,
> establish an organic relationship with the community,
> develop a realistic and comprehensive theory of welfare,
> fashion a compelling and challenging vision of human destiny.

But it is very difficult for the part to reconstruct the whole, and the experience of our schools with such reconstruction through the direct confrontation of great social and economic and political problems has not been encouraging. That enterprise began in the depression years, and gathered strength and experience throughout the years of war and of crisis down to our own day. Do we want good citizens— the kind that Jefferson prepared for, that Horace Mann extolled, that Theodore Roosevelt celebrated? Do not follow the misguided principles or methods of a Jefferson, a Horace Mann, a Roosevelt, but teach civics directly; that will surely produce a generation of good citizens and enlightened statesmen! Do we want racial and religious tolerance, and an end to the racism which has stained our history? Teach tolerance in the schools, and then when the children grow up they will practice it, in the schools, in housing, in jobs! Do we want to banish cultural chauvinism and encourage cosmopolitanism in the young, so that when they are adults they will be truly citizens of the world? Teach world literature, world history, world sociology: introduce children to the arts and culture of China, of Russia, of Vietnam, of all those peoples who have so much to teach us, and understanding will take the place of misunderstanding. Do we want an end to war and to militarism? The proper study of history will solve that problem, the study of the history of all other nations so that we can truly understand their problems; that—with the support of UNESCO and similar international agencies—should usher in an era of world peace!

Rarely, if ever, in history have so many been exposed to so much with results so meagre. To judge by results—the results of the past forty years or so—this whole enterprise of relying on schools to reform society by direct teaching has been an unmitigated failure. After forty years of exposure to world cultures, world politics, world geography, we turned out to be culturally more alienated, politically more isolated, economically more reckless, and, on the world scene, more chauvinistic and militaristic than at any previous time in our history.

The explanation for the failure in what was, in effect, a case study of our whole problem, is twofold. First it is an illusion—a characteristically American illusion—to suppose that a straight line is the shortest distance between two points in the intellectual and moral realms as in the mathematical. The generation that created the American republic knew this instinctively. It did not rely on the teaching of current events to solve current problems, but took for granted that students familiar with the classics of literature, history, and philosophy would be wise enough to understand whatever problems might arise and resourceful enough to work out solutions. The second explanation is that the earlier society was culturally and philosophically harmonious. There was no such deep chasm between what was valued in formal education—what went into Jefferson's Commonplace Book or Washington's Rules for Civility for example—and what society practiced and exalted: Jefferson the educator and Jefferson the statesman were of a piece, and so too with John Adams, Benjamin Rush, and others who operated in both fields.

Our society boasts no such harmony—perhaps no modern society does. A society that is divided, disillusioned, and bewildered, that has lost confidence in its own character and its purpose, cannot expect to achieve unity through the schools. The very fact that we require our schools to do so much that society itself should do is an indication that we do not know what our schools should do and we are not prepared to do what society itself should do. One advantage of asking schools to do everything is that you then have a kind of experimental social laboratory in which to try out your ideas; another is that, as the schools are bound to fail, you then have a scapegoat and can yourself shrug off responsibility.

All this sounds like we are imprisoned in a vicious circle: The schools cannot reconstruct society and society has no interest in reconstructing itself along the lines that schools might find gratifying. The schools cannot reform education, for most of education goes on outside the schoolroom. Society, which created a dual system of education, seems content with the perpetuation of that system. Yet only if society recognizes, as I think it did in eighteenth century America, its responsibility to *paideia*—to the total education of succeeding generations—will it permit, and commit, all of its institutions to work in harmony with its schools.

This is part of our task—the task of those who participate in these discussions—to enlist all educational agencies in an enterprise of education which shall embrace the whole of society; to make clear that education is not something we hand over to schools and then forget about (except at football or basketball games, or graduation exercises), but is the responsibility of the family, the government, the church, television, newspapers and magazines, business (which might profitably begin the enterprise by using advertising for purposes of enlightenment instead of purposes of deception) and labor, the great educational organizations (such as the Office of Education, the National Educational Association, the AASA, for example), and the scores or even hundreds of private voluntary associations (ranging from the PTA to the League of Women Voters, the Masons and the Elks to the Rotary and Kiwanis, the American Legion, and the Veterans of Foreign Wars). Even the universities might cooperate by integrating with their schools of education (an absurd name, this, as if the whole university were not a school of education). This was one of the objectives of the TTT—pretty much the brain child of Donald Bigelow—an objective not realized; perhaps in the nature of things it is an objective which cannot be realized. Perhaps the only way of achieving that integration is to turn the whole university into a school of education—what else is a university? And does not the division within the university between learning and education mirror the division in our society between education and schooling? Should not the functions of schools of education be absorbed into all the branches of the university? I have proposed elsewhere that the only way to cure the malaise of the Vice Presidency is to abolish the office of Vice President; I make an analogous proposal for schools of education. I am too old to indulge in these simply as *jeux d'esprit*.

It would be euphoric to suppose that the Academy—even with the allies it has summoned here—could reform both the school and society and integrate them into a single and unified moral, social, and intellectual educational enterprise. All we can do is to act on the admonition of George Washington (and it is somehow symbolic of our problem that we do not know whether he ever really said it or not): "Let us raise a standard to which the wise and the honest can repair. The event must be in the hand of God."

References

Jaeger, Werner. *Paideia: The Ideals of Greek Culture* (3 vols.). Trans. Gilbert Highet. Oxford: Oxford University Press, 1944.

PART II

Core Functions for the Schools

Commentary

Implicit in the charge from the legislators and in Professor Commager's keynote was the issue of the place of the schools, or perhaps more accurately of "schooling"—the formal educational enterprise and institution—within the broader social definition of *paideia*. What are the schools now, and what should they be? Since they are only part of a large, complex, self-regulating social system, how much freedom of action do they have? If they cannot reform society, can they at least reform themselves? If they cannot reform society, why do we go on behaving as if they could? What is within the power of the schools to change, or even to do?

Before the opening of the Southampton Summer Sequences, a number of position papers had been drafted. Some of them showed a remarkable convergence on the problem of "schooling," its place within the crossfield of social forces. They attempted to take on the issue of whether such a thing as a core function for the schools could in fact be defined. And if it could, however tentatively, some of the papers tried to suggest how the schools be organized more effectively to promote this core function.

Traditionally—when formal education was still directed toward a relatively defined elite, within the structure of a relatively stable and consensual society—education could be defined as the transmission of culture. In practice, this meant the passing on of society's ideal values as expressed in its "high culture"—its most respected and enduring artistic and literary artifacts. Culture, in Matthew Arnold's famous definition, was the study of "the best that has been thought and known." In contemporary America, such definitions of culture, and hence of education, are impossible for at least two reasons: first, because education is not only for the best, but for all, and cannot hope to be pertinent if it concentrates only on high cultural artifacts; second, because high culture has always held an uneasy position in American society, and is not necessarily democratic in its implications.

If we cannot answer our questions about the function of the schools with repetition of traditional definitions of the study of perfection, is it possible at all to locate and describe what schooling should be about, and then to specify what institutional and curricular arrangements should follow? The essays grouped here—written from a wide variety of perspectives and out of widely differing careers in education—suggest that some measure of consensus may be possible. All the essays are, first of all, committed to the idea of a core function in education, a belief that it can be and must be defined, and that a coherent pattern of schooling must be constructed on its basis. There is a striking degree of unanimity in the call for a rededication of the schools to a concern with matters primarily cognitive. This call does not appear to be motivated by a nostalgic or an abstract love for "culture," but rather by a strong belief that an educated and democratic citizenry more than ever needs to be provided with the tools for making sense of its complex, tension-laden, and often oppressive environment. Although the different writers give different names to their core concern, they appear to be in general agreement that it must mean primarily the fostering of those intellectual qualities of analysis that allow men to respond critically to the pressures of their environment, to understand the distinction between legitimate and illegitimate demands upon them, to be free.

The concern of these essays then becomes one of making the schools themselves free—free from illegitimate social pressures and bogus functions—to foster more effectively what schooling can foster. Although many divergent proposals are advanced here, and various kinds of new institutions and noninstitutions are considered, there is no argument for "deschooling" society, no implication that what goes on in the schools is unnecessary, or susceptible of being carried out in other ways. On the contrary, all the essays suggest that formal schooling, redefined and rededicated, is more than ever indispensable. And that is why argument about the nature of the schools, their function, and the responsibility for their future direction, matters so much.

The four essays printed here naturally divide into two sub-groups, the first (including the essays by Martin Green and Peter Brooks) mainly concerned with defining a "Core Function for the Schools"; the second (essays by Page Smith and Theodore Sizer) largely addressed to the curriculum that might best express the core function, and the institutional rearrangements that might foster it.

The first set of essays (both written by university teachers with long-standing interest in all aspects of education) probes the question of function and definition. Martin Green calls on his own experiences as teacher and as student to reargue the importance of instruction, of the time spent in the classroom—if rightly understood and carried out. He is led to define the function of education as, in the most general terms, the teaching of criticism. By "criticism," he really means a certain stance, toward knowledge and toward life: a stance of awareness, of informed scepticism, the capacity to dissent from dominant mythologies, and to address all questions with informed, analytical passion. If most of his examples are drawn from the sphere of higher education, the implications of this central stance, and what goes into its making, extend to the whole of education. Peter Brooks, on the other hand, is talking specifically about the schools, arguing (in a theme that recurs often in this volume) that they have been overburdened by the aspirations and tensions of American society, charged with reforming through its children what the parents cannot or will not cope with, and hence turned into a social battleground. Brooks suggests that the schools need to withdraw from some of the social responsibilities placed on them, in order to rededicate themselves to a core function that can most simply be stated as teaching and learning to read: to use language, to interpret human sign-systems of all kinds, to read in critical awareness the messages of the contemporary world. The "critical reading of reality" that he sees as the major aim of education on all levels does not differ greatly from Green's stance of "criticism." His essay does suggest somewhat more specifically what must be the components of a schooling that is to foster this goal, and he argues that all else that the schools are now called on to perform might more usefully be turned over to other paraeducational units or groups within the community.

Turning to the second set of essays, Page Smith's carefully argued paper starts from the premise that educational systems and curricula traditionally derived from the religious beliefs of their societies, passing on the values that the society deemed essential to its survival. The question then arises, what organizing principle can be given to education in a secularized, post-religious society? On what can we ground an ideal curriculum, running from kindergarten through graduate school? Smith's answer is original and in many respects compelling: he argues that for contemporary American society the ordering principles are to be found in law and medicine, which constitute continuing experiences throughout life, and embrace a large portion of what we must know about societies, their defining principles and rituals, and about the human organism and its environment. The essay is consciously utopian in its prescription of a totally rethought curriculum. More modestly, it is a criticism of present arrangements, and provides a reasoned basis from which to consider what a society must teach if it is to survive.

Smith considers the possibility that his universal curriculum might be taught in a variety of settings, without walls, in the community. Release from the sense of imprisonment produced by so many of our current schools is a theme in several of the papers here. It is specifically the focus of Theodore Sizer's blueprint for a system of complementary schools. Contending that education encompasses different kinds of learning, involving different techniques and calling on different characteristics and capacities, personal and social, in students, he calls for a diversified system that would include neighborhood schools devoted to teaching the "cognitive core" operations, and a variety of regional institutes, apprenticeships, and field programs. What is needed is a flexible system of options that would further education in basic skills and also bring the experience of cultural and social diversity. Sizer brings to bear on his argument his experience with the "complementary" program he has instituted as Headmaster of Phillips Academy, in Andover, Massachusetts. But his ideas have large implications, and suggest ways to satisfy at once the need for neighborhood schools and for broader social interaction, the demand for recommitment of the schools to basics, and the demand that they be open to the realities of American society.

Together, the four essays presented here suggest that there may be a basis for the informed participation of educators and legislators in mapping out a coherent future.

Peter Brooks

3

The Social Function of Education

Martin Green

Prologue

I have been told that this paper will characterize me as the most hardened kind of reactionary unless I let people know that I have earlier espoused democratic values in education quite enthusiastically. So I offer, by way of credential, a couple of passages, one at the beginning and one at the end of the paper, taken from my book, *Mirror for Anglo-Saxons* (1960).

This scheme of development, this kind of personality [the "gentleman's"], are of course in essence quite compatible with the keenest intelligence, the greatest vigour, the deepest satisfaction. But they have today become clichés; today only stupid people can use their phrases without irony; intelligent people, if they share their feelings, are condemned to self-deprecation. Above all, these characteristics, this manner, are now unreasonable and unseasonable, out of all relation to every contemporary or future reality. It is an aristocratic manner. And our only future is democratic.

I sometimes think people don't realize that enough. Whatever our personal aptitudes or preferences, whatever society we would build if we had a choice, we are committed to democracy. Our fathers and grandfathers committed us. It is natural to rebel at the moment we realize we are committed to the banal; we all know the absurdities and indignities of democracy, we could all be brilliant reactionaries; but nature also demands that we quickly accept what is necessary.

We have got to learn how to make real democracy work, with all its disadvantages. There is no other decent future . . . . If a democratic mind is to be born, the hierarchy of values will have to be maintained and fed from sources different from those of the past.

Education Is To Instruct

The primary function of education, even when seen in relation to society as a whole, must surely be to instruct. Of course there is more to it than that; after we have narrowed down the protean suggestiveness of "education" to mean "system of schools," we still expect a lot more from students than the acquisition of knowledge. For really young children, knowledge in the formal bookish sense must be quite a small part of what they acquire there; and even for the students I teach, including the graduate students, there is a lot more to the transaction between me and them, not to mention the transaction between the whole campus and them. There is social training, of various kinds; there is the imitation of models, in tones of voice and gesture as well as opinion and aspiration; there is the transmission of taste; and there is the whole social world of the students' peers, a world often more potent in all these spheres of education than the teachers are. Nevertheless, all these kinds of education cluster around the classroom and the teacher standing there to address a class with a book in his hand. (Maybe he is running a movie, maybe they are sitting in a circle and all talking to each other, maybe two or three are performing something for the rest, but all these are temporary variations of that first pattern. By some teachers, these methods are *regularly* used. But those teachers are variations of the usual pattern.) Thus seen in terms of *form*, the primary function of education is to instruct. And I think that a system of schools cannot be healthy if that particular function loses its primacy in feeling as well as in form. If the other functions of education are given the primacy, so that the hour in the classroom, and the teacher instructing with book in hand, does not feel central, then education will be unhealthy, because the role of the teachers will not be dominant enough, and so the teachers will not be proud enough. You cannot have good education without proud teachers. So education must be organized for the teachers' benefit.

I hope that by saying where I stand so definitely I do not seem to refuse discussion with people who hold a quite different point of view. The things I am saying sound slightly shocking in my own ears—leave me, too, uneasy. But I think that a position paper should take a definite stand, and map one of the geographical directions of the subject. I want to see the *tendency* of my own thoughts, which are usually cut short in caution or tact, and enmeshed in the details of particular cases or of other people's ideas to which I am reacting. Here I want to trace them out more nakedly so that I can see where they may take me.

If instruction is education's primary function, then the decisions about what to teach and how to teach it are matters of great social importance. That is, they become important when they are in dispute. Ordinarily, of course, it is accepted that one teaches reading here and nuclear physics there, and an innovative way of teaching anything is to be discussed as a matter of purely *local* importance. As teachers, we give the students access to that knowledge which crystallizes the achievements of culture as we understand them—in English literature or engineering science—according to the methods of study we think best. These decisions usually become of importance only when there is a dispute between the teachers and some other group about what or how to teach. There have been times and places even in American history when the state or local community has interfered—in the teaching of evolutionary theory in biology, for instance; or a church has interfered; or the trustees of a university; or the parents, particularly when the students in question were young children.

In all such cases, the teachers must react vigorously against such interference, if education is to stay healthy. (This does not preclude the possibility of the teachers being wrong about the particular issue, but in general they must be right to protest against interference from outside. If they were wrong to begin with, they must take over the right view and make it their own.) The outside force that has most recently exerted pressure on what gets taught and how has come from university students. There have been many innovations in the past few years: in books taught in a particular course; in methods of teaching them and testing knowledge about them; in kinds of courses and requirements for a major, etc. Such changes have usually been made in response to, or on behalf of, the students. And they have, on the whole, slackened the discipline of education, made its standards vaguer and more variable, made it seem that anything goes, or rather that anything that is going goes. This has happened sometimes in response to firm demands or pressure from students, but just as often as a result of teachers acting out those demands in advance of their being made. The academic world in many ways overcompensates for the crimes of the larger society, leaning the other way in some pathetic hope of redressing the national balance with its purely symbolic weight, so that the whole social boat may not capsize. Of course there are some insensitive rigidities in the campus world which might not too ludicrously be compared with those of the outer world, but the requirements for a major were not among them. The softening of such and similar requirements has exemplified the lack of pride in the teachers, a failure in health of education in America.

So much for the primary social function. But it is the secondary social function that interests me much more. It is what I want to call criticism; critical techniques and a critical attitude, within the subject matter taught, which extends itself to the world outside.

It is comparatively easy to say what this means in the teaching of the humanities. For example, the social function of education in literature, from this point of view, begins by enabling students to make an imaginative identification with the rebellious heroes of novels and plays. In the case of modern literature, just about all the heroes or heroines are rebels against some aspect of society—that is precisely what makes them heroes. And in the case of poetry, the persona of the poems, the voice of the poet has a similar character and calls for a similar effort of identification. Just to recall the names of the great writers of this century will demonstrate this point; D. H. Lawrence, W. B. Yeats, James Joyce, Ernest Hemingway, Samuel Beckett, and so on. The act of rebellion against society has been so radical a constituent of the writers' vocation that, for the student to appreciate their work, for the teacher properly to teach it, the student must go quite far, imaginatively, towards an outright repudiation of modern Western society, including some of those achievements of which even liberals are proud. This is not to say that the work of great writers is sheer rebellion; the act of writing itself is an act of cooperation in the cultural enterprise of that modern Western society, and great writing is one of the most self-committing of all such acts. Nor am I saying that the teaching of such writing can be, or should be, sheer rebellion, socially. But it can and should contain elements of rebellion combined with other, opposite, elements; for instance, appreciation of form, beauty, wit, or intellectual tradition, all have ideological affiliations unlike or opposed to those of social rebellion. It is the combination of those clashing affiliations or tendencies which has the social function I call criticism. As you learn to read the great novels and to sympathize with their rebellious heroes, you should come to form the habit of very complex sympathies with and revulsion from many of our society's main features.

In the same way, in the teaching of history, or political science, one's attention is bound to be arrested particularly by the innovators, the rebels, the passionate heroes of the historical process. One cannot teach the history of modern times without teaching Marx, and what he had to say about nineteenth century "democracy"; and one cannot teach the history of those times in England without examining the Labour Party and the way it combined Marxist ideas with more native and evangelical criticisms of society. Again, history itself cannot be made to carry the clear message "rebel," and the teacher should not neglect those other aspects of the record, like the triumphant functioning of great men in accord with their social context. But, like literature, history is essentially (though not totally) a record of great individuals in conflict with the kind of society we live in; and of other kinds of society, again in potential or actual conflict with our own kind. Any adequate teaching of history must convey to students some sense of the alternatives to the way we live now, and of the costs of the way we live now. Some disturbance must be set up in the student's mind, some process of reflection which could issue in the act of rebellion, and which should issue in the act of criticism.

I have been speaking, of course, out of the experience of a college teacher; and though it is easy enough to see how the work of a high school teacher is analogous, it may seem that teachers of primary schools can hardly think of their work in comparable ways. But in fact the teaching of a passionate concern for plants and animals, at a primary or even preschool level, already carries within it a commitment to values which our society has ignored or affronted. And in the same way the teaching of adventure stories and adventure history, about knights on crusades and quests, or of pirates and highwaymen, can carry values significantly in conflict with—and potentially critical of—those of our society.

The science subjects, and even more engineering, are often felt to have more conservative affiliations than the humanities. But this is surely a historical accident of the stuffy and hidebound way they have been taught. Certainly when they are taught as humanities, that is with full attention paid to both the imaginative sources and the historical consequences of their great discoveries, they have ideological affiliations which foster "criticism." When the discovery is shown to derive from an intellectual personality and imagination, and when its consequences are shown for the lives of other people, then the history and philosophy of science (which should be taught as part of science) become resonant with criticism in just the same way as history and literature. One vivid case of the relation of the theory to the personality is given in Arthur Koestler's biography of Kepler; many examples of the historical consequences of science can be found in J. G. Crowther's books; and the way science has been used in the West—the development of nuclear fission theory from Gottingen to Hiroshima, via Los Alamos—is one of the most critical pieces of twentieth century history. (I have given my ideas on this subject at length in my *Science and the Shabby Curate of Poetry*.)

There are two examples of criticism at work within education, within a system of schools, which I would like to say something about, because they come from my own experience. They were the best part of my own education, and they are the source of my faith in "criticism," which is itself the source of my faith in education.

The first one refers to my own training, when I was an undergraduate studying English literature at the University of Cambridge in England. Although I worked under five or six tutors while I was there, and attended many courses of lectures, I had only one *teacher*, in the important sense of that word, and that was F. R. Leavis. He lectured on the appreciation and analysis of literature, what I. A. Richards called Practical Criticism; on the great critics of the past; and on the nineteenth century novel in England, what he called the Great Tradition. He had been notable in the 1920s for his early acknowledgment of T. S. Eliot as both poet and critic, but while I was there his enthusiasm went mostly to D. H. Lawrence (then, in the 1940s, largely disregarded) and he attacked Eliot because of the latter's hostility to Lawrence.

However, the impact that Leavis had on me, and on lots of young people like me, did not derive from particular literary judgments, nor even from his great gifts as a literary critic, but from his passionate criticism of the rest of Cambridge. He was an isolated figure, who scorned most of his colleagues—at Cambridge and at other English universities—and in nearly every lecture he let this be known. Such a personality will always attract attention, but Leavis also attracted intelligent devotion, because he convinced us that he was both deeply serious and largely justified in that scorn. He persuaded us that the literary-intellectual scene in England as a whole was decadent, and that he was isolated because he would not fit himself into it and insisted on standing alone, as the only inheritor and continuer of the great traditions of Victorian England. Moreover, although he refused to extend his ideological scope beyond literature and literary criticism—that refusal was an important part of his ideology—he yet had an ideological meaning for us which went beyond literature. He disapproved of Marxism as he met it, as manifested in the Marxist poetry and criticism England had so far produced; he disapproved of Surrealism and all cosmopolitan modishness, in aesthetic philosophy as well as in creative work; he stood for a moral and purely English tradition, with clear affiliations to Bunyan and Blake and Ruskin. He was what is sometimes called a puritan and more illuminatingly a populist.

Leavis's nay-saying made sense out of my education for me. It was large enough in its bearings to justify the privileges and seclusions of Cambridge as a university. (There is a paradox here. Leavis made *nonsense* out of the leisures and pleasures of Cambridge, in that he scored the garden party atmosphere there. But he made one see what such a place could be like, which none of the other dons did.) He put his finger on what I still think was wrong with England's literary-intellectual scene, which had consequences for the social and political scene. He gave me a sense that being an English teacher could be a job worth doing.

(And perhaps I should say that my response to him was in no way a unique or merely personal thing. Out of his influence sprang a whole movement, involving hundreds of teachers of English whose major impetus derived from his example, and many thousands more who knew him indirectly, through his disciples or his books. His criticism has had a demonstrable effect on the life of England as a whole, and a *large* effect on the life of everyone connected with literature.)

But when I began teaching, curiously enough, it was not Leavis but Orwell I made most use of. This was because I began teaching in America, and the course I taught was Freshman English, to which the letter of Leavis's work was not applicable, although the spirit certainly was. But in George Orwell's essays I found what still seems to me the ideal material for such teaching.

Orwell's life was lived in opposition to England's literary-intellectual establishment as much as Leavis's. It was in the obvious sense of adventure more *actively* opposed, since he first served in the Imperial Police in Burma, where he acquired his intimate knowledge and detestation of the British Empire at work. Then he sank down through the stages of poverty to destitution in Paris and London, and lived the life of the very poor, the homeless, the beggar. And then he went to fight against Fascism in Spain. The essays and books describing these adventures, interpreting and evaluating them, provide admirable models for students of a mind fully engaged in criticizing the society it lives in; resisting, rebelling, accusing, but at the same time complexly aware of other aspects of that society, of its own pleasures in that society and its own ambiguities of motive.

In a different sense, Orwell's life was less actively committed against the system than Leavis's, since he moved outside the system, and talked to the book-reading public—talked to the components of that system in their off-duty hours. Leavis remained inside the system while he protested against it. He remained a lecturer at Cambridge even while he attacked all his colleagues and all they stood for. That is another reason why it was easier for me to use Orwell to my own purposes. Leavis had already used himself, translated what he stood for into academic or educational terms, and ones that did not fit the Freshman English situation. But my purposes were an adaptation of his purposes, only I could better use Orwell's essays as my means.

Thus I taught "criticism," as I have been using the term here. I taught reading and writing, but in such a way that they had ideological resonances, relevances for social and political issues. I did not teach attitudes to events of the day, or even analyses of them. (Of course I did refer to such things, but in such a way as to indicate that they were discontinuous with the work of the class.) And so did lots of my friends among the teaching fellows at Michigan. We taught criticism, as the social function of teaching literature. And that is what I still believe in—still practice, although in a slightly different way now.

Criticism is quite a different thing from the radicalism which has been a good deal advocated in the last few years. An essential feature of this last is to deny that there can be, or should be, any discontinuity between the work of the classroom and current events of social or political importance. This radicalism (which might be called revolutionism) wants every teacher to teach his own kind of political analysis and political action. I can see the logic of this, once one says (as such radicals often do) that the present situation, in this country, is intolerable, is unlivable. Then each such teacher must in his own way renounce academic objectivity, denounce it as a liberal illusion, provoke clashes with teachers of opposite views and with the administration of the university and ultimately of the country—must expect, at first, to be fired, and, finally, to be held responsible for ruining the whole system. Education, as a system of schools, must become an intolerable hypocrisy in such a political situation. No one who sees the situation in that way can continue to be a teacher, at least a socially established teacher.

But that is, obviously, all dependent on your making that enormous act of decision, that enormous judgment. If you don't make such a commitment, if you continue to believe in education, then it seems to me that you mustn't teach radicalism as the social function of education, but criticism. Certainly you must make being a teacher, building a life-career out of studying and appreciating culture, into an *alternative* to full participation in your society; a firm and whole-hearted alternative, a life-option in the major mode, not a minor *pis-aller*. But in effect the profession of teaching must be a loyal opposition to society's dominant forces—implicitly abiding by the social contract (unless the political situation becomes intolerable, when the profession too ceases to be feasible) but entering a protest against it. Education must stand to one side of society's main institutions, and contain a different atmosphere, the cool atmosphere of criticism. And this is only to be realistic, for though I want to describe education in such a way as to foster the pride of teachers, I can't engage in any romanticization of the teacher as type—he is not, after all, an essentially heroic type. It is a cool atmosphere which criticism generates, both in the good sense of being bracing and independent and dispassionate, and also in the less gratifying sense of being not romantically or heroically excited.

For we must return to the preliminary fact, that teachers are people who instruct students in some particular subject matter, some particular aspect of culture, and do so by the authority of their knowledge of that subject matter—of American literature, or English history, or nuclear physics. That passion is primarily what makes them teachers, and the social passion will be both secondary to that, and randomly distributed among them. Even where the social passion is highly developed, it will enter into combination with the intellectual passion only under special circumstances, and not always favorably even then. The two will easily conflict with each other, sometimes consciously, sometimes unconsciously. For that reason also, it is important not to lay upon teachers of tender social conscience crude moral obligations to make their teaching socially responsible. There are a dozen ways of doing that which will work out badly and will lead by reaction to a rigid subordination of the social function.

Teachers must have an intellectual passion for their subjects; otherwise the teaching will not be good and then education in that society will fail. These truisms must be kept alive in our minds and given the dignity of truths. Our concern with the social function of education must never be allowed to displace them from primacy. If one is thinking of the world of education as a whole, perhaps this danger is small and concern with it may seem absurd. But in certain times and places that danger has been substantial, and the last ten years of teaching English at American colleges has been such a time and place.

One consequence of these truths is that the subject matter imposes a discipline of its own, establishing what may and may not be said about particular issues, and that sometimes conflicts with a teacher's socially conscientious drives. The discipline cannot then be thrown away or ignored. On the other hand, almost every such discipline consists of a lot of totems and taboos with only a traditional or historical validity, which need to be interpreted before they become true here and now. Such discipline is, after all, not the product of the subject matter but of the passion for that, and it can and must be modulated, indeed modified, in each generation, by someone sufficiently in love with the subject to have the authority to do so.

But still it must be a passion for the subject matter, not for its social function; otherwise we shall get, in literature for instance, work that touches the book in question only at predetermined points, in predetermined ways, and gives us no sense of discovering it anew from within. Moreover, there must be discipline within the college and school, connecting the students to the teachers, and giving the initiative in classroom matters clearly to the latter. The recent fashion for handing that initiative as much as possible over to the students weakens effective teaching. So does the recent rash of innovations, alternatives, and variations in the curriculum. I believe even that some version of academic seclusion and exclusiveness is necessary—some social space between the university and the heart of society, to give a social dimension to the intellectual separation of the critic.

Such ideas are somewhat out of fashion today. Of course, they already exist as facts, in the form of the privileges and the conventions of the teaching profession. But that is not their best form: those facts do not express those ideas. At the moment, the privileges and conventions seem only like the trappings of some surviving feudalism or monasticism, like escapes from the duties and exertions other members of society have to face, like *inherited* privileges and *pompous* conventions. And they seem so because they are so, and will be, as long as teachers are not inspired by a positive passion for instruction and criticism. Reform is certainly necessary, but in the form of renewal, not revolution.

Thus I think that education has a social function. I think that teaching only becomes an exciting profession—only becomes what it should always be—when it makes much of that function. I think a society is only healthy when it has an educational system which practices criticism as I have defined it. But, on the other hand, that function must remain secondary; and the biggest threat I have seen to education in recent years has come from people who wanted to exalt that function to primacy and betray the intellectual passion.

One last word. I have been talking all along as if there were one "ideal" teacher involved in these questions; as if I were describing all men in one. In fact, of course, there are thousands of people involved in teaching college English alone, and I am describing what I think they as a group should do. I am perfectly happy to see lots of my colleagues come to choices unlike my own, as long as I don't feel that the profession as a whole has made such a choice. I am perfectly happy having some colleagues who teach in bland or grim indifference to the social function of education; and others who are political extremists and prepare favorite pupils for careers of heroic danger. I am happy to have both kinds of dissent, so long as I can persuade myself that my own position is the *central* one, the one that holds the rest together.

Epilogue

The second passage from *Mirror for Anglo-Saxons:*

Therefore what we need is a body of men, both fully democratic, un-aristocratic in sensibility, and still fully convinced of the values of the few, in key cultural positions, who might there form a sort of heart, a central ganglion of that mind. These men, if any, will make democracy possible. Where shall we find them?

In England, the only possibility attests the impossibility . . . .

In America? In America, it seems to me, one meets people who combine a simplicity and solidity of temperament with a genuinely adventurous mind, and sufficient shrewdness and self-confidence to keep them from disaster. And one finds them in the sort of place where they can do most good—teaching Freshman English Composition at the universities, for instance. At their best their keynote is a sort of determined ambition, a half-amused realization of being out on a limb, perilously separated from the mass. They have, in their personal and group past, all the huge unredeemed populace. Their ambition for the future has been, until they met it, education, culture, gentlemanliness. Now, as a satisfactory present and future, they have only each other, only more isolated fragments. It is up to them to make a new world; to explain and excuse to their parents and cousins and friends and pupils their differentness; to make the practical decisions that follow from their new insights, the votes, the agitations, the sympathies and apathies, palatable and influential in their communities.

Reference

Green, Martin. *Mirror for Anglo-Saxons.* New York: Harper, 1960.

4
Toward a Critical Reading of Reality

Peter Brooks

The Overburdened Schools

I have just spent a year in France, and my children a year in French schools. I was struck, as any American parent must have been, by the extent to which the learning process in which they were engaged was defined as acquisition of knowledge—represented by a growing number of carefully inscribed (and graded) notebook pages, by the memorization of poems, and of phonetic and grammatical rules. I was also struck by the extent to which the process of accultura- tion and socialization which they underwent passed through an apprenticeship to what we traditionally think of as "culture," particularly the national culture. School offered, that is, an accultura- tion in no way independent of mastery of the traditional elements of culture; with, as corollary, no questioning of the idea that schooling is the initiation in culture and the tools for its understanding, and need be nothing more. If it is true that in recent years the idea of education as transmission of the cultural heritage has come under attack in Western Europe, the demand of the critics has in essence been for an enlarged definition of culture, freeing it from its close identification with the intellectual past of the upper bourgeoisie, opening it to the complex demands and experiences of contemporary society. The basic notion that culture, and particularly its epistemological tools, is the proper province of education has not been at issue. A consequence of this conception of education, it appears to me, is the much more limited sphere of activity and responsibility assigned to school in France as compared to America. In France there is far less of a demand that schools be inclusive of "life," that they replicate its situations and solve its problems, that they provide total nurture. School is surrounded by a host of supporting institutions—sports clubs, musical groups, political societies, church groups—that supplement its rather stark definition of itself. One could argue about the specifics of some of these arrangements; what interests me here is the symbolism that emerges. School is resolutely school; the affective problems of socialization, the ideals of citizenship, the definitions of self in society do not fall within its purview. And no doubt partly as a consequence, the level of anxiety associated with the problem of education in America is infinitely lower in France.

Education in America has come to appear more and more the institutional expression of national anxieties. The schools stand at the tension-laden frontier between the ideal and the actual, responsible both for indoctrination in the one and training in the other. The pervasive democratic demand for a citizenry enlightened and enabled to participate in the affairs of the Republic through an education that both prepares them for "life" and raises their sights to life's "values" has placed a tremendous burden of responsibility on the schools, one that has probably grown intolerable as the gap between ideal and real has become more apparent, the myth of homogeneous values and goals more and more radically put into question. Paradoxically, and dangerously, as the society has become less and less sure of its consensus and its direction, it has asked the schools to do more and more both in mastering reality and in ameliorating it. Socialization by the school has been situated between an inadequate reality and an undefined future (with a nostalgia for a lost past). In the absence of any agreement on a core culture, or the school's mandate to transmit culture, acculturation has been assigned the impossible task of creating what it must convey, subsisting on the faith of a future coming-into-being of what it attempts to transmit. Education has been overburdened by the weight of aspiration.

Confronted with the force of an unmastered reality, it is close to collapse through anxiety.

The irreconcilable tensions that beset American education are in fact sensible in the document I received last April describing the Southampton Summer Sequences. As the "key assumption" of that document, it is stated that "neither educators nor the schools they staff can reform society," and that " 'reforming the schools' . . . will not greatly improve the education of our people" since the schools "are only a reflection of the larger forces controlling all our institutions." Then, a few pages later, we read that "Public schools have a mandate of a sort to see that young people are humanistically oriented and prepared to function as effective citizens in a democratic society," which is followed by the query, what is needed "to define (or even to develop) behavior appropriate to democratic society?" The statements pull in contradictory directions. The contradictions turn in part on the cosmic question of whether we in fact live in a democratic society that has any use for humanistic orientations. But they also point to the more specific paradox of asking schools to fulfill such a democratic and humanistic "mandate" while at the same time pronouncing them to be merely a reflection of large social forces, hence powerless to choose their mandate and powerless to provide through their own transformation a leverage on social change. The paradox is fundamental; American education has to some degree always been built upon its shaky basis, and today is agonizingly flawed by it. If the second set of statements—education's "mandate"— belongs to a tradition of liberal optimism that seems sadly inadequate today, the first, the "key assumption," seems to me too bleakly pessimistic, too much a depressive reaction to the manic hopes placed on education in the recent past. We know that the schools cannot directly transform society; and that schools, like any social institution, must reflect the state of the society. I nonetheless believe that there is a role to be played by formal education in dialectical relationship to the society, and that the proper definition of that role, and reform of what it is in the power of the educational complex to reform, can make a difference. I fear that in its sophisticated awareness of the interdependencies of school and society, a sector of progressive thought has talked itself into an unnecessary and retrograde abandonment of the idea of formal education.

We must ask a form of the question posed by the Stoics: What does it lie within the schools' power to perform, and hence to reform? We must then relinquish the effort to manipulate through the schools what lies outside their direct grasp. This seems to me the precondition to a release of the schools from the sense of anxiety and impotence wrought by the overburden of responsibility. We need to recognize that while education is a limitless domain and a continuing process composed of countless forces and experiences beyond the walls of the school, there is nonetheless something that can rightly be called "formal education" that has a vital role to play within certain limits. It is in drawing its limits—as the term "formal" implies—that its role can become clearer and stronger. The beginnings of a "solution" to the problems of the schools may have to start from their partial withdrawal from the social battlefield, their definition of their function and ambition in more limited, which also means more concentrated terms. This would imply their abandonment of the pretension to total nurture, and all the arrangements, curricular and institutional, that make the schools totalistic in a sense no longer tolerated by American society. In turn, this might mean the creation of any number of supporting paraeducational units around the schools, supplementing formal education and assuring the schools' freedom to pursue their central task.

I think that many university teachers who experienced the student upheavals of the late 1960s came to feel that the sins of the university often lay not so much in its failure to reach out to cover more realms of experience, to address and replicate more of the problems of "life," but on the contrary in its pretension to be what it was not, in the implication that it was microcosm of all the experiences, activities, commitments that lay outside itself. The view of the dissident students here was ambiguous: their analysis charged the university with failing to grapple with the real problems of society, yet simultaneously noted the university's lapses from fidelity to its own values and goals. I found the dissidents sympathetic to the argument that the university would do best to set aside its overweening ambition to total nurture of the souls in its charge, and to proclaim aloud instead that a university was equipped only to do certain things well; that these things should by no means be considered the totality of life or even of education; that the reasons for the university's existence, and for the students' presence there, were specific, having largely to do with matters cognitive, and the university experience should thus be accepted as partial, *sui generis*, and validated by criteria other than the replication of life and society. The dissident students were, I think, ready to accept a somewhat austere image of the university, for in this light it made sense as the place to form a dialectical critique of the real. Whereas a university that was too resolutely in the world, that promised direct access from its exercises to the manipulation of social realities, was from the outset compromised, the critical edge of its thinking blunted.

This particular analogy to higher education may hold some truth for the schools caught between their status as "reflection" of large social forces beyond their control and their "mandate" to educate for humanism and democracy. For if in this bind the freedom of the schools is clearly limited, the area of their freedom may lie in the same domain as it does for the university: the domain of fundamental cognitive tools and experiences. Through a retreat from some of its total ambitions, through a rededication to a minimal concern with cognitive fundamentals, education could strengthen itself both from within and from without. By renouncing a direct engagement with the pressures of social reality, it could become more truly the place for dialectical understanding of reality. The image of "withdrawal" need not mean that the schools be "closed" to the community, but it would necessarily entail a commitment to certain essential elements of curriculum conceived as relatively untouchable absolutes. On the other hand, all that the schools renounced handling might well be given over to parallel institutions (noninstitutions) directly under the control of the community, and characterized by a high degree of responsiveness and fluidity. This vision can be extended to the very concrete facilities: a school less totalistic in ambition than what we have now would not need to appear so threateningly close to a prison. Surely the mere size and physical vastness of our high schools, and the necessity for literal or figurative policing of all the activities carried on there, constitutes a major negative inducement to education. A narrowly defined school could be smaller, more subdivided, and make smaller claims on its students' total lives.

I am aware of some of the objections that come first to mind. Our schools, and our society, show no real consensus even as to the basic cognitive tools and how to teach them. And the image of a "withdrawal" may seem to make no sense when confronted with the fact of children dispossessed by American society, with their frustration, their injuries, their rage. In the face of such realities, one is tempted to heap scorn on talk about a core intellectual function of the schools. Yet I think it would be irresponsible simply to abandon the notion and to retreat to the more comfortable, currently persuasive, realms of sociological tinkering and general systems analysis. The idea and the fact of a curriculum, of training, of development and testing of the mind's capacities have brought us too far for us to give them up without the effort to rethink their possible meaning today.

Language as Power

In my experience as a college teacher, I have become more and more persuaded of the continuity of my function with the students' schooling from the very start, a continuity which comes down to the teaching of reading. I have, that is, become more and more convinced that, at my point in the educational process, I can really teach no more than reading; that I can of course do it best when it has been well done in the student's earlier education; and that the primary and continuing task in education really need have no other definition, and no other ambition, than the teaching of reading. By reading, I mean in the broadest sense training in the self-conscious manipulation of human sign-systems. This seems to me the absolute precondition of any grip on reality, any movement from impotence to mastery.

"Reading" covers the ability to decipher and interpret the messages transmitted through linguistic codes, from, on the most basic level, simple English sentences, to all the symbolic systems that man has invented. To be deprived of the ability to read is to be deprived of the primary leverage of human consciousness on the world around it, hence condemned to a position of frustration and exploitation. Our movement into a world where media of communication and propaganda other than the printed word become dominant only makes reading in the largest sense more important. The question of who controls and manipulates whom is more than ever a question of who owns and most effectively uses the word and the sign. The ability to read, interpret, and evaluate words, signs, and symbolic patterns—all based on the structure of language—is the very precondition of freedom. Only through the capacity to read the messages, benign or corrupt, proposed by the ambient society can one be in the position to judge and to choose in freedom. Only through the mastery of language, an understanding of the code and the messages formed from it, can the individual mind assert its resistance to the oppressive weight of "reality," and its transformative role in the world.

A massive concentration of resources on the elementary steps of reading seems to me the clear first imperative of any central curriculum. A renewed faith in the importance of the task might be created by a greater awareness, shared by teachers and pupils, of what language is and is for. Far from interfering with the teaching of the skill, a higher level of awareness of how language can be put to use should confer a greater urgency on the process. Along with the elementary mastery of the English language, one can begin to develop an awareness of other elementary sign-systems: road signs, for instance, or patterns of clothing, or the arrangement of pictorial signs in newspaper and magazine advertising. All of these are, like language, symbolic systems that have been invented by man to order and make sense of his world. They all have some sort of implicit "code" (to use the terms of linguistics) from which specific "messages" are formed. They have, in loose fashion, a syntax, and imply a grammar. Their symbols often have, like words, a primary level of denotation and a secondary level of connotation. What is most important to demonstrate is that all messages can be read—if one knows how to read them. Hence "learning to read" in school is, and should explicitly be, learning the tools which enable one to understand and to manipulate social realities. "The world is before us like a text to be deciphered," wrote Paul Claudel; it is, provided one has the tools to decipher it. From the elementary exercises of reading, one can and ought to move toward the critical reading of reality. It is here that "formal education" finds its dialectical position in regard to all the rest of education, the rest of life.

What I have been saying implies that initiation in reading at all levels must proceed with a certain degree of self-consciousness. This may sound elaborate and academic in terms of a school system where an alarming percentage of children never become functional readers at all. Yet it may be the only way to make the apprenticeship in reading important and worthwhile. Let me try to justify this through an excursus on what I have had direct experience of, the college curriculum. I came to believe a few years ago that the college-level teaching of literature had lost much of its force and its pertinence because it behaved as if the fundamental, the radical questions subjacent to the study of literature had been answered for all time. One proceeded with the study of a canon or an institution—the Epic Tradition, say, or English Literature in the Victorian Age—without ever providing a way to address, with the students, the questions: What is literature? Why do we have it, or need it? Why have men in all times and places made up stories? What function do they serve? We needed to turn our assumptions into questions, to reproblematize the objects of our attention. To see the range of the problem, it became useful to look beyond the confines of what is normally admitted under the head of literature, and to use the more inclusive term of "fictions," which from its Latin root (*fingere:* to fabricate, to feign) had the advantage of pointing to our two related senses of the "made-up." The range of fictions that one could study then extended over detective stories, comic books, advertising, political propaganda, day-dreaming, myths, riddles, TV serials, as well as Shakespeare. This gave an opportunity to perceive the constants in all fictions, which then could be followed by discriminations concerning their nature and kind, and it directed attention to the activity of fiction-making as a daily, normal, even indispensable element in man's life.

In our class discussions and analyses, we were repeatedly returned to a kind of basic situation: that man is consciousness in a world of nonconsciousness. He is different from what he lives amidst. His sense of difference is his self-consciousness, his awareness of his oddity in nature. He is hence obliged to use his sense of difference to process the world, to say its meaning to him and his meaning to it. This "processing" may take many different forms—the miniature replication of the world in model railroads, the re-forming of natural bodies in sculpture, the regulated replay of life situations in games—all of which tend to assert the grip of mind on things, its leverage on reality. Most basic of these forms, and to them, is language itself, our basic sign-system, a kind of made-up parallel world by which man names the phenomenal world, orders it, turns it into something that his mind can talk of, and hence master. In Adam's naming of the animals as they pass before him in Eden we have the emblem of man's necessary appropriation of the world through the sign-system, his transference of things into a medium—language—in which they signify, can be made to assume significant relationships, can be re-ordered and manipulated. We "make up" in order to "make sense of," and what we make up first of all is a language, which then opens the way to all sorts of other languages. Language is man's mark of meaning on nature. He can usefully be defined as *homo signiferens*, the bearer of sense-making sign-systems (see Brooks 1973).

As the English psychoanalyst D. W. Winnicott (1971) has argued, there is an area of experience neither wholly inner nor outer, subjective nor objective, but partaking of both, that is vital to personal growth and self-realization: the area of play. The capacity to play depends on our capacity to manipulate symbols, to move them around, recombine them, to entertain and explore the fictions of the world recreated through symbols. An awareness of the importance of play must lead to a recognition of the place of human symbolization and fiction making, its function as the basis of man's sense of freedom. To paraphrase Nietzsche, we need fictions in order not to die of the truth. And when we are aware simultaneously of our need for fictions and their nature and status, we are better able to exercise criticism toward those fictions which society or the state try to erect into myth, that is, into an all-encompassing, all-explaining "sacred" fiction, be it "the master race" or "national security." The critical reader of human fictions is in a position to resist the reductive, dehumanizing myths of reality.

I see nothing that prevents the teaching of an awareness of the function of human sign- and sense-making on the most elementary level, particularly in conjunction with the first self-conscious use of a sign-system, that is, learning to read and write. Elementary mastery of the sign-system can include playful manipulation of its components—not play that is extrinsic to the sign-system itself, an external coating of the pill, but that rather goes to its very nature, to show how the selective and combinatory axes of language function. Modern linguistics has more and more demonstrated the gamelike operation of language, and there is no reason to think that a primary level of linguistic exploration could not be present in the study of language from the start. Far from complicating the early stages of reading and writing, a consciousness of the reformatory, fictional, make-up possibilities of language should make the process more vital and important. The major point, I think, is that emphasis always fall on manipulation, on play as mastery, on the individual's capacity,

within the rules of the game, to invent and to create. The sense of
exclusion and frustration that often characterizes children faced
with learning to read and write can perhaps in some measure be
overcome by self-consciousness about the use of language, explorations of how and why man "made it up," and what you can do with
it. This implies on the practical level a constant accompaniment of
reading by writing, the most concrete demonstration of the play
possibilities of language. It might also imply the use of children's own
invented "nonsense" languages, and of course a constant reaching
toward analogies in other sign-systems, including those of computers
and the media. Use could possibly also be made of all the idioms and
dialects of spoken American English on the basis of their play with
the "standard" language.

To the extent that such a pedagogy of play with sign-systems
implies a previous apprenticeship of the spoken language, it no doubt
entails a greater emphasis in kindergarten and preschool on verbal
language games—a consequence we should embrace, since surely if
millions of Americans are to move out of their position of exploitation and impotence, the stakes must be set on the earliest possible
ages. My point is essentially and repeatedly this: if the schools can
teach such an awareness and manipulation of language, its uses and
possibilities, its *raison d'être* as man's stamp of meaning on the
world, his trace in nature, they need teach nothing else. Language is
our most significant sign-system, our most important tool to the
mastery of reality; it is inherent to our definition of civilized man;
and its mastery is the precondition of everything else.

"Everything else" is first of all the range of other sign-systems,
whether of mathematics, physics, computers, the cinema, whatever.
The central trunk of our contemporary "tree of knowledge," I would
maintain, can only be what in recent years we have learned to call
"semiotics," or the general science of signs. Semiotics is conceivably
what our society has elaborated that may best replace the earlier
organizations of teaching around a trivium or quadrivium or (at a
later date) around the evolution of species and genres. Semiotics
responds to the observed situation that man in the world finds meaning in things, and finds it by creating it through his signs for things.
Semiotics addresses itself to the nature and process of this meaning,
to ask from what materials and in what forms it is constituted.
Possibly, then, it offers the best basis and point of convergence for
what we most need to know and to teach.

This is not to suggest that our teachers, at any level, have to become professional semioticians, or to master the more abstruse questions addressed by modern linguistics and related fields. It is, however, to propose that a certain level of self-consciousness about language and its workings is necessary to pedagogy from first grade through graduate school, and that a teacher of any discipline needs to be aware of the peculiar nature and status of the "metalanguage"— the language about language—that he uses, its rules and possibilities, and its relation to other forms of discourse. The training of teachers and the retraining of those who teach them remain—whatever the shortcomings of the TTT Program—vital areas. One may suggest that here, too, there has been an overburdening with the anxieties of the society, an overinvestment in low-grade psychotherapy and communications theory, that calls for correction with a narrower concentration on the uses of sign-systems, a concern that necessarily implicates both subject matter and method. In part, the "professionalism" that marks all the upper reaches of our educational system must be put into question: professionalism comes to mean following, as the path of least resistance, the assumptions and the behavioral patterns set by the profession as corporation—its leaders, organizations, publications—which in turn means a refusal to address the radical questions, both of one's field and of the classroom. Equally, topical and thematic "relevance" as a superficial solution to the problems of student interest and commitment must be resisted, and particularly must be set aside by the new generation of textbooks in favor of a reworking of fundamentals made interesting in terms of their own problematics. This implies a mobilization of the country's best original thinkers for planning of curriculum and texts, a task that I believe could only be performed through an immensely strengthened Office of Education, a true Ministry of Education that could employ creative leaders from all spheres for terms of service, could propose model programs and standards. Since the concerns of the schools would be more narrowly defined, this would not impinge upon community control of all the ancillary functions of education, particularly its roles in socialization, which is probably what the community most wants to control.

Redefining the Role of Schools

American education, like American thought in general, is tyrannized by the sociological mind. No decision can be made without polls and studies, no program can be continued without evaluation, inevitably premature, no theory can be tested without immediate assessment or, at worst, preliminary cost-benefit analysis. That so many pilot programs should have been scrapped before they could possibly work changes in the human spirit is one consequence of our passivity before the measurers and accountants. That major recent studies of higher education—the Carnegie Commission reports, Parsons' and Platt's *The American University* (1973)—should present their visions of the future purely on the basis of an institutional analysis, analysis of current trends and forces, is another. To sociology, systems analysis, and cost-benefit decision making, we need to oppose philosophy, by which I mean simply hard, imaginative thinking about education and what we most want it to do. Among the many causes contributing to the pessimism of the Southampton Program's "key assumption" is no doubt the failure of a certain American liberalism, represented by the "best and the brightest" and the holocausts they created in the name of presumed ideals. The failure of liberal solutions and ideals may lead one to seek refuge in the study of social systems and behavioral processes as the best means to assure change. Yet such study cannot point the direction of change; this can come only from critical, philosophical scrutiny. We must not, then, abandon the ideal of intellectual and critical mastery, both as a goal for education and in the analysis of education.

I come back to what I described as the contradictions of the document presenting this conference: its pessimism about the results of reforming education, its ritual gestures toward humanism and democracy. We are all aware that we cannot have a truly admirable education until American society becomes more just and more free. Only in a society that desires the realization of human potential can there be an educational system really designed to liberate. Yet in the meanwhile—a meanwhile that may last a long time—there is an irreducibly important role to be played by formal education, a role that is not going to be fulfilled by the parallel school of life, by encounter groups, the media, community organizations, a role that would be sacrificed, at too great cost, if we were really to deschool society. What formal education can teach is language, the tools for a critical reading of reality. It can teach the elements of a dialectical relationship with the demands of reality. Hence the schools themselves can stand in a critical dialectical relationship to all the other educative experiences of life. But they can do so only if they define their function around a hard core of cognitive concern in which they believe and which they are, by their nature, equipped to deal with.

The discouragement legible in the Southampton Program's "key assumption" testifies to a disillusion born of our overweening ambitions for education. We have all lived in the characteristically American expectation that right education of the children will absolve the sins committed by the parents, particularly those of social and racial inequality and exclusion. But the beginnings of salvation for the schools may emerge only when we begin to understand concomitantly that direct solutions of social problems are indeed beyond the reach of the schools, and yet, that there is an area of human progress and liberation that formal schooling can address. When liberal thought has reached such overt discouragements, we near a situation where the idea and justification of formal education seem threatened with imminent collapse under the weight of bad conscience. We need to reaffirm the importance of formal education rightly—narrowly— conceived, to encourage those engaged in it, to unburden their task, to provide them with visible goals and leadership.

References

Brooks, Peter. "Man and His Fictions: One Approach to the Teaching of Literature." *College English* 35, no. 1 (October 1973).

Carnegie Commission on Higher Education. *Reports.* New York: McGraw-Hill. See also Donald McDonald's critique in *The Center Magazine* VI, no. 5 (September/October 1973).

Parsons, Talcott, and Platt, Gerald. *The American University.* Cambridge, Mass.: Harvard University Press, 1973. See also Peter Brooks' review in *The New York Times Book Review* (December 9, 1973).

Winnicott, D. W. *Playing and Reality.* London: Tavistock, 1971.

5

The Universal Curriculum

Page Smith

I suspect it could be shown (and probably has been) that all systems of education from the tribe to far more complex civilizations have grown out of and rested on the religious beliefs of the societies of which such systems or principles were a part. Whether we are talking about the initiation rights of a simple nomadic people or about the great universities of the Arabic or Western World, all "educational" ventures have been originally conceived of as a means of discovering and stating the ultimate truths which gave order, coherence, and meaning to a particular society. Education was not something for the individual but the passing on of values and attitudes considered essential by the society. It was not the disinterested pursuit of truth; it was the means of survival.

The Reformation, as derived from Calvin, was the basis of education in America: to know and to do God's will, to know God's will by reason and revelation unclouded by ignorance and superstition.

It followed that the curriculum was shaped and given its purpose by these ultimate ends. The community could not escape worldliness and corruption unless the young were taught those truths which confirmed and authenticated the society. The actual content of the curriculum was incidental. Or, to put it another way, the curriculum was simply the bearer of the community's values.

By the end of the nineteenth century the curriculum had become secularized. It had broken away from its origins in Reformed Christianity and been established as a separate, independent value, as a procedure by which people were trained in *skills* and *techniques*. Values of course still dominated the curriculum, but they were now practical, secular values: good citizenship, getting ahead, Americanism, etc. The system of primary and secondary education, moreover, had so much momentum that it carried its subjects—the pupils—along with it for several generations. In the face of waves of immigration it also performed a vitally important socializing role, but it appears in retrospect that the assumptions on which it had originally been based withered away and were replaced in rather random fashion by an odd amalgam of ideas, values, and practices which had very little coherence.

All of this is familiar enough. It seems increasingly clear that the basic institutions of contemporary American society are in an advanced state of demoralization and, perhaps, of disintegration. Education, one of those institutions, is obviously suffering from the same disease that has affected all other institutions.

This abbreviated tour of the educational scene, past and present, brings me to a question first posed by my colleague, Norman O. Brown: Is a secular education possible? If, as we have suggested, all methods, procedures, or systems of education have had their origin in the religious doctrines of a society, one is inclined to speculate at least that secularization must bring with it disenchantment and confusion as to the real nature and purpose of education. From this proposition follow two obvious conclusions. One is that we have reached a new stage in human development where reason unencumbered by superstition (religion) is able to take over and guide society. Thus the primacy of religious values in education need (and should) no longer be true. This proposition is, in fact, the one that has dominated the educational scene since the latter decades of the of the nineteenth century. Perhaps it is the only option available to a "pluralistic" society. Be that as it may, it is plain enough that American education is at present in a sad muddle and this conference is evidence of that fact.

The other conclusion is, of course, that any genuine education is impossible in this particular era and that we have no choice but to struggle along until some new "order" with a new or renewed set of religious imperatives emerges in the name of which education can be once more given direction, order, and coherence.

There is another possibility, however, and that is that there is a still largely unexplored territory between "knowledge" and "skills"— between essential truths and simple mechanics—and that this territory needs to be mapped.

At this point two further things need to be said. One is that education is a process that cannot be separated into stages called "elementary school," "secondary school," and "college" or "higher education." A large part of our problem stems from the fact that we insist on talking about these three parts of a single process as though they were independent entities. Thus we speak about the reform of higher education, secondary education, primary education, as though these were autonomous or semi-autonomous entities (as unfortunately they seem to be in our society). And different people talk about the reform of these different entities. It seems to me a simple enough proposition to say that until we all talk about the reform of education as though it was part of a single continuous process we will get nowhere. Subjecting students to three separate kinds of sequential educational experience, each dominated by a different philosophy, is clearly preposterous.

The second point I wish to make is that the American university as we know it today took shape in the period after the secularization of education. It thus embodied secularism in an extreme form. Where important residues of the earlier religiously oriented education lingered on in the atmosphere if not the curriculum of elementary and secondary schools (represented by such notions as making good citizens of the students), the college and university became centers of "value-free," "scientific" research and teaching. Any possible coherence was destroyed by innumerable specialized "courses" which were represented as containing the truth or truths—now scientific and scholarly rather than religious—of a particular field or discipline. The new dogmatism was as rigid as the old and, what is more, it was disintegrative rather than unifying—a thousand independent dogmas instead of one. The shift was, among other things, from morality to what we might call "operationalism," from what was right to how things worked.

The only problem was, as it turned out, things did not work that way. Outside of the area of "natural sciences" the new, value-free, scientific scholarship proved, if anything, less capable of explaining and shaping the world of human beings than the old humanistic-religious scholarship.

What I wish to emphasize is that the domination of our common intellectual life by the colleges and universities with their "system of orthodoxies," as rigid as those of any religious zealots, affected every level of the educational experience in the United States. What thus developed was, in fact, a highly segmented educational "system" or nonsystem that was held together, not by a dominant philosophy directed toward certain clearly perceived and generally agreed-upon goals, but by a nightmare of often conflicting philosophies and assumptions. Elementary school became increasingly preoccupied with shaping a "creative individual," the secondary school avowed its intention of producing a "good citizen" (which more and more gave way under the pressure of preparing students to be admitted to the college or university). The university, or multiversity, prided itself on disinterested, objective scholarship, on advancing "the frontiers of knowledge," or serving the practical needs of the larger society for trained experts in a wide variety of fields.

It was thus in the area of higher education that the disintegration of traditional values proceeded at the most rapid rate. Along with their system of orthodoxies, the colleges and universities (the universities were the real culprits, the colleges tagged along behind for the most part) exercised absolute tyranny over secondary education by prescribing what high school students must study (and how they must study it) in order to be admitted to college.

Put another way, the specialized graduate education developed by the universities determined the nature of undergraduate education (segments of specialized knowledge encapsulated in "courses"). Undergraduate education became, increasingly, a by-product of graduate education (and a generally neglected by-product). The nature of undergraduate education determined the nature of secondary education while elementary education turned increasingly into a kind of playground where, it was hoped, a "creativity" might be planted in the students that was strong enough to resist the debilitating effects of the arid zones ahead.

It is necessary to state these propositions in order to even begin to talk about the reform of education on all levels.

Leaving aside for the time being the question of whether the assertions are true, let us consider what might follow from them if they are. We must agree, for example, that reform of education should start from the bottom rather than be dominated from the top. I believe graduate education to be so thoroughly discredited at this moment that we can safely turn our backs on it. Thus we can free ourselves of the notion, stated or unstated, that the goal of "lower" education is to prepare students, ultimately and ideally, for graduate school. Next we can ask ourselves what do we, inhabitants of the United States, need to know in order to exist in a modern industrial, technological society? How, for example, can we become reasonably independent once more? Interdependent we must be but wholly dependent we need not be.

The second question I would pose is: Assuming we cannot tolerate an educational process devoid of any "ordering principle," what principle of order can we discover around which a so-called curriculum can be constructed? Ideally, this principle of order should be one that can start in first grade (or kindergarten) and be extended through graduate study.

Ideally, again, it would be a religious principle, such as to know and serve God better. But since that is manifestly impossible, we must find some other "principle of order." I propose one such principle; certainly there must be others. My principle is based on the need to bring education at once to the most direct and practical concerns of our daily life. Therefore, I would establish the study of law and medicine as the ordering principles of my educational system. My reasons are as follows: Law and medicine are continuous experiences; that is, the individual is acted upon and acts through law and medicine from his or her earliest consciousness. Law is simply the principle that there must be order in human groups from the family outward to nations. Law is experienced by the child in the family, by the citizen in the community. It comprehends politics (the means by which law is enacted), society, theology, economy, even, if you will, psychology—all the social studies. It appears, perhaps most strikingly, in the area of the dramatic arts. Law is the point at which all the complex relationships and forces of society are defined. The study of law is thus an organizing or ordering principle of, at once, the most practical and the most abstract and theoretical kind. It is, therefore, ideally suited to be taught progressively—that is, according to the development of the understanding and intellectual sophistication of the student, from the first grade through the last, whatever the last may be. The study of morality and ethics is, of course, an essential part of the law, not to mention history and anthropology. Through the study of law, abstract problems are rendered practical and comprehensible and practical problems are lifted out of the realm of the mundane and related to larger human issues.

With medicine the case is much the same. At certain points, indeed, law and medicine intersect. The young child is preoccupied with his or her body. Typically, he or she wishes to play "doctor" as a cover for this developing interest. Medicine is the human science which includes biology and psychology, chemistry and physics. By studying all these subjects as they relate to medicine (that is, to the health of the human organism) their conventional treatment as separate disciplines is overcome and many of the ethical problems connected with certain fields of scientific investigation (such as genetics) are, if not entirely avoided, at least brought within a specifically human frame of reference.

Another reason to make law and medicine the ordering principles of a new system of education is that both these great studies have been sadly abused in our era by their practitioners. Law (as witness Watergate) has been corrupted by being placed at the service of those willing to pay preposterous prices to have use of it for selfish purposes. Medicine has enriched its practitioners at the expense of their patients and is on the verge of becoming a nightmare for low-income Americans. Like law, it must be reformed for the good of the society. That is not, of course, the reason for placing law and medicine at the center of the new curriculum. They can be justified in their own terms. But it is certainly true that we must free ourselves of the tyranny of these overprofessionalized fields.

With law and medicine as the central disciplines of the curriculum, the rest can be highly unstructured. If independence from a technological society is a proper aim, a number of other subjects present themselves at once—motor mechanics and electrical engineering, plumbing and carpentry, horticulture, animal husbandry, elementary aeronautics, seamanship, communications, mountain and wilderness training.

Then, finally, there are the most important studies of all, the life-enhancing studies: dance, music, drama, pottery, painting, sculpture, architecture, arithmetic, story-telling, poetry.

In the new curriculum there are perhaps no school buildings at all. Or a complex of buildings used by five different schools on five different days. Education without walls or with a bare minimum of technical facilities (laboratories, studios, etc.) *must* come. Most of the education under the universal curriculum will take place in the community in which the student lives and without benefit of courses and credits. Old people, middle-aged people, young people, and children are all involved together in the educational process.

While law and medicine have "a curriculum," students master it at their own pace. In most of the other subjects students learn the rudiments and then continue or not as their interests and talents dictate.

The Universal Curriculum would seem wildly Utopian were it not for two facts: education is becoming ruinously expensive in the United States, and fewer and fewer people—students, teachers, or parents—feel that its accomplishments are worth its cost.

As to the question of whether the Universal Curriculum is presented as a serious alternative to the present unwieldy and deeply entrenched system of public education in the United States, I can only say that it is at least a point from which the existing system can be viewed and criticized; it thus serves as a means of engaging the subject. But beyond that, I believe that the Universal Curriculum could be easily and inexpensively initiated on an experimental basis. Only then could one begin to speak with confidence about whether it (or any other curriculum) can withstand the general intellectual and moral confusion of this period of history.

The prospectus of Project Open lists several questions for consideration. The first is: In an ideal society, what would be the social role of education? I have no truck with ideal societies, but it should be clear by now that in healthy and vigorous societies the "social role" of education is to teach what in the view of the society *must be learned* in order for the society to survive. The *must be learned* is crucial here (as opposed to what *may* be learned; what is interesting to learn; what leads to self-expression, creativity, etc.). The ultimate ends of a society have traditionally been expressed in its religion; however, we clearly cannot acquire the comprehensive religious faith that would give coherence to our education by wishing for it. Therefore, we must do the next best thing and seek, as we have said, "a principle of order" as representing at least a common goal and a substantial measure of unity. The moral issues will, of course, reassert themselves once we have stopped trying to exclude them in the name of value-free science.

One thing further may be said. Any new vision of education must be, in its essence, international. It should not be filled with pious observations about universal brotherhood (nor should it be hostile to or neglectful of one's own national tradition); it should take for granted that we are all part of an international community in the process of becoming, and everything taught should be taught from that perspective. I find it a sobering irony that this vision of our membership in a true international community, which transcends and makes all nationalisms look warped and parochial, is probably being transmitted most powerfully in Huey Newton's Intercommunal Youth Institute in Oakland, California, to a handful of black children. The school's philosophy is dominated by Newton's own unique brand of Marxism-cum-Christianity, and it is full of vitality and hope, more so than any school I have visited in recent years. Perhaps we need to attend the free schools being taught here and there around the country by radical blacks and chicanos. Maybe in these remarkable ventures we will begin to understand the requirements of a new education. I would certainly like to plant the Universal Curriculum in such soil.

6

Toward a System
of Complementary Schools

Theodore Sizer

My child goes to school.

Why not, my child goes to *schools*? Why must a child go to but one school at a time?

One gives up great variety by providing but one place and one staff for the formal education that society provides for each child. One also flies in the face of common sense, as the arguments for serving children concurrently with a diversity of schools are numerous and persuasive.

A pedagogical catchword today is "options," and the right of students and parents to have them, and to choose among them. However, most would have us select one option from a number. Why not arrange affairs so that a child could select two or three options simultaneously from a somewhat larger number?

The arguments for a system of complementary schools of varied character which, when put together for an individual child, are more effective than the sum of their parts, can be made from the perspectives both of politics and of pedagogy (which itself is a rare event).

First, a brief digression into the politics of education, and what troubles Americans about their schools.

The Politics of Variety

Scratch a citizen today to find the word that best describes the current state of American schools and he'll likely bleed, "busing." If you had scratched him in 1959, he would have bled "Sputnik." In 1965, the code word would have been "the disadvantaged." Given the dispersed and highly political nature of American elementary and secondary education, such slogans are frighteningly important, for public attitudes, national policy, and appropriations follow from them.

All three of these most recent code words have much behind them, of course. "Sputnik" meant a broadening of the conception of the Cold War, from a contest merely of arms to one of scientific and technological competition. The impetus was essentially optimistic, however: to make *us* wiser, better, stronger, rather than to force anyone else to be weaker. The public showed confidence in the schools, by giving them the responsibility and (albeit briefly) resources to make our children able to compete scientifically and linguistically with the Communists.

Lyndon Johnson's War on Poverty was also optimistic. Poverty was to disappear as we equipped individuals with the intellectual tools and self-respect necessary to break out of what was then thought to be a predictable cycle of disadvantagement. Schools were asked— as they often had been asked earlier—to be engines to drive the American Dream.

"Busing," however, is a code word soaked in pessimism, one signaling retreat, and it connects little with the American Dream. The root of the busing slogan is fear, fear of Americans to allow their children to associate with youngsters very different from themselves and distrust of the schools either to protect their offspring or to have any profound success at alleviating the hostility and resentment among racial, social, ethnic, and linguistic groups. Too many parents have seen too much physical and psychological violence among the young to have much confidence in the ability of understaffed schools, even if now patrolled by special police, to give their children an education.

Implicit in the urgent call for keeping the schools segregated is the assumption that the schools should try to do less than earlier conventional wisdom had preached, that they should concentrate on improving instruction in basic skills and in preparing for the world of work rather than taking on a social learning task—true integration of widely differing groups—of great difficulty and subtlety. Parents are saying, "Keep our kids where we can be near them, in classes made up of their friends, and teach them the basics." They fear an alternative, schools comprised not only of friends but also of those who may not (perhaps) be so friendly. They see "busing" as the means whereby this will take place.

With Judge Roth's Detroit decision—which would involve the suburbs with the central city in a plan to eradicate segregation—"busing" is an issue just beginning to strike the upper-middle class in suburbia. Many privileged Americans supported and still support the policy of class- and race-integrated schools as long as it is other people's children who do the integrating. In the North and rural South, the burden of school integration has, in fact, fallen disproportionately upon lower and lower-middle income families. Not surprisingly, they today seethe with resentment against the stereotypical "hip" but inconsistent suburban liberal, as Populist politicians such as Louise Day Hicks have long understood. But as the day approaches when the legal force behind school integration involves the suburbs or (as in a recent New York City decision) real estate practices, the fear and related distrust of schools has spread to a majority of the population. Provocative civil rights legislation such as Massachusetts' unique Racial Imbalance Act of 1965 is threatened, and almost surely will be changed. Suburban parents and politicians are no less fearful and distrustful than their less affluent cousins living in the city. As a result, American schools are likely to be as segregated tomorrow as they are today, and perhaps more so.

The fear of busing is justified. There *are* sharp antagonisms between youthful groups (as there are between their adult counterparts), though the clashes are provoked less by racial differences than by social class differences. Schools are poorly equipped, and teachers ill-prepared, to cope with a practical civics lesson as difficult and politicized as integration. Furthermore, the bitterness and enmities of the adults in the communities wash into the schools in ways that no educator can resist and combat. Ironically, just as the efforts to involve "the community" more fully in the day-to-day life in classrooms seems to be achieving some success, that very involvement may fatally infect the fragile structure of a socially diverse school.

How can teachers and principals who are threatened by adults expect not to be threatened by the children of those adults? The fear running in the schools is real.

However, if a national social goal is to use the schools to increase harmony among races and classes and to reduce prejudice among the population, and if there is substantial public resistance to forced integration of schools, why isn't the Solomonic solution to leave neighborhood schools as they are (for the most part segregated), and to create a complementary "system" of regional schools, which every student would attend a portion of each year, designed to foster intergroup understanding? That is, why not require a child to attend two schools at once, his neighborhood school primarily and a regional school secondarily? The public, hung up on the paradox of rhetorically supporting an integrated, open society and at the same time desiring to maintain their class, race, and group enclaves, might politically accept this middle position. Fortunately, this middle position is more than defensible pedagogically: it contains within it the seeds of an important and useful reform to improve what we offer for children.

Purposes and Pedagogy

While historical and professional literature is saggingly full of screeds on the purposes of education, three general lines of belief run strong through our culture. Formal schooling is to provide basic intellectual and social skills. Formal schooling is to provide the means of citizenship, in the sense of participation both in politics (as an intelligent voter and as a respecter of laws) and in the economy (as the secure holder of a job useful to the society). And formal schooling is to provide a sense of self-worth, of constructive individualism, of equality. To repeat: basic skills, citizenship and the means to make a living, and self-respect.

Big concepts, these—and ones easily ridiculed and pecked to death by well-meaning, myopic academic chickens. Most Americans *believe* these things, and they believe that schools should provide them. Indeed, many people (particularly those directly unaffected by the busing nightmare) believe that the existing schools provide them now.

Traditionally, three agencies were expected to meet these ends: the family, the church, and the school. Sometimes two other agencies were added: political life (the process of local government, for example, as an effective teacher of civics) and employment. Yet another agency must be added in modern times: the media, in particular television.

Again, traditionally, the school has been asked to pick up where other agencies failed or were inappropriate. For example, the family does not directly address the overlapping social illnesses of bigotry, inequality, and intergroup hostility and fear; the task was therefore passed along to the schools. Compulsory education became society's Mr. Fixit (which was especially useful because the parts being "fixed"— the children—had little say in the process).

Let us assume that the three traditional American purposes for schooling—skill training, citizenship and employment training, and self-respect—will remain. How can they most sensibly be approached pedagogically?

It goes without saying that many intellectual skills, if well taught, are readily learned in conventional classrooms. These operations are, however, essentially *individual* matters: one learns multiplication by and for one's self; one does not need anyone else in order to carry out this arithmetic operation. To be sure, working in a group often helps the process of learning, but at root this operation is internal to the individual.

Some other mental operations and most social skills, on the other hand, require interaction: they are, by contrast, *common* matters. One can learn little about friendship without friends, about other kinds of people without meeting them, about one's fear or self-confidence in different cultures without experiencing different cultures. Much of this kind of social learning goes on in schools, but schools are poorly designed to accommodate it for two reasons: their classrooms and teachers are organized primarily to teach individual skills; and few schools, most often for practical reasons, enroll children of wide enough cultural diversity to test one's willingness to understand and respect other cultures.

Other learnings are both individual and poorly learned in conventional school settings. An understanding of the limits of one's physical endurance requires settings to test that power. To gain personal self-confidence, one needs to test it against the unfamiliar. Taking a subway alone for the first time is such a test, and the exercise requires a subway. A rectangular classroom alone is insufficient for many of the experiences which children should have.

On purely educational grounds, then, I would argue for a system of complementary schools, some hard by a child's home to teach the individual intellectual and motor skills and activities, and others, necessarily of great diversity and far flung, to teach common skills and those individual matters that require unfamiliar settings. While I accept the obvious point that learning is never neatly divided up, and the individual and common learnings go on in a jumbled, idiosyncratic, and entangled way, I also argue that conventional classrooms reinforce individual learning, while a group effort (say, the building of a geodesic dome by a group) provokes social learning. It all is a matter of emphasis. We can teach and learn more effectively and efficiently if we draw on a variety of settings and experiences (see Sizer 1973).

Schools, Rather Than School

What, practically, would this mean?

For all children, say through the age of fourteen, it would mean a primary base in a neighborhood school. The work there would be well-focused and limited primarily to individual learning, learning that is essentially cognitive. The staples of this fare would be language study, mathematics, the individual arts, and the appropriate rudiments of the social and behavioral sciences. The emphasis would be on communication and on the development of the skills of discrimination, analysis, and argument.

That sounds grim, even unchildlike! Of course, it need not be so: such skills, if well taught, can be intriguing to the child's interest and personally joyful. The ability to think clearly, to understand, is greatly liberating, and the "ecstasy" (as George Leonard has called it) of discovery from using one's mind is peculiarly human.

To concentrate on individual learning in a neighborhood school does not obviate, of course, common learning. A youngster must learn to get along with his own kind before he is asked to cope with others quite different from himself, and the former would be an obvious concern of a neighborhood school. But what are cut back in such a school are emphases on broader social and civic learning, and the development of abilities to cope with change. These would be provided for by wholly different regional schools, attended in addition to the neighborhood school. These schools could be small and informal, special programs using the resources of a community and deliberately mixing in their enrollments students from various backgrounds.

Some specific examples may best describe the pattern:

A ten-year-old, restless and boisterous in classrooms, bigger than her age-mates and physically adroit; of average academic promise, but not working at this level; some interest in out-of-doors things. In a program planned with varying *months:*

Neighborhood school: basic program for 15 (of the standard 20) school days per month.

Regional sports program: athletics with a regionally recruited team, grouped with youngsters of her equivalent physical size and talent: 4 half-days per month, plus weekend practices.

Regional field science program (perhaps sponsored by a group such as the Audubon Society): 3 days per month.

A twleve-year-old, shy, somewhat withdrawn; of great academic talent, and resented by his age-mates because of this; special strengths in languages. In a program planned by *terms:*

Neighborhood school: basic program for nine weeks.

Regional residential intensive institute: in Russian language and culture, with students of equal linguistic ability, but drawn from several age groups: six weeks.

Regional health science aides program (perhaps sponsored by a group of hospitals): three weeks (the purpose of such an experience for this boy would be to lessen his shyness by giving him the experience of helping people).

A fifteen year-old, "turned off" to school and hostile to his teachers; on his own, primarily, and living in most respects independently of his family, though hero worshipping a brother who is in the Marines; quite into drugs, but not dealing; of good intelligence, using it in the street rather than in any academic field; waiting impatiently for a car and driver's license; on probation for a case of joy ride car stealing. In a program planned by *year:*

Neighborhood school: counseling and basic English and mathematics instruction: in some evenings and afternoons through the year, in classes also serving adults.

Regional auto mechanics apprenticeship: on-the-job training in specific skills, including some paid employment (perhaps run by a group such as OIC): mornings, throughout the year.

Regional armed services program: cadet training, emphasizing leadership, cooperation, and field craft (perhaps sponsored by reserve units): one meeting per week, throughout the year.

A seventeen-year-old, very "turned on" to school, especially the arts;

from a very protected environment and thus afraid of new ventures; of modest academic ability, but of great perseverance and commitment. In a program planned by *year:*

Neighborhood school: basic program for one term.

Regional arts program: employment as an aide and a student in a regional art/music program which sends artists-in-residence (plus aides) to elementary schools: one term.

Regional home-exchange program: exchange homes for two weeks with a youngster of equivalent age, but from a neighborhood different in character.

Several policies should be apparent from these examples. First of all, while all four youngsters are involved at least some of the time in racially mixed situations, the concerns relating to intergroup understanding—those promoting the fear represented by busing—are not dealt with directly, but implicitly. The means of lessening hostility and increasing human understanding are most effectively those of *shared experience,* the working together on a common project of self-evident importance. Direct discussion and confrontation of one's prejudices and fears is helpful for relatively secure adults, but easily confuses and disturbs a younger person. Thus the common learning provided in this system of complementary schools always has multiple objectives: the learning of a skill, or an attitude; the chance to have a new experience and to learn to master it; and the chance to meet, understand, and appreciate a group of persons different from oneself.

Secondly, membership in regional programs is not limited solely to students of a particular age group and their teachers. As countless commentators have noted, "youth" in this country increasingly is a separate caste, cut off from the main political and economic life of the society as a whole. Like most castes, youth suffers from this isolation, and means must be found to bring its members more directly and honestly within the mainstream of the culture. By involving youngsters with adults and with children younger than themselves, a better understanding of the interrelationship of generations and the meaning of each is possible.

Thirdly, an attempt is made in the regional schools to use existing institutions, concerns which already have financial support from the public. Creating wholly new entities, however exciting these might be, would involve an outlay of funds quite beyond the public's willingness either to pay or to accept something unfamiliar for its children. Most Americans do not want their schools fundamentally changed, and they will accept patterns such as those described here only if they feel that little of the status quo is being altered and that the additional programs presented are consistent with their basic aims of schooling. Using museums, army reserve units, business, and other such organizations is not at all threatening.

The plans set forth here are, of course, an administrative headache. One advantage of the current system (where the child attends but one school at a time) is that it is bureaucratically neat. One doubles the problems of attendance and coordination when one arranges for every child to have at least a second educational experience beyond his neighborhood school, and the difficulties increase almost geometrically as further flexibility and opportunities are provided. The danger that a bureaucracy would be spawned to run the system is very real, as one can already see in some school systems which are now providing outside options. What is needed is a flexible system of alternatives, independently as well as publicly managed, all accredited by, but not operated by, the state. Central management would squash the entire movement with the weight of well-meaning coordination and bureaucracy.

There are, of course, many models for such an open and flexible system, models from decentralized industry to the various American Protestant churches to provision in some states for special education under independently managed auspices. However, perhaps the best example is the system in higher education created by so-called G.I. Bill and other public scholarship programs that followed World War II. This system pumped aid *through the students* into public and private higher education. Unfortunately, many people today will connect this form of support with a number of the recently suggested voucher schemes promoted to create a "market system" in elementary and secondary education. A voucher scheme (or a contract scheme, such as used for special education in many states) is nothing more than a benign device to provide funds for education in a more flexible way, one more responsive to the user, than the direct-grant method seen in elementary and secondary education. Direct management or voucher schemes themselves are no better or no worse than the people administering them and the accrediting agencies reviewing the institutions at which funds may be spent. If one believes in variety, in flexibility (including the ability to shut down an institution that has lost its power and imagination), then some device other than direct public management, with all its attendant bureaucracy, is wise.

However, the use of nonpublic institutions as part of a system of complementary schools would inevitably cause political problems in some communities and constitutional problems in some states. While a Gallup Poll taken in the late 1960s shows broad support for the existence of nonpublic schools, at the same time resistance to public aid for schools not directly under public authority is very strong. Unfortunately, the public does not make a distinction between management and purpose. It is obvious that there are many publicly managed schools which do not serve the public interest, even when most generously defined; there are public school systems which in fact forward neither the interests of children nor the most elemental tenets of the American creed. At the same time, most Americans recognize that there are institutions which do not happen to be managed by the public but which nonetheless serve the public interest in a very direct way: few patients prefer the Boston City Hospital over the Massachusetts General Hospital, even though the latter is privately managed. Why could there not be an educational analogue in the elementary and secondary sector? Somehow the political point has to be made that the primary function of public schools is to serve the public interest, and not a private or class or special group interest, and that institutions managed by the public or by independent authorities can serve the public interest. The practical key is accreditation, most likely administered at the state level.

From another quarter, however, there are hopeful signs that increased options are wise for elementary and secondary education, options that could be the core of a system of complementary schools. In recent months several reports on secondary education have been published, one under the auspices of the Charles F. Kettering Foundation, another from the Panel on Youth of the President's Science Advisory Committee, and yet another (still in final drafting process) by a Task Force appointed by former U.S. Commissioner of Education Sidney P. Marland, Jr. The two that have been published to date (Coleman 1974 and Brown 1973), while disagreeing in particulars, both support the notion of alternatives to a school life wholly lived in rectangular classrooms, and to the use of the community and economy at large. The PSAC group, chaired by James S. Coleman, spoke directly to the matter of the control of such alternatives. It argued strongly for a loose system of accredited institutions, few or none of which were directly within the public school systems: "We feel that the benefits of incorporating noncognitive activities into schools are far fewer than those of organizing them outside schools. The principal benefit of the former path appears to be organizational 'neatness' and insurance that all youth will be covered by such activity. But the costs are the distortion of such activity to fit the organizational characteristics of a school, a distortion that strikes at the very heart of the activity" (Coleman 1974, p. 143).

What the CFK and PSAC commissions called for are options, the provision of varied ways for students to learn both in cognitive and noncognitive domains. The system of complementary schools suggested here, however, is more conservative than the CFK proposals in that it does not imply that compulsory education cease at age fourteen, a particularly controversial recommendation of that group. The basic structure of compulsory education would continue, but the routes of movement within it would be increased. While the tone of the CFK and PSAC recommendations are quite different, their general thrust is common; and the complementary proposal here being considered is consistent also with this general direction.

A Specific Example: The Case of Phillips Academy

How to proceed?

If one resides—as the writer does—in a specialized, nonpublic school, the strategy for experiment must be carefully focused. Phillips Academy is a well-endowed, residential secondary school, one which gives great emphasis to academic learning in the liberal arts. Traditionally it has been an "alternative" school, a place where youngsters enroll when provision for secondary education was not available in local communities (the case for most of Andover's 200 year history) or where for one reason or another parents wish their child to be away from home. This alternative function is a sensible and reasonable one, and should continue. However, there are many at Andover who feel that an additional complementary function is also desirable and defensible, particularly in this day of high-quality, mass secondary education.

The question posed for us at this school was straightforward:

What are the special qualities which make us distinct from day schools, particularly public high schools? First, the school's ability to provide a residential education makes it different from the overwhelming majority of other secondary schools. (Only four-tenths of one percent of U.S. secondary school students receive a residential school experience.) Residential education allows great flexibility: those who find an interest can pursue it with a single-mindedness simply impossible in a typical 8:30 a.m.-2:30 p.m. situation. Second, it allows for great diversity in the student body, which cuts across national, state, and local boundaries and provides a mixed community completely impossible in most day schools. Third, a residential setting, if well managed, can provide an intensity of experience which is also what economists would call (in their traditionally ugly jargon) "cost effective." One can learn deeply and quickly in a situation of intense involvement. In sum, the residential character so unfamiliar in American secondary education (though highly familiar in higher education) is a special facet of this school. In addition, Phillips Academy's focus on academic learning has led it to build a faculty skilled at teaching demanding and advanced cognitive (and certain noncognitive) skills and patterns of learning to youngsters between the ages of fourteen and eighteen. The school is well equipped with laboratories, libraries, computers, and the rest, at a level comparable to that of most small colleges.

Given these two strengths, the complementary contribution which the school can make follows quite simply: the provision of intensive academic training for a highly diverse student body for intensive periods, ones which are not excessively costly (either to the school or to the student), and thus open to many youths. Following this logic, the Andover faculty has identified a variety of academic subjects which are best learned in intensive settings and which could serve highly diverse groups of students for short periods of time. The school has created a short-term institute program offering four- to six-week institutes in observational astronomy, theatre, field geology, intensive German, intensive French, organic chemistry, advanced placement chemistry, statistics, and visual studies, the subjects to be taught in a highly concentrated manner to groups of twenty to thirty students and, in some cases, adults, particularly teachers. Given the availability of convenient facilities at the school and the sharp focus of the programs, costs have been kept quite low

($100 per student per week). The school is attempting to make these institutes—as well as its regular program and its six-week summer session—visible and available to students in public school districts and to provoke public as well as private financial support to make attendance possible for all who qualify, whatever their ability to pay.

A Word on Pessimism

Much has been said in recent months about the demoralization and retreat seen in elementary and secondary education, a retreat of ideals as well as of expectations and finance. Too many of us no longer believe that schools have important leverage on the profound social problems of the day, and we believe too readily recently published reports that stress the limitations of formal education. Rather than spurring us to self-examination and to new ventures in new directions, these reports have made us sullen and defensive. The educational establishment is in a period of relative immobility and scapegoating. It is not a pretty sight.

While one must greet this mood with dismay, at the same time one must understand it as a political reality. Radical reform is not possible in the present climate. Modest reform, carefully thought through, and quietly presented, is perhaps the rule of the day, and the system of complementary schools herein suggested seems to address this mood. It addresses in a fundamental way the most serious contemporary political problem that education faces—that of busing— and at the same time is pedagogically defensible and consistent with the growing demand for options in education. In a word, it fits.

No massive federal program similar to the Elementary and Secondary Education Act of 1965 is likely to launch such a system in a fanfare of trumpets. What must evolve is slow, steady work of individual schools and school systems determined not to be victims of the fear in our communities or to be demoralized by the scapegoating critics. The children deserve our courage and realism.

References

Brown, B. Frank, et al. *The Reform of Secondary Education.* New York: McGraw-
    Hill, 1973.
Coleman, James S., et al. *Youth: Transition to Adulthood.* Chicago: University
    of Chicago Press, 1974.
Sizer, Theodore R. *Places for Learning, Places for Joy: Speculations on American
    School Reform.* Cambridge, Mass.: Harvard University Press, 1973.

PART III

New Participants and the Shaping of the Future

Commentary

The essays in this volume have up to now mainly been concerned with the educational institution, from kindergarten through graduate school, its relation to the larger society and its needs, to the individual and his desires. At least implicitly, there has been a recognition that the present definition of the institution itself is open to question, and particularly that the issue of who participates in it, and in decisions about its future, needs much thought and debate. The essays in Part II suggested that the schools had too much become a social battlefront, that their core function should be given over to, or returned to, those mainly concerned with education itself. Chapters 7 and 8 bear witness to two different kinds of revolution in participation that are actually under way, though often unrecognized. The first concerns the kind of students participating in education: the movement toward adult or continuing education. The second has to do with new forces at work in determining future educational policy, particularly the yet unmeasured force of teacher unionism.

Elizabeth Janeway's report on new programs in adult and continuing education delineates a quiet revolution, one that is at present too modest, far from complete, but that promises to revise our notion of what a student is, of the place of education in the life cycle, and indeed of human potential and the capacity for self-renewal through education. Her observations take on particular relevance in the light of another report prepared for the Southampton Summer Sequences—which considerations of space prevent our printing here—by psychologists Seymour Sarason, Esther K. Sarason, and Peter Cowden, on aging and the nature of work. They discover a high degree of dissatisfaction with the definition of job and role among the most successful professionals. They hence imply the need for increased opportunities for recycling, mid-career retraining, and continuing self-examination through education. They suggest that we must cease to educate in such a way that people feel themselves channeled and trapped in defined jobs and social roles. What is at stake is the free realization of human potential in a society uneasily groping its way into the postindustrial era, where the breakdown in traditional patterns of self-definition and self-fulfillment has not yet produced new, freer patterns of self-processing. Ms. Janeway touches on the area where some of these new patterns may be forged. With the skill and humanity of the practicing novelist—and a thoughtful contributor to the liberation of women—Ms. Janeway brings together observations from many hours spent on campuses of all types in all corners of the country. The result is a progress report, in many ways encouraging, on an area where America has been retrograde in comparison with many other countries—where something is at last in motion, and where much remains to be done.

Jonathan Messerli's subject is quite different. As Dean of the School of Education at Fordham University, and a student of the history of American education, he is intent to explode some of the dominant myths of our educational establishment. He is particularly concerned with the belief in the power of the educational system to reform itself, and to produce social reform. He shows how the "educationist" establishment historically formed itself as a relatively isolated power bloc, resistant to change despite the attacks of influential academicians, yet strong in influence with the state departments of education. Then he traces recent shifts in the balance of power as the teachers themselves, more and more strongly organized into unions, assert their right to be the policymakers. He points, in other words, to the centers of power that have largely determined the shape and content of the educational institution, and to the shifts in participation in this power.

The "real change" that he delineates is of uncertain outcome. As he looks forward to the next decade, Dean Messerli predicts an effort on the part of the organized teaching profession to unburden itself of the role of social reformer, and to define the limitations of what it can be expected to accomplish. He sees the teaching profession as more and more determining the rules and standards by which it should itself operate. In the most optimistic view, this new controlling participation by the teachers could lead to a revaluation of the classroom discipline. Pessimistically, it could lead rather to the worst, narrowest, most self-protective aspects of American unionism or professional guildism. Dean Messerli suggests that we stand at a great divide in the history of American education, and that no abstract thinking about future blueprints will mean much unless we take account of the centers of power involved, and the actors participating in future decisions.

Both his paper and Ms. Janeway's have the virtue of turning us from abstract and utopian considerations—admittedly dominant in this volume—to human questions, particularly to the question of who has been excluded up to now from education or from determining what it is to be (and of course there would be much to say about other sectors of American society excluded in these two domains). They suggest that thinking about the future cannot ever be in-dependent of thinking about who is to participate in that future.

It is in this perspective that we include here Michael Rossman's "Edutopia," an essay which addresses the issues of core function and curriculum raised in Part II, but extends its grasp to a radically revised conception of the place of education in life, and the nature and forms of participation in education. One of the most thoughtful exponents of the American counterculture, Rossman has sought to reflect on the deepest meanings of the upheavals of the 1960s, and to draw from them lessons concerning the realization of human potential through education. It is striking that, for all its wholesale repudiation of present schooling arrangements, Rossman's essay keeps faith with a fundamental American optimism about the value and capacity of education. There is no proposal to withdraw from the idea of education, but rather a joyous and imaginative multiplica-tion of its possibilities and its forms. Society is not seen as "de-schooled," but totally schooled, with a flexibility and a variousness that put technological advance at the service of a poetry of work and competence. The essay is frankly utopian, implying not only a total reform of education as an institution, but also a sweeping change in social arrangements and mentalities. Yet the vision is tough-minded and pertinent. It cannot easily be dismissed. And any more modest attempts to reform education ought to stand accountable to such visionary thinking.

Peter Brooks

7

Continuing Education: A Life-Long Resource, A Unifying Force

Elizabeth Janeway

Adult education *per se* is far from new in American life. It began as a response to an especially American situation—the immigration into this country, and specifically into its cities, of adults from Europe who possessed some skills but needed to learn, first, a new language and, second, the particular characteristics of our society and our culture.

It should not surprise us, therefore, to discover that social change has again brought an influx of students to the campus, for access to learning has been taken for granted as a prerogative of American citizenship. In the last few years this prerogative has come to be exercised more widely than ever before as older men and women have been returning for further education to institutions of learning all over the country. The effect they have had on these institutions is already apparent, even though it is also apparent that the full significance of their presence has yet to be understood and factored into the programs and purposes of our universities.

In some ways the new wave of eager adult students is providing a problem for the institutions: these students do not fit the pattern of teaching and learning which the institutions are geared to provide.

For one thing, many of them arrive to take noncredit courses. None-theless, more students than is generally realized do want to receive some kind of certification. This is a highly certificated society, and enough of the Puritan work-ethic survives for many of us to want to prove that our efforts at learning have achieved a success that can be attested. Moreover, a proportion of students who begin as noncredit learners decide to go on as candidates for regular degrees, or even graduate or professional status. It becomes important for them to be able to transfer credits from earlier work to regular programs. Faculties and administrations are already beginning to give thought to setting up some kind of "continuing education unit" with a standard transferable value into academic points toward a degree.

Unfortunately, in spite of this growing desire on the part of students to receive some kind of credit, and on the part of the institutions to grant it, the image of the returning student is still that of an interested but unfocused wanderer through the garden of intellectual delights, plucking here a rose and there a chrysanthemum, to make up a bundle of information too scattered to be dignified by any formal designation. In addition, many want to study only part-time; nor can they present the usual credentials recognized by self-respecting institutes of higher learning.

By the universities, then, the mass of potential learners is seen as a chaotic bundle of bodies who represent some sort of financial opportunity (and heaven knows that is desperately needed) but are hideously resistant to processing. How are they to be assimilated? Human nature suggests that those in charge of the learning process will do their best to fit students into the existent patterns of teach-ing, whether or not these match the needs and desires of those who wish to learn. This is certainly the first approach. But it is becoming ever more evident that there are just too many students in this new group to be handled in this straightforward but high-handed way. The great universities can do so because they can largely ignore them. "You had better," wrote one correspondent, "simply take Yale as a negative statistic." But the less than top-rank colleges need them. Assimilation of new, mature students will necessarily mean a compromise of some kind; but for colleges and universities in financial need, compromise may be the better part of valor. As I begin this survey, I would like to suggest that it may also be the better part of education, for experience indicates that the older student, drawing on his or her store of knowledge and judgment, can and does enlarge the context of teaching and consistently relate it to life.

This is not merely my own impression. Older students and women in particular often approach a re-immersion in the learning process with embarrassment, timidity, and even fear; but this does not last. Writes Wendy Musich, Counselor for Adult Student Programs at the University of Wisconsin (Parkside): "Most adults believe that they lack the necessary intelligence to keep up with their younger classmates. But mainly we find that the reverse is true because of the adult student's maturity, life experience, and focused motivation." (This last trait is one to which I shall return.) Florence Howe, of SUNY (Old Westbury), speaks of the freshness of approach which her older students bring to the discussion of literature; far from being the victims of "received ideas" they judge for themselves the material they read on the basis of what they know. Diane Kincaid of the University of Arkansas (Fayetteville) remarks that although "virtually all of the returning women find some way to communicate to me their lack of self-confidence, they then virtually all go on to complete the course [political science] with an A or B grade."

I have raised this point—the value to the institution of the older student—so early in this paper because unless it is accepted the whole question of continuing and nontraditional education will remain in the limbo it now occupies. Adult education is already a massive movement, but it is extremely difficult to come up with any reliable figures on its extent. A run-down in *U.S. News and World Report* last year offered an estimate of thirty-two million students overall during the previous twelve-month period, and this is echoed in *The Chronicle of Higher Education,* reporting on the findings of a panel commissioned to study nontraditional education. Dwarfing even this figure is the panel's estimate, from a sampling of interviews with 3,000 adults, that more than seventy million Americans would like to attend some sort of class on some sort of subject, if these were available! A hard figure of what is available is provided by *The New York Times Guide to Continuing Education,* which covers 2,281 schools in fifty states offering more than 50,000 courses for adults, but even this is not complete. The study of the topic which Dr. Helen Astin of UCLA has undertaken for the Carnegie Foundation will be invaluable—when it is published; but it has just begun. At present, one feels inescapably that continuing education has been, like Topsy, born under a cabbage and left to "jes' grow." Whether (to mix our folk-tales) this stepchild will turn into a Cinderella is something that the future will show. But undoubtedly, from the point of view of the institutions' development, the teaching of adults in innovative ways is going to play a larger and larger role.

Now, if these mature students are regularly regarded as second-class citizens, not only they but the institutions which supposedly serve them will suffer. Unfortunately, such a view is too general, for adjustments to accommodate the special requirements of adults are made with reluctance and seldom imagined ahead of time. "Is it necessary," writes Patty McNamara, Dr. Astin's research assistant, "for a middle-aged woman or man to pass a swimming test and two years of gym courses?" Residence requirements are clearly inappropriate for mature students, but getting them waived or removed is often difficult. Courses tend to be scheduled with the needs of full-time resident students in mind; and even when some flexibility is introduced here, support facilities are often not available at times convenient for commuting students. Bookshops close, counseling centers close, registration is difficult, mere information is hard to come by, so that (for instance) some students who might be entitled to financial aid find it almost impossible to discover how and where to apply for it. Most telling of all, experimental and nontraditional programs are usually the first to be cut in any financial pinch.

All these examples are evidence of the pervasive attitude that continuing students are less worth the time and effort to teach than are the bright, middle-class eighteen- and nineteen-year-olds. Older men are often regarded as being motivated and ambitious, but intellectually second-class. Older women are assumed to be dilettantes, returning to the campus to amuse themselves with noncredit courses in areas that will enrich their personal lives—languages, art history, smatterings of literature. In part this is true, but though many women still return to college with the modest intention of enriching their minds and satisfying their curiosity about the workings of the world, they increasingly tend to switch to degree courses and to pursue studies that will qualify them to undertake a vocation or profession. I shall have more to say about these older women. Here let me emphasize only that many of them are motivated by a double purpose: to raise their earning capacity *and* to enjoy mental stimulation. These goals should not be thought of as opposed. They are complementary. Nonetheless, the idea that older women can be serious students and not "nice ladies filling empty hours" is far from universal. Aside from the unfortunate effect of this condescending attitude on the students, it also invites the faculty teaching them to view themselves as catering to an inferior element—a viewpoint that is surely to be deplored.

My own feelings about these campus changes are quite the contrary. I believe that the surge of returning students is the inevitable—and greatly-to-be-desired—effect of profound social changes in our ordinary lives, which affect both men and women, though in rather different ways. Both sexes are touched by the vast speed-up in technological change and scientific advance, but men feel it more directly. Even highly skilled professional men may find themselves in need of refresher courses to keep in touch with developments in their own fields. Some may find their chosen fields narrowing, while others beckon with new opportunities. The mid-life career switch is not yet common, but it is certainly becoming much more common than it was. It has been accelerated by the early-retirement programs of many bureaucracies, including the armed services. The returning-student movement includes twenty-year-and-out men from the army, retired policemen and firemen in their forties, airline pilots considering new vocations, and retired executives in their fifties, looking for new professions as well as "something to do in my retirement." Again, these last two aims are often complementary, not opposed. In addition, there is a psychological shift which can be felt better than it can be measured. People are much more ready to consider doing "something else" than they used to be. They are less dedicated to a lifelong, unchangeable commitment to a vocation or a profession. In view of the rapid shift in the backgrounds of our lives, this is a useful and adaptive reaction. It means a rising, long-term demand for additional education for adults.

The returning woman student is very much part of this movement. She tends to arrive at a slightly different period of life from the male returning student, "bunched," as Dean Dennis of Columbia General Studies puts it, "between the ages of thirty and thirty-five," but she is even more indicative of the massive effects of social change. The last generation has witnessed the movement of women out of their homes into all kinds of involvement with the world, but most extensively with the world of work. Women in the labor force now stand at more than 40 percent, and the percentage of women in their forties who hold jobs is as high as that of the old peak of female employment that was reached at about age twenty-three. No longer is it true to say of young women, "What's the use of training them, they'll only get married and quit!" Some of them do indeed quit to have babies but, increasingly, they come back. The lengthening life-span, the decline in the birth-rate and in family size, the greater ease of housekeeping due to the use of appliances, of convenience foods, and of outside services, have all contributed to this movement.

Even more important, the rising cost of living has supplied its own powerful incentive to women to work: many families need a second paycheck to keep their heads above water. These factors operate to bring women back to college for training and retraining. For some, it is still a matter of personal stimulus, but for many women college is becoming a stop on the way to employment in a profession or in a career. Even more than for men, the kind of certification which a degree can give will help a woman reach a higher earning capacity than she could without it. In the business and professional worlds, it is very hard indeed for women to move up to decision-making positions without some sort of guarantee of their capability. Until affirmative action programs are no longer needed, women are going to be looking for training as a means of signifying their abilities to potential employers.

Once more, this job-oriented approach to education is only part of the value expected and received. Testimony to this effect comes from the students themselves.

"I wanted to continue with my college studies because of (a) mental stimulation and (b) increased employment potential," writes a 39-year-old wife and mother, who clearly sees no conflict between these aims. She sums up a wide reaction.

Other women speak of increasing self-confidence, of realizing their own intelligence and enjoying the use of their minds, and also of the warmth of companionship across age-levels. While these are formulated as personal rewards, it is clear that they bode well for the ability of these students to function effectively in the world of activity outside the home. The learning experience, that is, is teaching these women more than the materials given in the courses. It is helping to end the isolation and the passivity which has characterized the middle-class, middle-aged wife and mother far too long, wasting her energies and talents. By so doing it strengthens the network of individual relationships on which social action depends.

This is true both of middle-class women and of those from a working-class background. An analysis of low-income women in special adult programs at Brooklyn College reports both a growing self-confidence and an increased earning potential. Major reasons for going to college are summed up as:

1. Options, meaningful work, get out of dead-end jobs, satisfaction, do "something I enjoy."
2. Better pay, financial independence.
3. Professional status, authority.
4. Change of career.
5. "Ticket" credentials (that is, certification), security in competitive market, background (for further employment) when special government-funded programs end.
6. Helping people, righting injustices, community service, sense of mission, conception of mother as teacher.

Of the many personal reactions to their experience, a few—given in their own words—follow: "I can feel myself growing." "You forget how bright you are." "I feel very much alive, my whole life has meaning to it now—purpose, direction." "I didn't think I'd enjoy it as much as I have." "The horizon is much wider." "I've become a better mother because I feel better myself." "I was very, very lonely. School stimulated me. It makes me feel really good." "School opened a whole new world." "Going to school has given me the security to think that if I do think something, it is real for me and I'm free to express it." "I take more interest in the political things that I ignored before because I see how they affect me."

Clearly, these women have diverse purposes in seeking more education, but it is hard to see that these purposes differ in any significant way from those we find in students of the usual age. Perhaps, only their aspirations and ambitions are not so vaulting as those of the young. But if we make this judgment on them, we must realize from how low a point of self-esteem they start; or, to put it another way, what their realistic appraisal has told them about their place in the hierarchy of power in our society. These are low-income women, who have been working in dead-end jobs they want to leave. Many of them are minority women. Few of them have truly sup- portive families behind them—middle-class women are more fortunate here, though even they speak often of fighting surprise, indifference, and outright hostility from some husbands and relatives. Many of these low-income women are carrying three loads—they work, they look after families, and they study, some of them on almost a full schedule, though the work has been arranged so that they need attend classes only two evenings a week. It is hardly surprising that few of them can really imagine their goals as the lofty ones which Ivy League students set themselves. Within the limits of what they can imagine for themselves, however, the intentions match closely the aims of the advantaged young. Perhaps it is worth offering one more quotation, this one from a summing up of the interviews and study of these women by the authors of *Project Second Start* (p. 236):

> Trained from birth to step into their roles as wives, mothers and unpaid houseworkers, the women we saw, like millions of their sisters, also knew that they would have to join the paid work force immediately after, if not during high school, and that they would continue to work or seek work outside the home most of their lives. Having been trained early either for a paid vocation or for the unpaid professions of mother and houseworker, they knew they would have little choice about the kind of job they would get. It would be a job that would enable them to survive and keep the family going.
>
> College was for someone else, off limits, unobtainable; something for which they didn't have "the right background," the proper preparation, or the money. It was a luxury. Hadn't their parents said "Sociology? Psychology? How are you going to pay the rent?" or "College is a waste of time. Get a job. Get married and have babies."
>
> Having met all the basic requirements (production in and reproduction of the labor force), the women in the Study Group had done something which was *not* expected—they had signed up for a college degree. They had decided to change their lives, to redefine themselves, and they were paying the price for having stepped out of their assigned roles—or for taking on an unpopular one. They were now being accused of being selfish, ugly, crazy; neglecting their children and their husbands; of breaking up their marriages; of wanting to determine the kind of work they did and the kind of life they would lead. They were, indeed, taking a giant step, committing a radical act.

It is possible, I am sure, that some of the participants in these seminars will feel that these women were indeed "neglecting their children and their husbands; breaking up their marriages." So—in fact—did many of the women themselves. So do many, many other returning students. It is a constant concern. Even the middle-class women at Alverno repeat their worry about "neglecting the children" and, be it noted, Alverno has an excellent program of child-development (not simply day-care) where students' children can stay, close to their mothers, at a charge of only fifty cents an hour, twenty-five cents for each additional child. The one thing you cannot accuse these women of is not being serious about their work. They are desperately serious about it; serious enough to put up with recrimination ("My mother thinks I'm crazy"), and with arguments from their own consciences. The picture of the part-time dilettante does not fit these facts. True, the part-time dilettante exists—and why not? The *U.S. News* article I cited at the beginning of this paper quotes a Bronx auto dealer as typical of "the new breed of 'fun learners.'" Who could wish to discourage him when he says:

"With me, there is a constant craving for new knowledge. I am not tied to any one field and will move into an area that interests me. I have two worlds: my everyday business world and my academic world. This academic world is the same to me as a golf club or yacht club or gin game. This is my extra life."

But "fun learning" is far from being the only goal of returning students, and the universities will profit from understanding and assisting the many serious men and women who see their studies as increasing their engagement with life, not simply as enhancing their leisure time. If only we begin by assuming that these mature students are with us and will continue to be with us, and that they are as valuable and worth teaching as young men and women of traditional college age, we can go on to consider their institutional needs.

One urgent need is greater flexibility. First, as to admission standards. Students desiring to enter regular degree programs are at once faced with the need to present credentials that are often not readily available, and are out-of-date once obtained. One authority writes, "A fifteen-year-old high school transcript or a transcript from sophomore year in college when the person was in the process of dropping out to be married won't look very appealing to admission officers. Entrance tests are designed for high school students who are taking related course work, not for a twenty-eight-year-old mother or a fifty-five-year-old executive who wants a new career." In addition, it must be noted that one of the great hangups of returning students is taking examinations. I expect that a large majority of adults (and I am no exception) has been plagued from time to time by recurrent dreams of an approaching exam which one is not prepared to take. Obviously, returning students who want credit towards a degree must be prepared to meet standards, and that means taking examinations; but they should be rather different examinations from those aimed at high school students fresh from concentrated work on particular subjects. A university which really wants to enroll older degree students should work out special, general knowledge examinations designed to establish learning capability rather than merely a grasp on some particular body of information. In addition, preparation for taking examinations could well be provided by short orientation courses, prescribed reading, or preferably a combination of the two.

This brings us to another need of older students, namely, better and more imaginative counseling than is usually provided. The special problem of older women is lack of confidence in their own capacities. It is certainly a product of the self-image offered the older woman by her traditional role and position and it can cripple her ability to perform until her experience overcomes it—as it so often is shown to do in the woman's later reactions. But older men face a problem as well, in the embarrassment they fear if they do not do well on examinations, an attitude which is partly a product of the traditional male role. A woman, in fact, will sometimes be more willing to try an assignment at which she may fail (or thinks she may fail) than will a man who cannot afford to see himself as a possible failure. In short, pre-admission counseling seems to me to be as useful a support as post-admission counseling. I would like to suggest that it may often come best from fellow students. Of course this would need supplementing by trained back-up people, but very often much help can be obtained emotionally from someone who has been through it, and lived to tell the tale.

Some institutions are giving credit for life-experience to older students. This is certainly worth consideration, though difficult to quantify and probably more suited to some disciplines than to others. If, however, a regular student at Temple University in Philadelphia can get credit for working for a semester, it is hard to see why a returning mature man who has worked for twenty years should not. One would hope that the experience of colleges offering such credits could be pooled and reported for the benefit of others.

Certainly flexibility in allowing noncredit students to move into degree programs would help those who had hesitated to undertake degree work immediately, but found themselves drawn into it as they continued their studies. Here the proposal to set up some kind of standard of continuing education units would help to transfer credits not only within one institution, but those gained at another. We all know that America is a highly mobile society. Students who have accumulated credits in one institution should be able to transfer them, if they (or their husbands) are transferred themselves.

It has, in the past, been extremely difficult for part-time students to obtain any financial aid at all. Some state programs are now easing this bind, but it is still difficult for many older students to receive financial aid. Counseling on this crucial point is vital. Benefits to veterans are now much less adequate than they were in the past. This will either mean that only middle-class veterans will be able to use their GI benefits or that they will have to work to supplement the grants, which will very often mean that they will want to study only part-time.

Women students are in urgent need of child-care facilities. The number of programs available is totally inadequate, and many of them do not operate at night, which is of course a time when working women most often wish to attend classes. Universities might well provide not only evening care, but rosters of available babysitters. Increased social mobility plus the decline of the extended family has left a woman with less and less traditional help to call on in raising children. At the same time, her work has become more and more necessary—and so has her ability to train herself to work. The idea that she is not entitled to such training until her children are grown (unless she can provide and pay for their care by someone else) is socially irresponsible. What is a single parent, male or female, to do? Child care, by itself, is expensive. But why should not some universities, at any rate, set up instructional courses in child development, early child training, child nursing, and child care? They would then be able to provide facilities for children, and instruction in a field where it is badly needed and hard to come by.

Older students need informed and pragmatically inclined counseling, for they do not have time to experiment. This means the opportunity to discuss not simply job options, but the sort of training that will direct these students to fields that are not overcrowded and underpaid. Too many older women contemplate getting their teaching certificates, at a time when the teaching field is not expanding. Sensible counseling would suggest other fields where there are likely to be more openings. These fields should certainly include those that are not traditionally "women's work" in the case of women, or "men's work" in the case of men. The very act of undertaking further education in middle life points to a readiness on the part of at least some students to consider vocations that are not humdrum, orthodox, or sex-linked.

Centers where older students could gather would be natural places for counseling, both from staff and from other students. Until the middle-aged student has been at college for a while, he or she is apt to feel slightly out of place with the young. Special centers and gathering places will reinforce the older students' growing feeling that they have a right to be on campus. So many returning women speak of their pleasure in finding friends and companions and in joining discussions that the impact of these experiences must be regarded as a vital part of the value of continuing education. Men no doubt feel something of the same sort; but women, in their traditional place and role, have been so isolated from each other, encapsulated in the nuclear family, that the simple experience of sharing is felt more immediately. It is, of course, an invaluable part of student life at every age.

Many universities and colleges are already alive to the need for imaginative and innovative programs. It is impossible to do more than mention a few, but such mention may prompt responses from others. Thus, SUNY through its division of Empire State College, and the University of South Florida via its program for a Bachelor of Independent Studies, offer students who can spend almost no time on campus the opportunity to do degree-oriented work independently, reporting by mail to an instructor and spending a minimum of time in residence. Many universities, and not only those operating with an open admissions plan, will accept students who cannot supply even a high school equivalency certificate. This is done on the basis of examinations, and credits which are given toward a high school diploma will usually also count toward a college degree. The colleges of the City University of New York, which do operate under an open admissions policy, are actively recruiting students from backgrounds very different from the traditional. Community colleges welcome older students. At Queens Community College, those over sixty-five may attend any course free, if they are working for a degree (which means associate degrees, though these will qualify them to go on elsewhere to four-year colleges). Free courses for the elderly are also offered by the University of Denver, Ohio State, and Seattle Pacific—and there are surely more.

One of the most exciting programs for education for the retired man or woman deserves special mention. The New School has invited retired professionals to attend not simply to study, but to teach. For a fee of $200 a year, these students are entitled to take one course a semester, which is the standard rate; but they are then provided with quarters and facilities to conduct courses themselves, Monday through Thursday every week. The School has managed to accommodate 550, and has had to turn thousands away, to its sorrow. So enthusiastic are these students, who range in age from fifty-five to eighty-five, that more than half of them are present every day that the sessions are held.

Other institutions are actively involved in educational projects in unexpected milieus. A professor at Auburn Community College is teaching at the maximum security state prison with which (as he puts it) "Auburn is blessed." In the fall of 1973, ninety-four student inmates took 450 college credit hours. "To characterize the experience as different would be an understatement," he writes, but does not—I'm sorry to say—elaborate. In addition, Auburn is offering five-week mini-courses on a remarkable mix of topics: contemporary American poetry, the metric system, how to take tests (which relates back to my suggestion that such programs should be available to returning students), expressive drawing, women and work, gourmet cooking, and calculus. Students completing the five weeks receive one credit hour, representing one-third of a course credit.

Fort Campbell, in Kentucky, a large army base, has set up an educational program which it calls Eagle University. Faculty are drawn from nearby institutions. Though vocational learning is featured, other courses can be pursued at colleges in the region on a released-time basis.

I mentioned in passing the conferences which many colleges are holding, designed to attract the interest of the communities in which they are located. Morningside College in Sioux City has been very active in this field. Speakers address a college-plus-community audience, and panels drawn from faculty and community then discuss the topics raised, both in large groups and in small sessions. These are not single meetings, but continuing seminars—for example, ten weeks of discussion of local affairs, open to students at the college and to community members. Another seminar was centered on youth and its problems, and a third on pragmatic views of the future over the next generation. Some conferences are run by students, as one at Tulane, in New Orleans, now in its ninth year, and another at Emory and Henry, in its fifth biennial meeting. Both these festivals profit by television coverage and newspaper reporting, and draw on the community for attendance. As for Alverno College in Milwaukee, its new curriculum of teaching by modules calls on community members active in professions to judge students' achievements and qualifications throughout their college attendance.

Some general conclusions are in order. To a considerable degree I have been talking about the needs and desires of students returning to college for further education in middle life, rather than the needs and desires of the institutions to which they return. Designedly so, for I believe that the student body is the *raison d'etre* of the university, rather than (as it sometimes seems to be considered) raw material to be processed by the university. Too many instructors are of the opinion that education is a one-way enterprise, with faculty passing out information and values from its special hoard to passive instructees. Writes an official of the National Coalition for Research on Women's Education and Development, on the topic of institutional insensitivity: "If anyone can figure out how to crack ingrained faculty-administrative attitudes that result in the God complex, viewing all students as uninformed, unformed sponges subject to an identical set of intellectual rules, we will all be grateful."

Cracking that attitude—that learning is to be doled out as we, the learned, see fit—can only profit our institutions of higher learning. They, like the rest of us, exist in a world of profound and continuing social change. In this world, the hoard of learning they possess is invaluable. The ability of the human race to pass on its experiences and judgments to posterity is what makes us human. As Nobel Prize winner Sir Peter Medawar says so well, our bodies are still caught in the slow processes of Darwinian evolution, but our minds can proceed by accelerated, Lamarckian evolution, so that one generation can profit from the knowledge and wisdom of its elders.

But, by the same token, the repositors of knowledge cannot know, as those abroad in the world know, what is most needed out of this store. The demand for relevance comes in here. I think that almost everything we have learned in the past is in some way relevant to the present situation—but the task of defining priorities is an individual matter. The best education will be provided by those institutions which respond to the cries for help and the demands for relevance from the world outside: because that world is where people live and feel and act. Now, superficial responses are not enough. Educators should call on their own understanding of the learning they possess to relate it to the demands made from outside. What I am urging is a continuing, imaginative dialogue—neither the teaching of a curriculum chosen only by educators, nor the teaching of one desired only by students, but the setting up of new ways of teaching old things that reveal their significance, and the willingness to fit the new subjects and topics into an older structure of knowledge. Does this mean that I would welcome a course in astrology? Of course not. It does mean that I would encourage the departments of literature, psychology, philosophy, anthropology, and probably history and sociology to include in their programs a study of the occult and the interest it holds for humans: of the witchcraft craze, of Giordano Bruno's magic world view, of the Greeks and the irrational (to steal Dodds' title), of the provenance of myth, of comparative religion—and so on.

The fact that our society is feeling the need for more education throughout life should be enormously encouraging to our institutions of higher learning. They can now see themselves as a resource not simply for the young, not simply channeling preprogrammed instruction into the heads of those who have not yet made contact with the great world of events and action, but as possessors of knowledge useful to the mature as well. The need is great. I have dwelt on the millions of women, leaving their old-fashioned dependent role for greater participation in society, who see further study as a powerful instrument and support, and their number will grow. Writes Elizabeth Cless of the Claremont Colleges:

There are nuances far more important than bare facts. What should be said, for example, to a thirty-five-year-old stenographer of great potential who wants to get her R.N. on top of her B.A., and then go on to qualify to teach nursing? Her husband . . . refuses to give her his moral or financial support; her two-year-old has no collegial child care available; she has been accepted at a private university—no scholarship funds. But you know, she *will* do it. I can't imagine how, but she will. After one has seen dozens of people each year who overcome equivalent obstacles, the statistics about continuing students pale.

And I agree. These students with a vision of what they want out of life are going to storm the universities as if they were the Bastille—because learning is for them, the students.

Dean Dennis of Columbia General Studies speaks of the man, not the woman, who has reached middle life and finds himself shelved, in a routine backwater job at a level that can run from blue-collar to middle management. Why should not working men and women (and that includes women who work at home, accumulating life experience) win credits against college tuition—to be paid for in part by industry, or funded in much the same way that Social Security has been funded? These credits could be accumulated at a rate that would run with pension plans, and be transferable too. I think we have hardly scratched the surface of the ways in which our universities can begin to interact with society, through the individual interests, desires, and needs of adults who want to supplement their store of knowledge.

In closing let me suggest that this continuing interaction could do a great deal to close the gap between town and gown, and more important, between "high culture" and the great interested majority of citizens. We know each other too little. We are not really very different—but we have slightly different manners and ways of speaking, and as happens so often between cultures, we put each other off, even frighten each other. Mature students from all sorts of backgrounds (Temple University reports on the astonishing capabilities of welfare mothers as students) can work as mediators and missionaries to help us get our society a bit more put together than it seems to be right now.

Reference

Robinson, Jolly; Paul, Susanne; and Smith, Gloria. *Project Second Start*. New York: John Hay Whitney Foundation, 1973.

8

The Real Change Taking Place
in American Schools

Jonathan Messerli

Without an assist from the apocalyptic, only gradually and with greatest reluctance do we sever the cord that ties us to our favorite myths. Of these which Americans have nurtured as self-evident, none has become more deeply imbedded than our belief in the triumph of the American public school as the means for eradicating poverty and injustice and ushering in a new golden age of prosperity and domestic peace for one and all. For historical convenience, we can chart the beginning of this development with Horace Mann's crusade for the common schools in the 1840s. Then, driven by a democratic secular evangelism, our belief in a system of formal schooling, which was supported and controlled by the public, won over an entire nation of converts after the Civil War. The wealthy, many of the poor, the new immigrants, and both the more aspiring and more defensive within the middle class all embraced this institution as the best means for gaining economic security, equality of opportunity, upward mobility, and a republican consensus of ideals and social norms. The millennium was on its way, and it was to be only a matter of time before the world would see the superiority of the "American way." Rarely, perhaps never, has one nation placed so much of the burden of its hope for the future upon a single institution. Max Lerner spoke for many and said it well when he concluded that "Americans have an extravagant reliance on education. It is a piously repeated truism that some concrete social problems—capital and labor, Negro-white relations, anti-Semitism, juvenile delinquency, war and peace—can only be solved by education" (1957, p. 733). See also Cubberley (1947); Bailyn (1960); Cremin (1965).

This conference, which avowedly challenges such a belief, quickly gives back with the left hand what it has attempted to obtain with the right. Starting with the premise that "neither educators nor the schools they staff can reform society," it seems to define a more realistic, if circumscribed, role for our schools. Yet the ambivalence by which we approach such an iconoclastic task is illustrated by another premise presented to us which asserts that "public schools have a mandate of a sort to see that young people are humanistically oriented and prepared to function as effective citizens in a 'democratic society.' "

To be sure, we have done great and unparalleled things through our schools, but for more than a century, we also have indulged ourselves in a heady inflationary spiral of educational expectations. Most frequently these expectations have come from politicians, social reformers, teacher educators, journalists, and parent groups. Moreover, they have been accepted by the general populace. Although not leading in the creation of these unrealistic hopes, until recently the classroom teacher has willingly gone along with this mainstream of public opinion, reassured by the enhanced status this promised to bring to the profession.

It is doubtful that teachers had any alternatives. When compared with doctors and lawyers, they had little power to set their own standards and define their professional role. However, with the dramatic (and for some school boards, traumatizing) success of teacher unionism and collective bargaining in the 1960s, the relative organizational impotence of teachers has come to an end. Through the National Education Association and the American Federation of Teachers, they have gained a strong voice in determining the terms of their accountability and under what conditions this will take place.

In this paper, I will argue that more than all the writings of liberal reformers, social commentators, and academicians, this success of teacher unionism has set in motion the beginnings of a significant change in American education. Although too early to plot out many of the details, even at this stage it is possible to recognize that one of the outcomes will be a painful but healthy devaluation of our sense of the social productivity of our schools and the re-assessment of what we realistically can expect. In order to help understand why this is coming about, I will sketch some of the origins of our expectations for teachers, outline some of the reasons why they have been unrealized, and conclude with several hedged predictions on how the current and future actions of the organized teaching profession will shape the mission of the American public school.

Background

Since colonial times, the view of many Americans who have thought more than casually about the classroom teacher has been blurred by a split image which frequently confused the real with a romantic notion of the ideal. Some of our earliest writers on the subject, like Benjamin Franklin and Thomas Jefferson, suffered from the fewest illusions. Franklin thought that the "poorer sort" of students in his Academy were at least "qualified to act as School-masters." Jefferson assumed that those who could not complete their education in his plan for Virginia would drop out and become teachers. See Larabee (1961, pp. 34-37); Lee (1961, pp. 92-97). Admittedly, in their day there were great teachers like Ezekiel Cheever and Christopher Dock, but the talent and dedication of these two men was the exception which substantiated a widely accepted fact. An additional minority of teachers did possess good will, common sense, and at least marginal pedagogical skills. The vast majority, however, seem to have been incompetent and insufferable pedants who rightly deserved the indelible caricature penned of them by Washington Irving.

Civic leaders, editors, and clergymen all bemoaned the state of affairs. A few even put forth plans for a more systematic preparation of teachers. (See Carter 1826; Rudolph 1965.) Their proposals held public attention for a time, but it was not until the emergence of the normal school movement of the early 1840s that an institutional basis was laid for a sequential program for training the American classroom teacher. Although gaining minimal acceptance before 1860, the movement caught on after the Civil War with state after state founding normal schools as paraprofessional institutions with a yet-to-be-defined relationship to the burgeoning system of public colleges and universities. See Borrowman (1956, pp. 35-37); Gordy (1891, pp. 2-55).

Within these first schools, particularly in those schools fostered by Horace Mann in Massachusetts, one finds four rudimentary elements for the training of teachers which remain with us today. The first three included a mastery of the subject matter to be taught, pedagogical instruction on how to teach while keeping order in the classroom, and supervised student teaching which attempted to apply theory to practice. The fourth element came less from the formal curriculum and more as the result of an ideological osmosis at work. Through the normal school experience, Mann, Henry Barnard, and others expected their novitiate to become indoctrinated in the belief that teaching was the holiest of all callings. Cyrus Peirce, a normal school teacher, would close each day with the admonition, "My pupils, live to the truth." Clearly he saw in his work the means of fulfilling Isaiah's prophecy that "the eyes of the blind shall be opened, . . . the tongues of the dumb shall sing." (See Norton 1926, pp. xxv, xxix.)

All too quickly, these reformers realized they were attempting to fashion professional elites out of limited human resources. Although their original plans called for a two-year period of intensive study, their recruits refused to stay in training. Instead, they often remained for no more than a few months, picking up whatever techniques and bits of knowledge they could, and then accepted a teaching post at a salary higher than their "untrained" competition.* With these "summer enlistments," as one frustrated normal school principal labelled them, the reformers went on to mount their campaign against ignorance and vice.† Not easily discouraged, they believed that progress was still possible with such raw and undisciplined recruits. If forced to concede the limited intelligence and

---

*A typical wage for teachers in the 1840s was four dollars per week for women and ten dollars for men. Rural positions paid less in cash, but provided "boarding round" privileges which enabled the teacher to live with one family for a week before moving on to another. See Messerli (1963); Butts and Cremin (1953, pp. 283-85).

†As Samuel Newman, one of the first normal principals, described the problem: "The plan of receiving some 25 or 30 new scholars every term, most of whom are to remain 3 months only, has been, as it must be, ruinous to the whole concern." See Messerli (1972, pp. 368-69).

commitment of their students, they never doubted the rightness of their cause or the reliability of their curricular model.

This model was based upon three important assumptions, not widely held at the time, but soon to gain an acceptance down to our own times. The first assumption stressed the importance of formulating the correct *input* into the process of training teachers. This was to be of two kinds. One was the none-too-promising group of students who wanted access to a proto-profession. A second was the formal curriculum. Quickly disabused of their belief in the qualifications of their students, the reformers placed a growing reliance on the efficacy of systematic instruction. They depended on the curriculum to bring about the necessary intellectual and behavioral changes in their trainees. See Harper (1939, pp. 30-32); Elsbree (1939, pp. 315-19).

Their second assumption grew out of the first. With the right subject matter in hand, they believed they could *manipulate the process* to ensure the achievement of their objectives. To be sure, they did not use some of our current managerial terminology, but they did see the training as a process that could be engineered and monitored. This led in turn to their third assumption. By a rational preparation of the curricular input and an intelligent manipulation of the process, it was possible to achieve *predictable outcomes,* and with economy and efficiency for good measure. Understandably the process would work better with able students, but the virtue of their system was that it would also work with *hoi polloi* who neither aspired to, nor were capable of, college instruction. If these reformers reluctantly came to accept Franklin's or Jefferson's earlier judgments on the caliber of potential teachers, they at least proposed a more remedial response.

At first glance, this looks similar to the management of factory production which was, at the time, turning out muskets, clocks, and peppermint sticks with unprecedented speed and profit.* But the normal school advocates did not see this as a problem. For them, as

---

*Perhaps the most unvarnished advocate of the factory method for education was DeWitt Clinton, who described the Lancasterian system of instruction as doing for learning what the factory was doing for material production. (See Campbell 1849, pp. 309-27.)

with many others, the factory was a new instrument for bringing greater material benefits to all. Welcoming its technology as a humanizing force which would relieve men and women of some of the age-old drudgery of hard physical labor, they did not comprehend its total human cost. Paradoxically, while the reformers continued to describe the educational process largely in agricultural metaphors, a favorite term being that of "cultivation," their procedures increasingly emulated the model of the factory.* Troubled little by the prospect of regimenting pupils into a lockstep system, they were dazzled by a vision of the common school which would enable every American child to realize his or her birthright and become a consumer of all that could now be made available in education. And the key to the entire process was a trained and dedicated corps of teachers.

As they pushed their instructional model forward, the reformers may have been viewed as impractical amateurs and dreamers, but hardly a threat to those in higher education. If one were to describe the attitudes of college presidents and professors at the time, it was the admixture of casual curiosity and diffuse good will towards a phenomenon far removed from them, such as they might later direct toward the Salvation Army or the YMCA.† And they were right in their own time. Normal school advocates, although envisioning a great educational triumph, did not anticipate the day when their institutions would become part of the first rung in the ladder of higher education. Neither did they expect all classroom teachers to possess the minimum of a baccalaureate degree. Such developments were even beyond the scope of their expansive social idealism which anticipated a new golden age of education bringing opportunity and social mobility to all.

Only later, following the rise in the status of the medical and legal professions, and the subsequent incorporation of their preparatory training within university graduate schools, did normal school education also seek a place on the college campus. No detailed attempt to explain this process can be made within a short space

---

*My conclusion concerning the use of agricultural terms and metaphors to describe the process comes from a random sampling of educational writings in the *Annals of Education* (1832), *Common School Journal* (1839, 1841), and the *American Journal of Education* (1855, 1860).

†What opposition there was, was more likely to come from those within the academy movement. See Edward Hitchcock, *The American Academic System Defended: an Address Delivered at the Dedication of the New Hall at Wiliston Academy Seminary* (Amherst, Mass. 1845).

here, but for the purposes of this discussion, it is sufficient to note that practitioners in both medicine and law were able to convince state legislatures that the public interest was best served by allowing the profession to regulate itself. For their own purposes, they were also able to co-opt part of the apparatus of higher education in order to limit the number who would enter their ranks. Following this strategy of graduate training and more rigorous admission standards, they went on to reap the twin rewards of money and status for their professions.*

No such successes accompanied the efforts of teacher educators. Unable to emulate their medical and legal counterparts and utilize only post-baccalaureate education, the "educationists" soon became embroiled in jurisdictional disputes with the undergraduate arts and science faculty. Parvenus within the academic establishment, and teaching students with questionable credentials, they lacked both the status and confidence to alter admission standards which would control the number of students training to become teachers.

For its part, the arts and science faculty often vacillated between an expedient embrace and an intellectual disdain of the new arrivals, with expedience most frequently carrying the day. Both they and the educationists needed a growing number of "student equivalents" to justify their existence. With undergraduate college enrollments in the twentieth century including as much as 40 percent preparing to become teachers, more than a few college presidents learned that regardless of their intellectual preferences, growth and a favorable public image required them to be in the business of training teachers. (See Pangburn 1932; Harper 1939, pp. 129-59; Jencks and Riesman 1968, pp. 231-37.)

Even once established on the campus, the educationists continued to experience an intellectual ostracism. Faculty debate and institutional in-fighting often revolved around the false dichotomy of knowing what to teach as opposed to knowing how to teach it. For the most part, neither faction gained a clear advantage. At best, the first four decades of the twentieth century witnessed a gradual institutional

---

*The celebrated "Flexner Report" of 1910 has been credited with closing down a number of substandard medical schools while making medical training unequivocally post-baccalaureate. A concomitant consequence of this usually overlooked in the histories of higher education was the severe limitation it placed on the number of practitioners entering the profession.

accommodation, often in the form of an armed truce, with the adversaries carrying out their functions behind departmental fortifications. Where campus skirmishes did occur, they were not sufficiently important to draw the attention of the public press.

Yet insecure in their new academic position and impelled by a sense of social reformism, the educationists could not settle for such a stalemate. Accordingly, while holding the academicians at bay on the campus, they tried to out-maneuver them through a campaign waged on a second front at the state capital. Setting their sights on state departments of education, they lobbied for a system of licensing that would legitimatize teaching as an officially sanctioned profession and require a growing number of professional or "education" courses.

In this campaign, the spokesmen for the arts and sciences were markedly the inferiors. Elitist and uncomfortable in a more political arena, they were no match for the more populist educationists who, in negotiating with state departments of education, were working with their former students and associates from the old teachers colleges. Also coming to the aid of the educationists were the classroom teachers, especially those active in the National Educational Association and its state affiliates. Seeking their own improved status and better compensation, teachers consistently supported the notion of additional professional courses sanctioned through state certification. The result was a *troika* of educationists, teachers, and state department of education officials based upon tangential and mutual interests but arrayed in a common cause against the academicians. (See Wesley 1957, pp. 342-68.)

It was this which first drew the attention and then criticism of Arthur Bestor (1953), James B. Conant (1963), and James D. Koerner (1963). More closely allied with the arts and sciences, their sense of intellectual rightness was exceeded only by their amazement at the near-invincibility of the educationist establishment. From their desks came attacks on the system, ranging from carefully weighed strictures tempered by the patrician gentility of Conant to broadside muckraking fired by the righteous indignation of Bestor and Koerner. On paper and from the lecture platform they often made a convincing case for the lack of intellectual rigor in teacher training, but they failed to mount a political offensive which would change what they castigated as a self-serving "monolithic establishment" or a "copper-riveted bureaucracy." In the paper war which followed the publication of each of their volumes, the critics and their academic allies found themselves winning the intellectual skirmishes, especially in the pages of the New York *Times* and the *Saturday Review*, but more often losing the battle for significant changes in the preparation and certification of teachers.*

Eventually, when editors moved on to other campaigns and the arts and science faculties needed to concentrate on a rear guard action, contending with class boycotts and pressures to justify the social relevancy of their own offerings, the teacher educators remained in control of the field. For all of the verbal exchanges, teacher training was still an amalgam of information drawn from the intellectual disciplines, a conventional wisdom and folklore on how to teach which was partially validated by a minimum of scientific data, and an anxiety-ridden baptism of fire on how to survive the first year in the classroom. What curricular change had come about since the days of Horace Mann was merely one of accretion in subject matter, pedagogy, and student teaching. (See Sherwin 1974, pp. 3-56.) Thus, through a slow historic evolution, the educationists had erected an annex connected to the main structure of higher education which a series of critical and frequently persuasive books might shake, but could not bring down.

Although Conant's work was still being discussed by the mid-1960s, and Koerner had yet other books to write, the triumph of the educationists seemed virtually complete. More than 1,300 institutions of higher learning in the United States had teacher education programs enrolling 38 percent of the undergraduate population. Congress was making educational appropriations of unprecedented generosity, and the legislation was being signed into law by a president who took special pride in once having been a school teacher.

If the victory was real, it was more in terms of acquiring institutional goals and legal sanctions than in closing the gap between public expectations and the actual quality of professional training. To use an insightful comparison which Herbert Gans (1974, p. 9) has applied

---

*For example, compare the pro-Koerner reviews in the *New York Times Book Review* (May 26, 1963), p. 3 and the *Saturday Review* (May 18, 1963), p. 77 with the *Harvard Educational Review* (Winter 1964), p. 96, *Teachers College Record* (October 1963), p. 83 and *School and Society* (March 1964), pp. 135-39. Since Conant's book was less polemical and more constructive, its reviews were also less partisan.

within a different context, the educationists had achieved a "merit-ocracy of *credentialing*" if not a "meritocracy of *performance*." As a group, students majoring in education continued to be less intellectu-ally able and frequently felt snubbed by their arts and science instructors. When compared with their pre-medical and pre-law counterparts, those who planned to become teachers suffered from a low professional identity on campus. Instead of enjoying a sense of exclusiveness maintained by pre-med students, they seemed indis-tinguishable among the masses. Furthermore, far outnumbering them were those who, failing in their vocational or matrimonial objectives, could always "pick up a few education courses and teach." (See Clark and Marker 1975.)

For all their efforts then, the educationists were but partially successful in raising the status of their cause above that of a low prestige academic endeavor. One reasonably clear index of this could be found in the comparative investments made in academic programs. Historically, undergraduate instruction had been allocated less than graduate programs. Within undergraduate education on the campus, teacher training remained a low-cost activity with large classes and routine instruction. Thus, even into the present, it has continued to suffer the compound fiscal jeopardy of being one of the most im-poverished among the academic poor.*

That portion of teacher training conducted in the public schools had even less institutional status. Compared with other clinical instruction and internships, student teaching offered little more than a brief apprenticeship in how to get by the first year of teaching. Crippling what might have been effective cooperative venture is what two authors have recently called the continuing "guest-host relation-ship" of the college and the school (Clark and Marker 1975). The cooperating teacher is given a pittance for his or her services and the

---

*Dean James Doi of the University of Rochester, a scholar of note in the study of higher education, has warned that such a summary statement is subject to numerous qualifications. While he agrees with the generalization, he also points out that the relative costs of undergraduate courses in the biological and natural sciences are much higher than those in the humanities and behavioral sciences. Then, too, the cost of upper division undergraduate instruction is generally higher than that in freshman and sophomore classes. Within teacher education programs, the cost of training music teachers and those in secondary school sciences and modern languages is much higher than the cost of training elementary school teachers. Dean Doi also warns that our analyses of comparative costs are relatively crude and require much more refinement.

college has little functional control over the quality of the field experience. Yet even with such handicaps, beginning teachers have consistently singled out practice teaching as the most valuable portion of their training. If their arts and science instruction and education courses seemed largely irrelevant, at least their field work gave them a survival kit with which to negotiate within the lonely environment of the American classroom.

Perhaps Bestor and Koerner were right in part. Teacher education had become bureaucratic, but a monolithic establishment it was not. Instead, it had become sufficiently fragmented so as to make it difficult to fix any clear responsibility for the education or miseducation of the American teacher. Far from some idea of shared participation by higher education, the schools, and the teaching profession, the education of teachers had become an undertaking confused by overlapping jurisdictions held together by academic, professional, and legal red tape.

The Real Change

Ironically, Charles Silberman (1970, pp. 412-69), the most recent critic to complain of the invincibility of the establishment, failed to recognize that it had already begun to come undone. Had he seen this, he might have been longer on proposals for reform and shorter on entertaining but often irrelevant vignettes. Public school systems needing an ever-larger portion of the real estate tax dollar to meet their burgeoning current budgets, now all too easily overlook their long-range interest in improving teacher education. Meanwhile, the most coerced and least compensated participants, the "cooperating" teachers, have begun to insist on changes in the partnership. From the political base provided by their associations they are insisting upon the right to establish professional standards for entering and remaining within the profession as ironclad as those enjoyed by medical boards and bar associations. What began as a hesitant whisper a decade earlier has swelled into a national call for the profession to govern itself. At its 1974 Chicago convention, the National Education Association stated its unambiguous position by asserting that "Members of the profession, through professional standards boards and professional practices commissions, must set forth and enforce standards of license, practice, ethics, and competence." This alone was sufficient to shake the coalition of interests in the area of professional governance which had been skillfully manipulated by the educationists operating from their higher education base. (See National Education Association 1974a, pp. 18-20, 30.)

To make the dissolution more complete, the guardians of the public interest in state departments of education made their dissatisfaction with teacher education manifest by championing the so-called performance-based teacher education movement. By their mixed responses the educationists gave evidence of a division in their ranks. While their national organization, the American Association for Colleges of Teacher Education, generally supported PBTE through a series of monographs, the deans of two leading schools of education spoke for themselves and others in raising serious reservations about the movement. (See Griffiths 1973; Atkins 1975.) Quite clearly, the fragile hegemony gained by the educationists from their merging of interests and fashioning of a series of institutional accommodations could not survive in its present form.

Of these changes, the most dramatic has been the shift in policy and program of the organized teaching profession. If teachers now seem less professional to some, most would agree that they are far better organized. For a century and more, they had been lauded as the architects of a new American society, yet throughout this period they had continued to be paid something less than bricklayers. Frustrated by the 1960s as never before, they gambled status and public esteem for money and professional power. Through militant action which took them to the collective bargaining table and sometimes beyond to the picket line, they won salary increments and a strong voice in determining their working conditions, both not thought possible a decade earlier (see Braun 1972).

Then, flushed with their initial victories, they drew aim on state departments of education, insisting on the right to set licensing standards.* In addition, they have gone for what some teacher educators consider their lifeline, the accreditation of college programs. Insisting on and gaining representation within the National Council for Accreditation of Teacher Education (NCATE) equal

---

*The NEA position is clearly documented in a number of publications including Darland (1969, pp. 135-49); Knispel (1974); National Education Association (1974b, pp. iv-vi).

to that held by the colleges through their membership in the AACTE, they have served notice of their intent to exercise a strong role in accreditation. No surprise attack here, the teacher educators were amply warned. As early as 1970, the President of the NEA ("Report of the 108th Meeting of the NEA," San Francisco, July 1970) had announced that the organization had long dreamed of controlling "who enters, who stays in, and who leaves the profession . . . . Once this is done," he continued, "we can also control the teacher training institutions." For the University of Oregon, this dream became more of a nightmare when the re-accreditation of its secondary programs was denied, largely at the insistence of the NEA members in NCATE. (See the Eugene, Oregon *Register-Guard*, August 1 and 31, September 29, October 17, 1974.)

Also potentially threatening to the colleges have been the "Teacher Centers" similar to those in Great Britain, proposed by teachers' associations. (See Shanker 1971, 1973; Kemble 1973.) To date, however, more has been printed than put into operation. Furthermore, endeavors of this sort will be viewed as wrong-headed even by those within the profession. In their continued efforts to narrow the quality gap between teacher training and that of medicine and law, removing higher education from professional training is an anti-intellectual step towards apprenticeship training. The uncertain future of teacher centers notwithstanding, we can be confident that teachers will not relax their efforts to determine the entry criteria for the profession, and *ipso facto*, the content of their teacher training. The result of this, although not recognized by most academicians at this time, will be a shift of the power base away from the campus and an accommodation which will allow the organized profession to pass on curricular decisions.

To back up their demands, the largely *sotto-voce* partners have become both vocal and active. In most states, they have become a force with which politicians must reckon. In the 1974 elections, teachers gave money and rang doorbells for their candidates. When the votes were tallied, more than 75 percent of those they supported were elected, including the leading members of several important Congressional committees.*

---

*In the House, 229 of 282 NEA endorsed candidates were elected. In the Senate, it was 21 out of 28. For a complete summary, see Grotton (1975).

Finally, and most important in its long-range impact on the changing role of our elementary and secondary schools, the teachers are insisting on participating in determining the educational outcomes for which they are to be held accountable. No longer will they accept the chimerical mantle of miracle worker while being encumbered by a ragtag collection of monitorial assignments. If they are to be held accountable, they are also demanding a more defined specificity of their responsibilities and a greater voice in determining how these are to be carried out.

In addition, I believe that we can look for the following developments within the next decade:

1. Teachers will refuse to be held accountable for creating the good society when so many other forces in our country are frustrating the achievement of this goal. Attempting to limit what they are expected to accomplish, they will work for contractual arrangements which more clearly prescribe their functions and objectives. The day is past when any unfulfilled desire or unexpressed anxiety of the American parent, taxpayer, and employer can be shifted to the shoulders of the classroom teacher.

2. Teachers will make more explicit efforts to raise the quality of those entering the profession as a means of controlling the supply of teachers. If they succeed here, it will rightly mean the demise of weaker institutions which have exploited teacher education to keep their other academic programs solvent. For others it can mean a cutback in faculty and budget, unless the limiting of students will be accompanied by reforms requiring a far greater investment in instructional resources in those who are in training. For those institutions that have known only growth and a relative independence in setting admission and graduation requirements, the efforts of the profession will be perceived as a threat to institutional autonomy and academic freedom. Others may seize it as an opportunity for genuine reforms.

3. In their attempt to limit numbers and raise teacher qualifications, the profession may come to endorse, if not insist upon, a fifth year of graduate professional work including student teaching followed by a sixth year of carefully supervised teaching internship. One consequence of this would be a shift of most, if not all, educational studies out of the undergraduate sequence. Advisable though this

might be, it should not prevent new experimentation with under-graduate and graduate programs in which the integration of pro-fessional and liberal arts instruction is attempted throughout the college sequence.

4. Politically, the relationship of the organized teaching pro-fession and leading graduate schools of education will be similar to that of bar associations and the major law schools. Although this marriage will be more forced than voluntary, it should prove an enduring one. This accomplished, teacher educators will no longer woo the support of the arts and science faculty. Tiring of pursuing a mistress who never accepted them, they will find more to share with the profession. Here, too, the history of law school faculties may be illustrative.

5. With their new partners, teacher trainers will rely more heavily on field-based and clinical instruction. The "guest-host" relationship will disappear, the cooperating teacher will assume a more functional role in preparing the novitiate, and the entire arrangement will be based on a more solid fiscal basis.

6. On the state level, the organized profession will have much more influence in setting licensing standards. In some states, they will control and process and exercise a power similar to that enjoyed by medical doctors in setting their standards of practice. At the outset, the profession will face two difficult problems. The first will be the relative emphasis they will place on raising professional standards as measured against their concern for establishing greater job security for their members. The second will be their success in working cooperatively with, rather than alienating, the leading gradu-ate schools of education.

7. The influence of foundations on reforming teacher education will be further diminished, if there is no change in their past strategies. It is hard to conceive of their launching reforms in legal education by first attacking the bar associations, yet in their efforts to alter education practices in elementary and secondary schools they have often followed the lead of outside *Wunderkinden* or self-styled experts who have gained press by antagonizing the very classroom teachers who can make or break their schemes.

8. Although working for a more realistic, albeit circumscribed, mission for public education, the organized profession will not accept diminished support for the schools, any more than the medical

profession would endorse a cutback in expenditures for hospitals and other health services. Teachers will also oppose public funds for alternatives to our present institutions such as "store front" academies, the voucher plan, and various imported and exotic plans. With these, their response will be similar to that of the medical profession's official stance on acupuncture, chiropractice, and yoga.

Some of these developments are well under way, even though the more general intellectual community, and teacher educators in particular, have not comprehended their significance. Liberals and conservatives will find common cause in opposing them, but for differing reasons. The former, ever ready to embrace enlightened institutional intervention in the lives of individuals and groups, cannot endorse a lessened role for the public school. The latter, ever alert to the abuse of power by collective action, will hardly welcome the entry of a new power bloc into the field of public education. Meanwhile, on the campus, what will be taken to be the rise of trade unionism in the NEA and AFT will only reinforce the pseudo-snobbery of many arts and science professors who have thought all along that teacher education was casting false pearls before real swine.

I suggested earlier that we sever ourselves from our favored cultural myths only slowly and with great reluctance. Yet since it is crucial to shaping public policy, the demythologizing of our expectations for the public schools and the shedding of the false security these brought us, can no longer be postponed. In so doing, however, we also cannot afford to embrace some of the current rhetoric of educational change, innovation that would impose still greater educational burdens for the schools, nor follow the pied-piper claims of others who advocate a deschooling of society. Actually, once west of the Hudson and east of the San Andreas Fault, there is little support for this latter simplistic notion.

However, even if we are to free ourselves both of the heady image of our schools as social panaceas and the romantic fantasies of Ivan Illich and others, we must comprehend and come to grips with powerful and professional, albeit not necessarily intellectual or ideological, forces shaping the future of public education. To do so will require a rethinking of the mission of our schools and the role teachers will exercise within them. Neither incompetents nor miracle workers, neither docile servants nor transient pedants, they are willing to measure up to reasonable criteria and devote a lifetime to their vocation, even if this also entails their submission to far more organizational discipline than given by their predecessors. If at times they have doubts about the new course they are following, these are easily set aside by their recognition of what they are achieving through collective action. It now remains to be seen whether, after having won impressive gains in the immediate area of job security, they will go on to create a professional organization, akin to the guild system of the American Medical Association or the rank and file unionism of the American railway worker, or will yet develop a hybrid alternative that will better serve their own needs as well as those of the greater public.

References

Atkins, J. Myron. "Professional Leadership and PBTE." *Regaining Educational Leadership: Critical Essays on PBTE/CBTE, Behavioral Objectives and Accountability*, edited by Ralph A. Smith. New York: John Wiley & Sons, 1975.

Bailyn, Bernard. *Forming of American Society*. Chapel Hill, N.C.: University of North Carolina Press, 1960.

Bestor, Arthur E. *Educational Wastelands*. Urbana, Ill.: University of Illinois Press, 1953.

Borrowman, Merle L. *The Liberal and Technical in Teacher Education*. New York: Teachers College Press, 1956.

Braun, Robert J. *Teachers and Power, the Story of the A.F.T.* New York: Simon & Schuster, 1972.

Butts, R. Freeman, and Cremin, Lawrence. *A History of Education in American Culture*. New York: Holt, Rinehart & Winston, 1953.

Campbell, William W. *The Life and Writings of DeWitt Clinton*. New York: Baker & Scribner, 1849.

Carter, James G. *Essays upon Popular Education, Containing an Outline of an Institution for the Training of Teachers*. New York: Arno Press. Reprint of 1826 edition.

Clark, David L., and Marker, Gerald. "The Institutionalization of Teacher Education." National Society for the Study of Education, 1975.

Conant, James B. *The Education of American Teachers*. New York: McGraw-Hill, 1963.

Cremin, Lawrence A. *The Wonderful World of Ellwood Patterson Cubberley*. New York: Teachers College Press, 1965.

Cubberley, Ellwood P. *Public Education in the United States*. Boston: Houghton Mifflin, 1947.

Darland, David D. "Preparation in the Governance of the Profession." *Teachers for the Real World,* edited by B. Othanel Smith. Washington, D.C.: AACTE, 1969.

Elsbree, Willard. *The American Teacher.* Westport, Conn.: Greenwood. Reprint of 1939 edition.

Gans, Herbert. *Popular Culture and High Culture.* New York: Basic Books, 1974.

Gordy, John P. *Rise and Growth of the Normal School Idea in the United States.* Washington, D.C.: U.S. Government Printing Office, 1891.

Griffiths, Daniel E. "Intellectualism and Professionalism." *New York University Education Quarterly* V (Fall 1973): 1-6.

Grotton, Martha. "NEA Pushes for Teachers' Rights." *Change* VII (February 1975): 17-20.

Harper, Charles A. *A Century of Public Teacher Education.* Westport, Conn.: Greenwood. Reprint of 1939 edition.

Jencks, Christopher, and Riesman, David. *The Academic Revolution.* New York: Doubleday, 1968.

Kemble, Eugenia. "Why Teachers Want Teacher Centers." *New York Teacher* (November 11, 1973).

Knispel, Margaret. "What Can Be Done?" *Theory into Practice* XIII (June 1974): 210-21.

Koerner, James D. *The Miseducation of American Teachers.* Boston: Houghton Mifflin, 1963.

Larabee, Leonard W. (ed.). *The Papers of Benjamin Franklin* (vol. IV). New Haven, Conn.: Yale University Press, 1961.

Lee, Gordon C. (ed.). *Crusade Against Ignorance: Thomas Jefferson on Education.* New York: Teachers College Press, 1961.

Lerner, Max. *America as a Civilization.* New York: Simon & Schuster, 1957.

Messerli, Jonathan. "Horace Mann and Teacher Education." *Yearbook of Education, the Education of Teachers,* edited by George Bereday and Joseph Lauwerys. New York: Harcourt, Brace & World, 1963.

Messerli, Jonathan. *Horace Mann, a Biography.* New York: Knopf, 1972.

National Education Association. *Resolutions and Other Actions.* Washington, D.C.: The Association, 1974a.

National Education Association. *Teacher Standards and Practice Commissions.* Washington, D.C.: The Association, 1974b.

Norton, Arthur O. (ed.). *The First State Normal School in America: The Journals of Cyrus Peirce and Mary Swift.* New York: Arno Press. Reprint of 1926 edition.

Pangburn, Jessie. *The Evolution of the American Teachers College.* New York: AMS Press. Reprint of 1932 edition.

Rudolph, Frederick (ed.). *Essays on Education in the Early Republic.* Cambridge, Mass.: Harvard University Press, 1965.

Shanker, Albert. "Where We Stand." *New York Times* (December 26, 1971 and July 22, 1973).

Sherwin, Susan S. *Teacher Education: A Status Report.* Princeton, N.J.: Educational Testing Service, 1974.

Silberman, Charles E. *Crisis in the Classroom.* New York: Random House, 1970.

Wesley, Edgar B. *National Education Association, the First Hundred Years.* New York: Harper, 1957.

9

EDUTOPIA, or, 266 Suggestions for Change

Michael Rossman

Three men came to do foundation work on our house, or rather two men and a lad of fifteen. Out my window I watched him running the cement mixer, shoveling sand, not with a man's experience but competently, and for hours. I joined them for coffee break; we cussed the economic situation for a while, and they instructed me in the mysteries of J-bolts and form-stripping. The kid listened, serious, intent—not so much to the tricks of the trade, though he picked up some as they were explained to this outsider, but to the rituals of intercourse between us men. I tried to draw him out, with no luck; he would not yet join in our joshing humor, but went off to clean the mixer.

"How long has the kid been working with you?" I asked.

"He's my boy, my son."

"He works good."

"He does that. And it's nice to have him with us. But I worry."

"Mmmm?"

"Oh, he dropped out of school a couple of months ago. I asked him what he wanted to do, said he wanted to work with us. It's good, him learning a trade and all. But I think of him pouring concrete under houses all his life, and I dunno. He said he just couldn't

take school any more, all the B.S." We both grunted ruefully.
" 'Course, it's his life; I don't think it's my business to tell him what
to do. But I wish there were some other way. . . ." I was silent,
thinking about the options for him. There wasn't much to say.

So much of what he was learning in his apprenticeship was useful, precious, strong, and beyond the reach of the schools to teach.
Why should his father have regretted it, as leading him into a dead
end? But I know why. Manual labor is lower class, and the myth of
social mobility is indeed a myth. The kid will be lucky to be doing
foundations when he's middle-aged; more likely technological advances will put him on the welfare rolls. And once you jump off the
educational train, it's hard to get back on to go somewhere new:
only some of the strongly motivated manage, and for them it is a
struggle.

I try to imagine the conditions of society, of education, that
would make what that boy was doing with his life truly okay. I
imagine them from his perspective, as an exercise in social biography;
I will call him Horatio.

At fifteen Horatio found himself entering manhood, and grew
impatient with the closed routines of the classroom, which many of
his friends had already left. Without fuss or stigma he took leave of
his schooling and put his learning record in the out-student registry.
There it was added to from time to time (at his request) by Mary, a
teacher he had grown friends with, whom he came back occasionally
to visit in the hours her job provided for such relationships.

Mary gave him the usual advice, about the wisdom of a solid
vacation between the discipline of school and the discipline of work.
In some months, the school's triennial contracts with the furniture
factory and the supermarket association would both come round
again, offering him a choice of basic industrial apprenticeships, two-
year trainings to teach him their full cycles of routine operations.
Horatio's patience was more tempted by his friend Jeff's proposal to
wait until spring and take a farm apprenticeship together; but the
fortune of a place opening in his father's crew won out.

Like any apprenticeship, his had a broad curriculum. He learned
a body of industrial knowledge—the use of tools and their care, the
properties of structures and materials in considerable pragmatic
detail. He learned the rhythms of cooperative work; its processes of
beginning, duration, completion, and aftermath; the cycle of

destruction and creation—not in arbitrary exercise, but in the course of doing something essential for the community, something real and substantive. At seventeen he found himself usefully competent, able to swing his weight in the intimate society of work beneath a house, and through this in the larger society. Some sense of this was recorded in his out-student file; more was reflected in his feelings of self-sufficiency, and his confidence in his ability to learn and do certain kinds of things in the future.

Meanwhile the passions of adolescence moved in him. Not school but the rec center centered his social life, although he had to ride its special buses till he was old enough to drive. He hung out mostly with his peers there, though the center's health maintenance operation brought him together with all ages in his aikido training and its supplemental nutritional course. He met his first love on the mat; it lasted three months, by which time he had run through enough of his wages to force his parents' anger. Consumer training, from elementary school on, had taught him the essentials of money management no less than his contemporaries, but love is a wild force, and he knew as yet no compelling reason to save.

He soon found one. Winters are slack in the foundation trade. During the first one he mooned around the rec center, waiting for evening and his friends, dreaming of the sun and the beaches of Mazatlan. When the second winter came he took an intensive introduction to Spanish at the learning pavilion. Self-guided media access made up for the days he missed, working while the sun shone, and he learned enough to audit a night course in Latin American culture the university extension gave during the spring.

His friend Manuel took him to hell around in the Chicano barrio; I will pass over his brush with the cops, except to say that the community's power on the police review board was real, that its programs of instruction for officers and judges were humane and effective, and that Horatio took his sentence like a man. Indeed he enjoyed it, all but the coercion. He was surprised to learn how much he knew about foundations, and what rose above them, in the course of conducting school classes of various grades with their teachers on tours of building sites; besides which, explaining things to the kids gave him his first sustained practice in conversational Spanish.

By the time he finished putting in his hours, he felt less abused of the pay he was missing. He found himself in his first serious tutoring relationship, with Isabella, ten, who had pestered him with questions on an early tour, and had gotten her teacher (with Horatio's assent, and his guidance officer's) to let her meet Horatio at the learning pavilion one morning a week to accompany his tours. He went back to his own teacher Mary for help in writing the report for Isabella's learning file. As his first student Isabella remained special, and their formal association continued sporadically; years later he would have the pleasure of working with her for a summer on a construction crew, and having her tutor him in architecture.

More important to Horatio at the moment than this nascent friendship was the new image of himself as teacher, or rather its social currency. As he grew familiar with the operations of the learning pavilion's registry, and as the teachers who accompanied him helped him learn how to connect with their classes, he saw that the role of adjunct teacher was open to him, as surely as it was to any other citizen who had learned enough about something to teach. When his sentence was up, Horatio asked Mary, Isabella's teacher, and his boss/father jointly to certify him for the instructional work he had been doing, and his name was entered in the registry, to be activated later if he wished.

Meanwhile he had been scheming with Manuel after work and on the sly, until time let them make their fantasies open. With a long spell of freedom in mind two more seasons of work passed quickly, Horatio's nest egg accumulating, and also his linguistic capital. Came the third winter; he was ready. His loss was no blow to the work team in rain, and the usual apprentice shift was two years anyway. Horatio kissed his parents and his girl of the moment goodbye, and took off with Manuel for Mexico.

To be on one's own at seventeen is scary and glorious, and an education in itself; but I am concerned here with what can be institutionalized. After six months Horatio dipped back across the border, to dodge the Mexican rains in the open dorms at Arizona State. Like many of the other out-students staying there, his interest was more social than academic, and he resisted his friends' invitations to share in their classes. More often during the days he was to be found at the public garage, learning to make sound the ancient VW that had failed so expensively in the desert. He besieged the resident mechanic with questions, far out of proportion to his use fee, recognizing the learning as a prudent and basic investment.

At the end they offered him an apprenticeship, touting its advantages: public machine maintenance was dependable work, with hours as flexible as anyone's need for employment. But Horatio was already grounded in one such subsistence skill and not minded to cut short his freedom. The rudiments of personal competence were enough, and he took care to certify this for his learning record by spending his last week in Arizona cramming the texts the mechanics lent him, till they rated him "pass" on the basic knowledge-and-proficiency exam. Armed with manual and toolbox, he resumed his Mexican adventure, this time alone.

The day before his nineteenth birthday he came home to San Jose, with a guitar and a moustache. After some months he got bored with his anecdotes and just hanging out, and set about putting his educational affairs in order, transferring his learning file to the college center and finding a first advisor there in one of Mary's friends. His conversational proficiency in a foreign tongue was no trouble to certify, but Horatio's literacy was spotty, and he elected a course in Latin American literature, nourished by the fantasy of some day traveling farther south.

Most of Horatio's studies were generated in like fashion from his recent experience. His seminar in composition and personal growth gave him opportunity to express his adventures in writing, and encouraged him in the self-reflection that brooded beneath the moustache. Such rituals of travel were common among his coevals, and he found many peers in his comparative anthropology course. Grounded in the experience of another culture, and with new perspectives of his own, he found its focus on American suburbia to his taste; and the graduate student who helped him through the basic readings in theory commended Horatio to his advisor.

Horatio found himself less at home than he thought in the survey course on Housing, which had seemed like a mickey; he realized how narrow his view had been under the houses, and how little he had understood the factors governing indigenous Mexican constructions. It was as much this chagrin as his work experience that led him to register Housing as his concentration field, connect with a concentration advisor, and accept the invitation of a girl he met in class to move to the low-cost student facilities and make the fourth in her study commune.

They were fortunate to draw a bungalow, rather than co-op

housing in the reconverted dorms. Horatio still had enough of his nest egg to forgo the option of working off costs in the campus maintenance service; after four years away from school, he wanted to focus his energy on study. The commune held together for two years, working on one course in common at a time and sharing their individual explorations in their joint concentration. Horatio was satisfied with this; concentration was a long haul, and for the time being he was more interested in completing his basic education credential.

The credential's job relevance had eroded further with the general swing to apprenticeship and work-skills certification, and many concentrators chose to neglect it until middle age. But Horatio had no burning aim, and saw the sense in qualifying himself for the basic adult educational rights of unsponsored facility access, the job learning tithe, and sabbatical support. Work and travel had left him confident of himself in new situations, and finding the right level to engage his remedial studies was not difficult. He completed arithmetic by himself and went on through algebra to calculus; the computer programs were excellent and bungalow-serviced, and his roommates knew enough to spare him the necessity of hunting up a liaison in the math center to supplement them. But literature was not to be explored in isolation, and Horatio found himself at first most comfortable in Mary's classes on his old campus, though the predominance of fourteen-year-olds made him feel somewhat incongruous.

By the time his partnership with Jane, who had invited him into the commune, had solidified, Horatio had much of his credential on file—a respectable spectrum of subject studies, and, more importantly, a sheaf of letters certifying that he knew how to learn with guidance in the humanities and the social sciences, and independently in his concentration. Natural science was more difficult to satisfy, its certification running more by the old norms of textbook accomplishments; Horatio worked on the human body core through the learning pavilion, but held off on the elective for two years, until the commune reached the normal parting of the ways. After Jane and he moved to a den in the barrio, they took geology together, spending spring weekends in the field and winter afternoons in the associated chem lab. On his twenty-second birthday, Horatio's advisor's committee judged his file as certifiable, and registered him as an educational adult.

Well before this, Horatio had returned to work. Part-time

employment in his own subsistence trade quickly proved incompatible with a steady study schedule, and his advisor suggested that he draw against future sabbatical support; but Horatio chose instead to activate his adjunct instructional registration. After some months the learning center assigned him to the education crew of a major government-housing construction project. Working three half-shifts a week, Horatio was able to serve as liaison to two dozen classes of various ages, conducting each on monthly tours from groundbreaking through completion.

His Saturday seminars with the project's senior educators served a double function, deepening Horatio's understanding of the many factors governing the project's design, materials, and social policy; and organizing the curriculum of his tours. Horatio found he could relate most of his concentration studies to the work it was his job to explain, and took his running discussions with the older classes seriously. After evaluating their papers at the completion of the project, he drew on them for his own survey critique of the project, with special reference to neighborhood impact. It earned him a major independent credit in his concentration, and a letter of praise from the senior educator who certified it for his advisor.

Shortly thereafter Horatio left school, for financial reasons, though he welcomed the change of rhythm, his credential being finally complete. Jane had been working half-time in retail foods, an early choice of subsistence apprenticeship that by now had completely lost interest for her; she wanted a spell of full studenthood to train herself productively in her concentration before starting a family. Her interest in the social side of Housing had led her recently into city planning with a focus on neighborhood social services, and though her academic studies were rooted in fieldwork, a paid apprenticeship was two years distant. Horatio went looking for a full-time job.

He did not look far. A contractor he had grown friendly with on the housing project invited Horatio to join his crew. After five years Horatio's hands welcomed the hammer again, and the renewal of his pride in labor. The old rhythms of building were comforting, and season by season he solidified his basic carpentry skills. The journeymen offered to apprentice Horatio in finish work, or grant him job leave for intensive work at the industrial skills center if he wanted a quicker way to complete the master credential in carpentry.

But Horatio was content with mastery of the eightpenny nail: more precision meant less space for introspection, and base scale was adequate. To remain a common carpenter, as he did for years, cost him no social loss or privilege, and his learning interests ran in a different direction.

The construction firm was too small to be subject to the Uniform Job-Related Education Act, except as its provisions automatically applied to contracts with local and higher governmental agencies and firms engaged in interstate commerce; but Horatio's firm honored them voluntarily wherever else it could, finding that the improved skills and spirit of its work crews more than offset the nominal disadvantage in competitive bidding. The learning tithe was flexible, and though throughout industry the general practice was to use it for a one-week skill or background intensive each quarter, at first Horatio tithed in the form of a paid afternoon each week attending a seminar on the City run by his concentration advisor.

As Jane's interest in neighborhood services grew more definite, Horatio began to pursue a slow convergence of their work. Studying the administrative face of his industry rarely brought him into seminar; rather he laid aside his tools at odd intervals to be present as an authorized auditor at the various interactions of job contracting, union relations, and architectural liaison.

For a while, acquiring background for his auditing at the video terminal took up so much time beyond the tithe that it cut heavily into Horatio's nights, straining his relationship with Jane and reminding him ruefully of how simple "learning the business" had seemed when he was under the house with his father. Finally Jane convinced him to overrule his old superstitions and take training in learning-trance at the out-student center, arguing that a learner without hypnosis was like a joist-cutter without an electric saw, and that a carpenter ought to know enough to patronize the tool shop. His absorption rate increased and the strain eased. But when the firm let Horatio undertake supervised minor bidding and troubleshooting, he credited his burgeoning administrative competence less to psychic and computer technology than to his solid grounding of experience as a member of the working crew.

By now Horatio's breadth of study and work in his concentration were sufficient to leave him a straight shot at residential construction management, and his father urged him to go through formal internship and enter white-collar practice. But Horatio was only twenty-six, and in no hurry to opt for a specialization. Also, like most of his male peers, he saw no reason to sacrifice family life to a profession. He wanted a child, and the time was coming; he knew it would leave him less than free to invest his full energies in a major turn of career.

Jane's own internship was in its second year; they banked the income against the times when neither would be working, and planned conception so that she would be in the third month when they took job leave and set off to winter in Mexico. For Horatio those months were sheer vacation, watching her belly swell in a strange dear land, undisturbed even when Jane pulled him from the beaches to serve as her interpreter as she explored the jungle of city agencies. On returning home she finished her comparative study and took her orals while her perspective was fresh. Both of the neighborhoods in which she had interned had filed requests with the San Jose Planning Council for her ongoing assignment, pledging their matching share of tax base, and with master certification her employment was automatic. In the eighth month of pregnancy she registered with the Civil Service as a neighborhood services organizer, based in the barrio, with a hold on active employment.

Horatio had done carpentry full-time since Mexico, and was glad when the paternity provision of the Job Education Act took effect in the ninth month. The reduction to half-time work left him free to finish LaMaze training with Jane during the days, and make a thorough job together of the pre-parent course at the learning pavilion. The pregnancy being normal, their instructor midwifed the birth, though as it was a first she did not ask to bring her mixed class of adolescents in on the ritual. When their friends left, Horatio put away his tools, and settled in to enjoy his baby Maria, watching her learn from the instant her lungs knew air.

His appreciation of her learning was sharpened by the pre-parent course; and by the time their three months of postpartum work-leave had passed, both Horatio and Jane were glad to go down to the neighborhood pavilion and play their part in forming an Early Education Group. Many parents preferred to dial guidance in private; and indeed the library video channels were far richer in information than any face-to-face could be, so that serious EEGers too drew on their survey readings. But Horatio found even the live program tapes too cool a medium. His conditioning to educational dependence, in the pre-adolescent schools which still tended to foster that attitude, had been largely undone by his later experience in the study commune, and at twenty-seven both he and Jane preferred to work in peer-learning pools whenever they could.

Often an EEG would form among a group of friends, using the pavilion only for skilled liaison, if at all. But Horatio and Jane were in the more usual position: of their good friends only one pair of parents lived nearby and were ready, and they knew only one other neighborhood couple working on a first child. They registered together, but it was two months before the group grew large enough to be assigned its skillpeople, as the pavilion was strict about observing the formal negotiations of compatibility whenever racial mix-matching was requested.

Their EEG opted for triweekly meetings, a schedule it was to maintain for almost three years, through several changes of skillpeople and the replacement of two of the original families when time came to organize the learning-play group formally. As the children moved beyond motor skills and speech into social relations, their parents followed and learned to anticipate, pooling their observations. In its meetings the group found the skillpeople as useful for their facilitant skills as for their specialized knowledge, even after learning how to use them effectively in this.

Horatio was always glad when his turn tending the learning-play group coincided with the apprentice's weekly visit, being grateful for company as well as advice. He enjoyed working with younger people. But after the Perkinses and their kid worked out of the tantrum game in three months of group focus without recourse to family therapy services, he saw the wisdom of the custom that led most EEG skillpeople to draw out their internship in child development over a period of years and many groups, and not function as senior resources until they had served in a parental capacity to some child through adolescence. And he and Jane took seriously their responsibility, as members of a registered EEG, to criticize and certify the work of each intern the pavilion matched them with.

Jane studied the skillpeople's work in the EEG with a double eye, as parent and as professional. Having a child gave her a natural vantage on neighborhood services, and in Maria's third month she activated her organizer registration, to quarter time at first and then to half as she moved afield. By then Horatio had returned to work as a carpenter, finding a firm in their quarter of San Jose with an open half-time slot in its crew. Like many parents they preferred this arrangement of work for the way it brought them into and out of the home, and the flexibility it left them to pursue their interests. At times their staggered schedules collided, but Horatio and Jane had little trouble finding care for Maria among their EEG's families, and rarely had to fall back on the neighborhood center; and when the learning-play group was organized each had time to share its tending. Often Jane would take the kids out to the greenbelt farms or on the simplest industrial education tours, while Horatio kept up his weekly concentration seminar as an out-student at the college. Less regularly she would tag along when he took them exploring at the pavilion, to observe or to sit in on an EEG reference seminar.

From such excursions Jane's first organizing project took form, as part of the general reintegration of childhood health maintenance then in progress. Though the socialization of medicine had made for equitable distribution of remedial service, the forms for implementing its other major component, educative service, were still rudimentary and in flux. Health instruction was well established in the pre-parent curriculum as a project of the midwife guild. But few people had been satisfied with the attempt to provide ongoing health liaison via the EEG skillpeople, whose training in any case brought the doctors no closer to the children's lives; and recently that policy had been voted down throughout the city. Jane viewed the ensuing consolidation of health education at the pavilion level as a retreat from decentralist philosophy, and feared that resurgent professionalism would under-mine even a neighborhood version of consumer control. Though the medical people put in their hours freely, her own visits to the pavilion clinic convinced her of how risky it was to connect with their teaching on a drop-in basis, and she found their evening lecture series stiff and alienating.

Maria's pediatrician was willing, and Jane soon found a nutritionist and an athleticist open to a cooperative project. Most of her difficulty in fielding the team came with the neighborhood funding council, which made them run the project out of job-learning tithe until Jane had brought enough other EEGs into the experiment to power the team's assignment through on a straight demand basis. The team spent more time helping with the learning-play groups than it did sitting in on EEG meetings. Their learning about in-context health maintenance was as difficult to quantify against other models as was the parents' learning, and Jane's first statistical support for the project took a year to assemble.

Her report of a small but definite shift in the ratio of consultative to remedial clinic visits, among the participant parents, put the project beyond all but advisory review. By then the children's familiarity with the team was bearing fruit, and in the older learning play groups it had begun introducing cognitive health curriculum. When her schooling cohort formed, shortly before Maria turned four, the pediatrician and the athleticist registered with full parent support for a joint adjunct instructional assignment there two mornings a week; and Jane had the pleasure of seeing two other teams fielded in the barrio, and the task of coordinating their evaluation.

Well before this Jane had taken on a project at the other age extreme, which was to bring her work and Horatio's to a first confluence. Their initial contact with the neighborhood's elderly had come about through the child care service. When its group of seniors, nearly as mixed between Anglo and Chicano as the children they tended, sought her aid in organizing refresher seminars in early education with bilingual emphasis, Jane followed up the pavilion work with an intensive survey of local senior services. Much was familiar from school; her main purpose was to establish the network of contacts that would ground her usefulness as an organizer.

Part-time work and the learning play group left Horatio free often to accompany Jane on her rounds, and he found a special poignance in talking with the men whose bodies would no longer serve them in labor. It was as much this as Jane's urging that they move with the politics of the time that led him to enroll with her in a year of half-time intensive study at the nearest metropolitan aging center. They decided also to pile up capital to underwrite some major future move, and Jane went through the formalities of drawing a half year of sabbatical support, which she promptly banked, to cover her studies. When Horatio's turn came he preferred to double in work, holding his sabbatical past his seventh adult year so as to be able to take two years running after they made their leap.

Senior class interests had been a remedial priority item at the level of national policy for only a few years. What little legislation had accomplished for the elderly outside the traditional areas of health and finance had come about almost accidentally, as a by-product of the belated recognition of the media as the "fourth school." The media's own popularizing of the society-as-school theorists had inspired a rash of suits by minority groups, criticizing the curriculum of public channels, and based on the community access regulations governing co-axial video systems.

When the Supreme Court ruled that the educative function of media extended to the private domain as well, and defined the instances in which licensing to print or broadcast was tantamount to licensing a substantive sector of the public school system and subject to equivalent regulation, liberals were sharply divided over the First Amendment question. But the evidence that governmental regulation had indeed been determining the content of the press, indirectly but massively, was too compelling; and in passing the Media Fairness Act, Congress faced directly at least a part of its responsibility. Though the Act avoided the question of equitable instruction in political philosophies, its antidiscrimination provisions applied broadly to media engaged in interstate commerce. In national advertising, and the reportage and entertainment it supported, the elderly, like other minorities, began to find themselves more present in the content of media, and more involved in determining its creation and presentation.

Though "reasonable progress" towards fairly democratic norms was difficult to enforce, the decreased stereotyping and increased representation of senior views were soon unmistakable. If they were not everywhere as remarkable as in the series of dramas on aged sexuality that Avon sponsored, still they were critical to revitalizing the wave of class consciousness among seniors, whose first thrust had gone largely to political potency.

Its second thrust was less for increased senior securities than towards a renewed social integration, and in Horatio's neighborhood the switch to senior predominance in the child care center had been seen as a model beginning. Even the Death Education Center, intimate though its inner rituals were, functioned beyond the age class it served; and though Jane could dial most of its presentations at home, she made a point of bringing Maria when she went with her parents to visit a friend who had chosen to die in public.

But senior power was active in more complex ways at the city level. When Horatio took on study of the aging with Jane, it was with an eye to the slow clock of urban renewal in San Jose, and in light of the recent example of San Francisco. The edge of the barrio came up for redevelopment sooner than he anticipated, and halfway through their year Jane found her working hours occupied largely in helping the neighborhood seniors' association learn how to implement its demand for project priority. Their suit stalled the project long enough for Horatio to finish his mini-internship; and by the time the city's appeal against the 40 percent senior quota was denied, Horatio, his old student Isabella, and an emeritus architect had prepared a preliminary design for a three-block residential redevelopment, brought in a preliminary budget, and gotten full neighborhood backing for the project with Jane's aid.

When the redevelopment agency ratified Horatio's nomination as co-coordinator of construction, his father could only whistle at how the lines of power had changed since his day, though he knew that the barrio resource planning board was careful with the rarer training opportunities and had put Horatio up for the high-level apprenticeship with an eye to future needs. Horatio worked closely with the advisory group convened through the pavilion's public call, even after he, Isabella, and the old architect had digested its revisions of the project's design for high senior density. The bidding for subcontracts was relatively cut and dried, despite the educational clauses that the neighborhood specified, which were common on major projects; and the learning registry filled the 10 percent supplementary apprenticeship quota straight from the barrio schools in time for most to work on the salvage operation that cleared the land. But the provision for senior instructors was a local first, and Horatio had to draw on the advisory group, Jane's web of contacts, and all the craft guilds before he could track down the last retired electrician.

Construction was two months along before the coordinative load eased to half-time, leaving Horatio free to take up a hammer on the job itself. He found the activity as essential for his sense of self as it was politic for one in his position, and regretted somewhat being interrupted when the old workers' presence brought problems. Though it was impossible to keep their participation strictly verbal, few were foolish enough to require medical attention; but old men do tend to lecture, and Horatio was called on to mediate more often than he had anticipated.

The days when the children came absorbed senior energy more

smoothly, and Horatio recalled his time on probation as he watched the neighborhood classes following the progress of construction. During contract negotiations he himself had been unsure of the child-participation provisions, despite the educators' explanations of the unusual mandate; but the extra instructional workers were in fact sufficient to cover them. And periodically, when he watched Jane attending Maria's group as they witnessed the tinkertoy miracles of copper plumbing at the feet of some greybeard Archimedes, or saw them at clean-up time gamely bearing away the antloads of refuse from the school facilities that would be theirs on completion, Horatio felt himself as a man fulfilled.

The physical decentralization of schooling had been accompanied by a conceptual decentralization of the school model even for pre-adolescents, and in the project's design Horatio's team had felt free to take a conservative approach to the need for a home base. Their choice to locate the four cohort base rooms together around a common tool core did cramp the full rituals of learning-visitation in the near-peer range, but they defended it in terms of the project's senior priority. The base complex and the intensive play park, landscaped for sound deflection, were the only child-dominated areas, taking up barely one acre; the larger part of the children's on-site learning that took place in the other seventeen acres was to be absorbed into the routines of the predominantly senior community.

In later years Horatio would sometimes arrive to find Maria in the garden, engaged in some transpiration experiment, or attending her favorites of the dozen elders who worked regularly with the children. More often he would have to trace her through base to the scattered craft rooms, or the quiet luminescence of the media pod, where he would find her insular in her earphones, intent as the elders around her.

Before construction was over, Maria's learning-play group had outgrown the weekly resources of its skillperson. Jane's EEG was already agreed with three others near the project site, and together they registered the children as a cohort reference group, requesting immediate assignment of a child-teacher. Rather than base at a temporary site, they kept him rotating until project's completion, and filled in after that until he could draw the cohort's complement of aides from the residents. Only the eldest of the other three cohorts had children drawn from the project, though fully fifty pre-adolescents lived with their families among the senior bungalows; for most of the residents had moved from nearby, and stable cohort groups were not broken up lightly.

Usually a new cohort would occupy the separate base of an old one dispersed by adolescence, and contract independently for its first teacher. But in the close quarters of a base complex, cooperation was critical, and Maria's cohort held off soliciting applications until the three older cohorts had made their choice of teachers for the new ground. One did not wish to work with the other two, and the replacement they suggested to his ex-cohort was accepted by the parents but vetoed by the kids. By the time a compatible three were contracted, Maria's parents were relieved when they suggested a fourth who had actually been among the dozen or so skillpeople who had worked with her EEG, and had gotten warm recommendations.

In Horatio's own childhood the assignment of four teachers to the hundred children who used the base complex would have seemed wasteful, even without the apprentices who often teamed with them and the less formal supplementation of their instruction by neighborhood residents. But the economy of education had changed considerably. Most administrative functions had been reabsorbed into processes of community learning, and the separate agency serving them had evanesced. Periodically Maria and her parents met with the rest of the cohort and its teachers to agree on use-priority for the part of the children's pooled voucher credit left over from salary and base maintenance. The same video-computer interlock that made it possible for them to contract materials and services directly from the city registry, and loan such scarce resources as their recording microscope to unaffiliated cohorts and the community, served also to hold (complexly privileged) what teachers and others entered in the children's learning records. Early on the children took part in these uses, and Maria knew how to file her first teacher evaluation all by herself after Jane helped her formulate it.

One of Maria's first drivers was a project woman from a traditional family, who had done nothing with her learning rights in the first decade after her children left home except dabble in pottery and take a smattering of courses which left her little but the belated ability to learn from print. Maria found Carmen often at loose ends in the media pod, and liked to use her rather than the console for aid with her readings. When Maria asked her to help a group from her cohort to learn about glazes, Carmen started hanging around the base, doing what she could with ceramics and driving, but more often listening. By the second year she had become a regular, if minor, member of the teaching team. Buoyed by acceptance, she tested out a trial apprenticeship with an EEG newly formed in the project itself, and then took the plunge. With its recommendation, and the base teachers', Carmen was accepted at the pavilion as a full instructional apprentice.

She was assigned as liaison to two additional EEGs, and her continued work at the base was formalized and contracted. Carmen split a sabbatical half-time over two years, to underwrite her supplementary learning. It took all her courage to attempt independent study of the books and channels, and she drew heavily on her advisor and the experienced teachers at first. For two years her apprentice seminar teased her about her hurry, but it had its point. By the time a pubescent Maria said goodbye to the base, Carmen had qualified fully, and moved in as prime teacher with a cohort formed around the project EEG children with whom she had been learning for three years.

In such ways as these, college teacher training and the bureaucratic structure it supported, as well as the administration of the lower schools and much of their functional support, had been absorbed and reconfigured; and though Maria received much more direct instructional contact from a wider range of teachers than her parents had as children, the overall investment of public energy in her education was not greatly increased.

The character of that contact, however, had changed strikingly. Maria pursued most of the standardizable curriculum by herself as soon as she learned to use the console, and took the usual pride in keying in to her skill profile each completed program's mastery. In time she came to strive for a balanced profile, though her initial pleasure with the mystery of numbers continued, and she was hard put to catch the other skills up. Her literacy did not fully unblock until the diagnostic metaprograms notified Maria and her teacher that they had narrowed the cause of her stylus' faltering cursive down to two possible metabolic deficiencies, bringing Jane to base to consult the nutritionist whose assignment she had catalyzed.

By then, her writing problem having been unrelated to the reading and speaking programs, Maria was well along in her Spanish, becoming as truly bilingual as most in her barrio school in preparation for her family's sojourn in Mexico. She liked the immediacy of audio-video feedback, and grew adept at making her voice match the prototype curves on the screen; on her return she went at sight-singing and then harmony with the same independent passion of mathematics. By contrast the testing programs, designed for her to check her objective knowledge against, were a drag, however neat they made her profile, and Maria didn't like to do them. Usually she had to stay home and clean her room, to get in the mood to cue the response circuits on the right channel; and on such days it became her habit to remain sprawled in the living room afterwards, dialing through the library channels and raiding the refrigerator, until the sun told her the late afternoon gang had formed at the park.

On most days Maria did choose to go to school, though some-times she would check in late. The base media facilities were fuller, and she did not like to dial strangers for advice, so she did a fair share of her solo study there. But mostly Maria was drawn to base by the prospect of learning-play with her peers. Much less of her teachers' time went to aiding her core curriculum study, as watchdogs and resources, than to the learning games and special demonstrations that engaged most of the cohort, and to tending the variety of small projects and investigations the children chose to engage in by twos and threes.

As lore had accumulated, open classroom style had evolved beyond the early unfocussed excesses of do-your-own-thingism and grown sensitive to the varieties of group ritual, and their place in the curriculum of moral education. Great texts notwithstanding, most of what we learn in institutions about how society should be and how people ought to treat each other is no more than what we see and do while we are in them. And so a fair part of Maria's teachers' training had gone to prepare them to make modest occasions of such events as the first rainbow, spring planting in the project garden, and the cohort's quarterly budget allocation meeting, with each child punch-ing in her own voucher and selection of supplies at the end.

The more personal conflicts of interest occurred without schedule, and Maria was not slow to choose fishbowl encounter, with or without a teacher, to focus on and sometimes resolve them. Ever since the early influence of skillpeople on her EEG, Maria's experience in family and out had been to treat conflict in deliberate ritual; and she did not share the inhibitions that still lingered among adults and led a few of her peers to prefer private dealing. Indeed she was merciless towards one teacher her cohort contracted, who was good at helping them learn the subrituals of teaching their projects to each other and of evaluating their own learning in group, but who could not conceal from the children's eyes his refusal to do more than play-act when they tried to lead him through self-criticism.

Here I take leave of Maria, Jane, and Horatio. In this sketchy fantasy about their lives, I count some 266 assumptions about how education in America might be changed for the better, and how it might then proceed. Some major changes I pass over casually, some minor ones I dwell on; a few contradict each other, and the whole set is far from comprehensive. Despite this essay's title, it is not meant as an image of an educational utopia, but as a speculative and partial answer to this more modest question: *How can "education" be institutionalized, to make it a flexible vehicle for the various uses of learning that people find worthwhile?* Though I like Horatio's uses, I've tried to sketch an answer that would serve quite different uses as well.

I imagine many other answers can be sketched; but the one above is neither random nor arbitrary. A few of its 266 changes are now spreading widely, and many others are based on real models being tried out here and there in America. Many more are afoot as proposals in and out of the "educational community," and the rest are obvious harmonious innovations. Together these changes point towards a reinstitutionalization of education that is coherent, systematic, and pervasive; that involves the learner more integrally in his learning experience, and the experience more integrally in society.

Behind this patchwork of fantasy is a small cluster of principles. *Autonomy, decentralization, power in the decisions that shape one's life, shared resources, maximum opportunity for diversity and individuation, voluntary involvement in a web of mutual responsibility—* these and a few others are pretty much my prescription for the ills of education, and of society in general. They may not be a sufficient remedy, but they are a beginning.

Had I begun with Horatio as an artist, short-order cook, or pool hustler, in Manhattan or on the farm, my scenario's details would be slightly different but their tenor much the same. Still, some of what I've left out should be mentioned. I have not dealt at all with the research/creation function of education. I've written in terms of the family structure that even now is disintegrating, and neglected the emergence of new structures. Touching lightly on the problem of race, I've ignored what we learn as women and as men, which may be even more important. Nor do I deal with how we learn citizenship in world society and how we can find our place in nature. I don't mention the problems of coping with change, or of surviving and growing in the social chaos that now enfolds us. Horatio and his family are paper characters: their lives do not include frustration, distress, trauma, dead ends, or injustice. Any reconfiguration of education must relate to all these topics and more. But it is not hard to imagine scenarios based on the same principles which begin to deal with them.

This entire essay is pitched at a certain intermediate level of the problem of education, one I rarely deal with. Normally I am much more concerned with extremes: with the intimate processes of people's learning, alone, together, and in small groups; and with how people learn to share the governance of society and be responsible citizens of a democracy. Here instead I stick fairly strictly to imagining a *form for the institutionalization* of the principles above. I describe the system from the user's perspective, rather than the managers', because to do so reconfigures the categories of the problem, and restores a certain clarity of purpose.

But I must say that this whole question of form seems to me not so very important. "Where there's a will, there's a way." In truth, institutionalized education reflects our institutionalized will about who shall learn what how. The problem in changing it is not so much in imagining new forms, as in summoning the will to begin to implement a set of principles suitable for a humane democracy.

PART IV

*Paideia, Culture, and
the Work To Be Done*

Commentary

We print here two addresses delivered at Southampton. The first is a keynote speech by William Arrowsmith, classical scholar, translator, and critic of education. The second is the summary comment read by Henry Steele Commager to the members of the steering committee following the last session of the Summer Sequences. Thus the two documents span the life of the conference. They do not really belong together, but together they suggest the range of the problem facing the conference, and facing us all, from the most global implications to the specific tasks of the future. Above all, they both call with fervor and anguish for a new kind of leadership in American education.

William Arrowsmith brings us back to the core notion of *paideia*. He examines the disjuncture between culture—a harmonious and total mode of existence where all the institutions and customs of society work toward an education in the society's necessary values, beliefs, and knowledge—and civilization, the technical mastery of the world. Culture is necessary to *paideia*, but we no longer have it. We have merely civilization. Among the many consequences of this situation is the degeneration of the concept of the elite, of the leadership necessary to advance the cause of humanity. Masquerading as an clitc, Arrowsmith contends, we merely have an old-boy network in sad disrepair, attempting to legitimize itself under the banner of meritocracy. Lost is the classical sense of *arete,* of competitive excellence, and responsibility for excellence. It is to the need for *arete,* for assumption of the need and the right to lead, and the moral obligations that leadership entails, that he would rededicate us.

Henry Steele Commager points to some of the lessons of the Southampton Summer Sequences, the conclusions to be drawn from what was said and what was not said. He reiterates the problems that derive from the American confusion of "schooling" with the whole of "education," and argues again the need to be clear in our own minds about what fraction of education schooling can be held responsible for—so that it may at least accomplish that. It is mere schizophrenia to hold the schools accountable for inculcating virtues which the society as a whole openly flouts. It is absurd to make the schools agents for the apprenticeship to equality and justice where nothing proves that American society really wants equality and justice. Yet this does not mean that the schools can do nothing. Professor Commager's litanies on the role of certain individual reformers in the history of American education hold up a model for emulation. His call for a history of American educational reform is designed to suggest how new breakthroughs may be accomplished. He calls upon the sponsor of the Southampton Summer Sequences, the United States Office of Education itself, to take on a more active leadership role, to provide the information and the collaboration that would constitute informed participation in future planning about education.

The whole message of Southampton is not here, and not in all the papers taken together. But it is interesting and appropriate that we end on the call for new leadership, as we began with the call, by legislative leaders, for informed participation. The problems of America in the last quarter of the twentieth century clearly have much to do with the crisis of leadership: the bankruptcy of old models and methods, the uncertain search for new. Many of the participants in the Summer Sequences left feeling that coming together to meet, to interact, to know one another was valuable, but that future progress depended on a willingness to take the risks of leadership, that participation could not mean collective decision making and the avoidance of responsibility. The country is no doubt suspicious of leadership, ready to shoot it down. Yet—and this is as much the case in education as elsewhere—nothing will be accomplished without people taking sides and raising banners in the name of which to do battle.

Peter Brooks

10

Thoughts on American Culture— and Civilization

William Arrowsmith

The world today speaks for itself: by the evidence of its decay it announces its dissolution. The farmers are vanishing from the countryside, commerce from the sea, soldiers from the camps, all honesty in business, justice in the courts, solidarity in friendship . . .

—*St. Cyprian (200-258 A.D.)*

Just fifty years ago, in medieval 1924, there appeared a remarkable essay by the linguist Edward Sapir, one of those penetrating and incisive works in which, like Freud's *Civilization and its Discontents*, the malaise of contemporary life was, brilliantly, with magisterial brevity set forth. Its title was "Culture, Genuine and Spurious"; not the least of its merits was that, with sympathy and clarity, it defined true culture (not traditional "high" Western), which it distinguished from a variety of competing shams:

A genuine culture is perfectly conceivable in any stage of civilization in the mold of any American genius. . . . The genuine culture is not of necessity high or low; it is merely inherently harmonious, balanced, self-satisfactory . . . the expression of a richly varied and yet somehow unified and consistent attitude toward life . . . a culture in which nothing is spiritually meaningless, in which no important part of the general functioning brings with it a sense of frustration, of misdirected or unsympathetic effort. . . . It carefully refuses to instruct its children in what it knows to be of no use or vitality either to them or its own mature life. Nor does it tolerate a thousand other spiritual maladjustments such as are patent in our American life of today. . . . Moreover, a genuine culture refuses to consider the individual as a mere cog, as an entity whose sole *raison d'être* lies in his subservience to a culture that he is not conscious of or that has only a remote relevancy to his interests and strivings. . . .

Sapir proceeds to contrast life in such a culture with the life of the modern telephone operator, employed for the most part in an efficient technical routine which bears no relation to her own spiritual needs. As a solution to the problem of culture, "she and her society are a dismal failure." We can assess the scale of the failure simply by contrasting her life with that of an Indian salmon-fisher in a culture of markedly inferior sophistication to hers. Indeed, Sapir argues, we must distinguish sharply between "culture" and what, for want of a better word, he terms "civilization." By "civilization" is meant the constantly increasing sophistication of our society and personal lives—"not merely technical and intellectual advance but most of the tendencies that make for a cleaner and healthier, more humanitarian—but not necessarily more humane—existence."

Sapir, of course, is not unique in observing that "culture" is often out of phase with technology or what is called, pejoratively, "progress." It is a commonplace that the spirit of a culture is not synonymous with its flourishing material existence. The fear that Christian (or simply "cultured") Rome might in fact conceal the features of "Babylon" is at least as old as the Johannine Apocalypse; when St. Jerome left Rome for his monastic labors of translation at Bethlehem-Ephrata, he left cursing the Roman "Babylon." The same fear, with varying emphasis, has haunted the modern world from the Reformation to Matthew Arnold and T. S. Eliot. Arnold, of course, feared inward Philistinism, a resurgent barbarism, and he associated these, as did Ruskin and Nietzsche, with bourgeois "progress" and utilitarian "happiness." But these are the official voices of High Western, crying out against the enemy at the gates—the new barbarians.* The voices are old. Look behind the grave figure of the Christian Eliot and you see the figure of the Roman senator Symmachus, warning that the removal of the Altar of Victory by

---

*As the Greek poet Cavafy observed, this tack had the advantage not only of externalizing the enemy, but of paralyzing all cultural effort: "Some people arrived from the frontiers,/ and they said that there are no longer any barbarians./ And now what shall become of us without any barbarians?/ Those people were a kind of solution."

Christians would mean the end of Rome, which is to say, the end of culture. With such official views of culture and barbarism, I am not here concerned. My concern is to move beyond them as swiftly as possible. For the problem, as I see it, is not one of preserving High Western but rather of protecting the rest of the world—which may still possess some lively vestigial culture of its own—against the Faustian West. *Against* Western "civilization," that is—civilization in Sapir's sense.

Civilization in this sense is *culturally indifferent.* But the distinction goes far beyond "material" and "spiritual," beyond "progress" too; it goes to the centrality in all true culture of human purpose; to the need for men to feel that they are autonomous, not cogs in a routinely aggrandizing system with no relation to their lives or human life generally. Constantly increasing sophistication of technical means threatens the validity of the culture which that sophistication presumably serves and diffuses. Modern and ancient applications immediately come to mind. Thucydides, for instance, recognized that the exquisite "feedback mechanisms" of the Athenian empire, the remarkable mesh between self-interest and expansion and the impressive "social" technologies (especially in the law courts) implicit in empire, inevitably seemed to erode the very culture, the *paideia,* which that empire existed to defend and diffuse. In a few short years, Athenian civilization fatally eroded the Athenian culture which claimed to be, in Pericles' words, "the education of Hellas."

Yet Athenian civilization was a comparatively modest affair; and so too was the American world described by Sapir. Sapir's purpose was to reprimand the champions of High Western for their arrogant and complacent assumption of cultural superiority vis-à-vis supposedly primitive cultures. What were the positive benefits of a culture which, in the name of technical sophistication and progress, stultified the lives of its own members? *Now,* fifty years later, it is clear that culture and civilization are not merely out of phase, but directly antagonistic. And the implications of this simple fact are as vast as they are unexamined.

To say that culture is threatened by material progress is to assume that culture is still *there,* still exists. But does it? How many of us have seriously—I repeat, *seriously*—asked ourselves whether we any longer possess a culture at all; whether the familiar apparatus humming and booming around us with such confidence of permanence and power (for all its malfunctions and nuances) is in any respect a culture at all? True, the *fiction*—the huge throbbing machinery—is still there. The citizen with a family, a job, pastimes, is constantly assured by the apparent solidity of the conventions, and the apparatus, by the general certainties of everyone else, that the culture *still,* however imperfectly, functions. But no sooner does one begin to *think* about it than the certainty crumbles. What, after all, *is* there in our lives which we can still point to and say, *"This,* indisputably, is culture; this is not civilization"? Society depends upon *socii,* a *community.* Where is the warm embrace of culture in our communities? What is left of religion, of locality, the deep individuality of places, sacred with their own rich particularity of lore, history, and persons? Is there, in fact, *anything* at all in our lives which is truly, unmistakably, culture—and not civilization rigged out in the borrowed clothes of culture? Only shards, fragments, a hazy residue of values, the fictive community of the English language, our industrial folkways—roads, cars, commodities, the habits imposed by planes and cars, the semiotic habitat created for us by the instruments we designed, and for which we are now more and more measured and fitted.

Everywhere one looks the civilization has effectively usurped the culture. The roster of instruments of which the civilization disposes are exponential by contrast: the world-wide mesh of international corporations; immense conglomerates devoid of any imperative except safely diversified profit and limited risk; immense data banks of computerized information; vast and ominous accumulations of fiscal and political power; an exploded bureaucracy operating in secret on the basis of low-grade systems theory; hospital cartels linked by television and computers; a vast network of research universities with wholly professionalized faculties (Riesman's safe-playing "revolutionaries"); agribusiness; managerial elites; comprehensive high-schools which obliterate old communities without creating new ones; huge learning corporations which have devoured the country's publishers; the emergence of the military as a sixth estate; the syndication of charity; and of course the relentless, mindless growth of all these things in a world incapable of offering principled or coherent resistance.

The effect of these changes on culture is incalculable. But the overwhelming *personal* fact is the sensation of having fallen out of culture into "mere fragmentary life," of having lost control. Whence the anxiety that comes of impotence and the old habit of meaning which men find it so hard to kick; of feeling responsible, even in the face of the civilization's daunting mass and scale. The individual may perhaps combat his conviction of helplessness by directing his energies to the correction of his own situation, but his impotence continues to grow, and with it the susceptibility to evasions and unconscious compensations. Despite the individual's efforts, the gulf continues to widen: between public and private; work and leisure; thought and action; literature and life; self and other. Convinced of his isolation, the individual may turn to institutions, hoping to lose his powerlessness and loneliness in what he imagines is their massive, collective purpose, their undeniable *power*. And at this point he frequently discovers the intolerable fact that these institutions function blindly and routinely, for very limited and limiting ends, and, further, that these ends have no bearing on his own anxiety, his sense that society is ultimately as aimless and powerless as he is. And at this point somnambulism begins, for the vision is even more intolerable than the world glimpsed by St. Cyprian which, after all, only proved that there was another, better world.

Paradise Lost

But here we are. On one side of us are the great engines of civilization, with their impressive material benefits and their frustration of individual purpose and meaning. On the other is the memory of a lost culture which almost nobody has ever known, but which still haunts us like some future Utopia or paradise lost. Once he had lost his culture, the Indian, according to Sapir, is indistinguishable from his destroyer:

> When the political integrity of his tribe is destroyed . . . and the old cultural values cease to have the atmosphere needed for their continued vitality, the Indian finds himself in a state of bewildered vacuity. Even if he succeeds in making a fairly satisfactory compromise with his new environment, he is apt to retain an uneasy sense of the loss of some vague and great good, some state of mind which he would be hard put to define, but which gave him a courage and joy that latter-day prosperity never quite seems to have regained for him. . . . He has slipped out of the warm embrace of a culture into the cold air of fragmentary existence.

In Christian myth the loss of paradise is explicit; the loss of culture is less explicit because it is so rarely recognized. Culture, after all, is what we unconsciously think we still have, the context of our lives, what we are *at*. But if this is an illusion?

Then we get compensatory "individual" culture, style without substance, the theater of diversity-for-its-own-sake, the semblance of pluralism unmoored from any defining norm or unity—the culture of shards. Mere eroticism; libertarian groupiness; the ceremonial perversion of art as social and cultural bond or "token of recognition"; the party of nostalgia and evasion; aggressively organized bad faith; frantic efforts to compose a culture out of fragments—bits of Zen, Lévy-Bruhl, sherry parties, Indian philosophy (mantra after mantra, sutra after sutra), the infantilism of flower-children-who-never-grow-old, and all the decorous and organized pretences of a civilization which provides the paraphernalia, but not the substance, of culture. For education, training; for knowledge, sophistication; for inner necessity, a series of decorative "lifestyles"; for morality, law or equity; for community, "groupiness" and collective isolation; for bread, a stone.*

The Civilized Universities

Too apocalyptic? Perhaps. The texture of the truth may be more gritty; it is also more revealing.

Take the academic world. What to my mind is missing from common accounts of academic mindlessness (to borrow Charles Silberman's all too happy unhappy phrase) is a full reckoning of the pervasiveness and range of academic *mauvaise foi*: its elegantly interlocking mechanisms; the prodigious bureaucratic beauty of its complicating organization; and the ramification of its effects and causes through institutions of higher learning to the national and supranational grids that rationalize and reinforce the institutional guilds. The function of this massive apparatus is to protect professions and scholars alike in what they do and do not do; but above all, I think,

---

*Compare, for instance, Sammler's remarkable homiletic aria in Saul Bellows' *Mr. Sammler's Planet*: "I was saying that this liberation into individuality has not been a great success. For a historian of great interest, but for one aware of the suffering it is appalling. Hearts that get no real wage, souls that find no nourishment. Falsehood, unlimited. Desire, unlimited. Possibility, unlimited. Impossible demands upon complex realities, unlimited. . . ."

from the jeopardy of imaginative vision and action and the real risk of freedom. In engineering jargon *mauvaise foi* is a form of dysfunction termed "suboptimization," by which is meant a high degree of efficiency in the production of an undesirable or irrelevant output. Its cause is almost always deliberate or careless inattention to any ends which are not simply marginal or proximate. Suppose, for the sake of argument, that an intelligent dean, perhaps an educator to boot, asks a chairman "to improve his department's performance"; the dean is exercised, it seems, about some intangible called "excellence." The chairman and his senior colleagues, faced with this exhilaratingly vague challenge, respond suboptimally—that is, in the ways they see normalized about them everywhere in the institution. They respond, that is, by mindlessly tightening up what they like to call "standards": the syllabus is reworked, a few subspecialties are deftly stitched in, dubious junior colleagues and "unstable" graduate students are sent packing; there is a flurry of memoranda on some timid "new" departure, memos on the best means of achieving greater "professional visibility" are circulated, and so on. The final illusion is that of a taut little ship, a sound professional hand on the tiller, sprucely sailing along with the favoring tradewinds currently blowing from whatever fashionable quarter, making briskly for nowhere.

In American universities nowhere is not an unknown destination. It is, in fact, a familiar port-of-call. It is a number—whose "worth's unknown although his height be taken." The number sought is a higher grade on the list of the top twenty graduate departments, all rank-ordered, discipline by discipline, in those lustral documents known as the Cartter Report and the Roose-Anderson Report. Published under the auspices of The American Council on Education, these documents were originally commissioned by three federal funding agencies: the National Academy of Sciences, the National Institute of Health, and the Office of Education. They purport to represent "expert opinion"—that is, the judgment of the professoriate on its own performance. For obvious reasons, their appeal is immense. In a milieu devoid of goals, they suggest the *illusion* of an end. To unimaginative administrators they are miraculously appealing simply because they assign a quantitative value to quality and provide models of imitable virtue and the road to preferment. Clearly a high ranking is as good as gold; indeed, it is gold. Even a slow-witted administrator can grasp the import of a high ranking on a rating list funded by those charged with the disbursement of public funds and accountable to unpredictable congressional committees. Even administrators, that is, can grasp, beneath all the plausible talk about the wisdom of having peers judge peers and the value of expert opinion, the profile of still another form of institutionalized bad faith. The responsibility for assigning public funds is a risky business; mistakes can be costly for a man's career. But the responsibility can be shirked by the simple device of summoning "expert opinion" (and since the experts are all anonymous, they cannot be asked to testify). A congressman angrily demanding to know why *his* university has been consistently scanted by a funding agency can be abruptly silenced or shamed by this published consensus of experts. The rankings, of course, are most warmly defended by those who have been ranked most favorably (and vice versa). But the effect of these reports is clear. They tend, first, to make the rich richer and the poor poorer; second, the example of the highly ranked is clearly a constraint upon the behavior of those institutions lower down the scale; and the effect of such constraints is to reduce diversity, penalize imaginative risk, and reward conformity. There is, I think, an obvious tendency to promote the prevalence of disciplinary dogma: linguistic analysis in philosophy, for instance, or structuralism in literature. They destroy diversity, they destroy that pluralism of talent and talent-in-community without which the mind cannot live its free or necessary life, without which we cannot, in any useful sense, really think at all.

The Synthetic Culture

Fifty years ago, then, Sapir, a man of genuine culture, warned that culture and civilization were in no sense synonymous. Now, in 1975, it is tolerably clear that civilization has almost wholly usurped the place and functions of culture. Civilization has *become* culture. The importance of this fact—so disastrous to both individuals and societies—cannot be exaggerated; obviously, it also involves radical simplifications. But no amount of reflection or academic caution deters me from the belief that what we call "mainstream" culture cannot in any meaningful sense be called a culture at all.

The civilization has effectively obliterated the culture it was meant to mediate. Once, it might have been held that civilization propagated culture (examples might be the invention of printing, American plumbing, the electric light, organized *Wissenschaft,* information-retrieval systems, or comprehensive high-schools). Now the medium has wholly, or almost altogether, become the message. The apparatus now flourishes for its own sake, relentlessly pursuing its own aggrandizing ends, and systematically sets about exterminating what little survives of genuine culture everywhere in the world. This mindless Faustian gospel is now consciously or unconsciously expounded by multinational cartels, Brazilian Indian-killers, academic departments, Father Moon, the publishers and teachers of Dick and Jane, and all the other organized expressions of coercive "civilization." In benevolent disguise, it appears as the lunatic consequences of Affirmative Action, or the Buckley Amendment, or the Cartter Report, and similar assaults on quality in the name of statistical science or social equity. It is the impulse behind all efforts at creating the *semblance* of community and quality—in short, synthetic culture.

There is perhaps no more articulate expression of it in American history than the nakedly Faustian gospel preached a hundred years ago by several of Grant's Indian commissioners to a group of Cayuse, Umatilla, and Walla Walla Indians:

> We white men have read books and they tell us the history of the red man. From the books we learn truths; they tell us that knowledge is power. The more man can do, the stronger he is; it has always been so, and always will be so. The weak people who have no books have always given way to the stronger who had books. No matter what color they were, what religion, what country. . . . Where are the Indians now? Their bones are mixed with the ground for three thousand miles. There is no wigwam in all that country. . . . And the white man melts the rock, and makes iron. The canoes have left the river and the white man's steamboats are on it. . . . Do you know why there are so many whites everywhere, and why they have so much more power than the Indians? I will tell you. The Indians are gone because they tried to be Indians always. Some of you Indians here are still trying to be Indians. All such will soon be gone to their fathers; but if the Indians listen to the white man's teaching and become like the white man, instead of getting fewer they will increase like white men . . . and can make a history for themselves. . . .

Here, unmistakably, we see a genuine culture in the act of being destroyed in the name of a synthetic culture whose confidence and missionary zeal conceal the ambitions and *hybris* of the civilization.

Everywhere, in everything we do, whether as groups or individuals, the startling emergence of civilization in the borrowed clothes and dignity of culture—the eclipse of culture by its own means—confronts us as the prime reality of the age. I offer the following examples of this reality in the knowledge that their very patness will render them suspect, but in the conviction that their pervasiveness and coherence cannot be accidental.

1. *"Locals"* and *"Cosmopolitans."* This problem, it may be objected, is particularly—unfortunately—academic, as well as familiar. But my point, here and elsewhere, is to suggest, in familiar contexts, usurpation of the culture by the civilization, and the consequent loss of community in areas (like intellectual life) where community is crucial to quality and humanity of thought. Besides, there is no reason to apologize for considering matters of apparently academic concern. In a "knowledge-society" the university and schools could not be more central. We inhabit, after all, a knowledge-society in which the formation (and deformation) of knowledge imposed by expertise are inextricably bound up with our cultural plight. And the possible role of the university as a redeemable community is one which therefore has immense importance to a society in which the indiscriminate application of knowledge has helped to destroy community.

It is a commonplace that the American campus is divided between those whose chief loyalty is to the local community—the colleges and its students—and those whose allegiance is to the national guild. The division is seldom absolute, but "locals" generally view teaching as their essential task, whereas "cosmopolitans" like to argue that teaching is a function of research, and that research therefore comes first. The rift reveals the failure of the college or university to reconcile its older task—teaching, the making of men and the moulding of character—with its newer, secular mission of research; and the conflict of missions, almost invariably resolved in favor of research, in turn reveals how deeply the cultural ends of education have been eroded by the civilization. Talk about "teacher-scholars" only serves to obscure the fact that institutions have transferred to their faculties the problem they cannot resolve. Theoretically, the difference is between those who see the college as a potential intellectual community—a coherent academic culture—and those whose true home is the national guild. But everywhere the locals are inferior, in power and prestige and, all too often, in talent, to the cosmopolitans. The chief reason for this is the pervasive operation of a national grid which rationalizes the civilization and administers its rewards with practiced discrimination. The successful cosmopolitan is visible because of his research; he is mobile because he is visible and desirable; his mobility and visibility combine so that his market-value prevails locally as well as nationally, and this in turn tips the balance even more strongly against the locals. It is the same with graduate students. Thus we reward the "superior" student (translation: a talent for independent research) with fellowships which require no teaching and are exempt from taxation; we in fact recognize the inferiority of the teaching assistant (and our own poor opinion of teaching) by throwing him sixty or seventy undergraduates to teach and then taxing him on his earnings.

My point is not to rehearse familiar abuses, but to emphasize the ways in which the civilization is academically imposed, and the difficulty, in such circumstances, of building a coherent intellectual milieu or culture. But the life of the mind, the escape from professional tunnel-vision, all ultimately depend upon creating such a milieu. ("Is not Community the dream of Bedlam?" Emerson asked. "Men are so discordant and of unequal pulse; and all excellence is inflamed or exalted individualism.") The problem is not really that an increasing number of professors are intellectual gypsies, alienated and mobile carpet-baggers of the mind ("I know them," said Nietzsche, "I'm one of them myself"), or that they care too much for money and power and too little for their students. The problem is that most of us have never known anything resembling a true intellectual community and indeed cannot begin to grasp the idea except as a mildly congenial faculty-meeting. The crucial thing is the absence of an enterprise which might liberate, in the effort to create a community or a common culture, the values crucial to it. In their effort to create institutions worthy of their imagination and love and aspirations, men liberate the values they will later house as their joint achievement. But no community or culture can be built which does not take care to defend itself at both local and national levels from the pressures of a civilization whose gridded influence grips even the reformer at his work and subtly bends him to its purpose. It is productive of purpose to have an antagonist and be required to struggle for a goal, which struggle helps to clarify and define. *Arete*— "always to be best, and to excel all others"—is inherently competitive, and even agonistic. In a time when competition is regarded as a threat to the general complacency of individual and society alike,* it is important to remember that no great human culture has ever been built upon the principle that the loser's loss is more important than the winner's victory†—which, in Greek terms, means the victory of the species.

2. *Minority English.* No problem is more vexing to minority communities, especially the blacks, and to teachers of English than the kind of English to be taught. We have, in black English, an amazingly vigorous colloquial English—a valid dialect by any criterion, yet one which condemns its users to severe economic and cultural penalties when they leave the community. On the other side is the great English of Shakespeare ("the language God learned," said Auden, "when he forgot how to speak Greek"). English in this sense is,

---

*The eclipse of competition in recent times as a major factor in cultural life deserves a book-length study as a revealing malaise in Western (and perhaps human) culture. But there can be no doubt that the prevalent egalitarian rage at work in American life and culture is the essential component in it, as well as the latest and most invisibly potent form of melting-pot assimilationism. Competition is of course disesteemed when the viewpoint is *individual*, rather than social and collective, that is, cultural. Thus it is almost a cliche in individual psychiatry (above all in its most bourgeois form, psychoanalysis) that competition is an unmitigated evil and a threat to individual happiness. But the distrust of competition conceals the deeper distrust of excellence, and heroic excellence in particular, perceived as an affront to the self-esteem of the ordinary individual. Thus Ortega y Gasset's "mass man" not only asserts his claim to the privileges of the old aristocracies, but rationalizes his claim by impugning the very *idea* of excellence. Even in the fifth century B.C. the radical democracy of Athens exhibited, according to a reasonable interpretation of Thucydides, a revealing distrust of leadership—the "envy of all superiority." And, Thucydides implies, Athenian democracy and culture paid the price of that envy of excellence in the bad faith of its leaders and the self-betrayal of the culture.

†Compare, however, the remarks of Eli Sagan (1974, pp. 129ff): "Cannibalism is aggressive; it is aggression because it implies that one person can be successful only if others are not. One does not have to kill or enslave others to domineer over them; one can do it in a civilized manner. This is the true meaning of competition: competition means that someone else must lose if I am to win; to be winners, there must be losers. To insist upon the necessity of losers is an aggressive act." The naive and ahistorical mindlessness exhibited by Sagan is not, I must aggressively insist, merely "pop" anthropology, but comes with a glowing foreword by Robert Bellah, proclaiming it as a significant contribution to the discussion of culture. But its significance lies, not in its thought, but in its fashionable advocacy of the New Quietism—a countercultural amalgam of Marx and revisionist psychoanalysis, designed to dethrone competition (persistently seen as a capitalist value) as merely "civilized" aggression. What Sagan persistently fails even to consider is the civilized, and civilizing, uses of both aggression and competition. Wit, for instance, said Aristotle wittily, is "civilized *hybris*" (*pepaideumene hybris*). Are we prepared to renounce wit (and slapstick—the extremest form of Hobbes' inherently aggressive, but profoundly human, notion of laughter as "a sudden glory" arising from felt superiority) in the name of Sagan's tranquilized civility? If the mindless egalitarianism of Affirmative Action requires an ethos, Sagan's mindless anthropology supplies it.

perhaps at the university level, the language of a functioning culture; but elsewhere in the society it is simply the civilization's *lingua franca*, a language condemned, like classical Greek in the Hellenistic Age, to increasing vulgarization and indeed barbarization as it becomes the *koinē* of the government—of business, law, science, the military—and, ultimately, a kind of world-Chinook. This English is the official language of the civilization, not the culture, and it is, as linguistic fact, even more oppressive than other instruments of coercive civilization. At present, standardization—the victory of *koinē* English—seems imminent. Minorities, understandably unwilling to be excluded by language disability from the economic advantages of membership in the civilization, have reluctantly acquiesced. At the university level the Mandarins of English have effectively—though not without bitter arguments—persisted in treating the potentially rich development of minority dialects or languages as a necessary sacrifice to the traditional "high culture" they represent.*

The problem—like the civilization itself—is of course not exclusively American. But the willful extinction of human and cultural "otherness," as that otherness is conveyed by languages and dialects, is one of the great scandals of a pluralist society. Many, if not most, Italians can, after all, speak both their own native dialect—dialects so distinct that they are mutually almost incomprehensible—and standard Tuscan Italian. Of late, because of the standardization of Tuscan imposed by the mass media and formal schooling (as well as the

---

*A colleague of mine, for instance, recently reviewed, in quite unfavorable terms, a collection of tribal poetry, largely American Indian, as irrelevant to the official educational enterprise; the poetry in question, it was argued, was not only "primitive" but, more important, not truly "ours," presumably because not written in "our mother tongue." Here I detect, a little too arrogantly for comfort, a professorial echo of that unconscious superiority with which assimilation is still pressed on non-English speaking and ethnic minorities; the same superiority with which nineteenth century white negotiators forced Indians to treat with them in English or a wretched pidgin trade-language, effectively depriving the Indian not only of his own eloquence but even the terms in which to articulate his case. It is, in any case, a very real question whether the poetry of Tennyson or the novels of Jane Austen have any true pertinence to American students in the twentieth century; we are, I would maintain, much closer in our cultural condition to the ancient Greeks or the Navahos than to the very peculiar and insular culture of nineteenth century England. In Pakistan, it was for me both astonishing and revealing to note that prospective civil servants were effectively being judged by their ability to discuss the novels of George Eliot—not, one would immediately suppose, the natural intellectual preparation for a clerkship in Hyderabad or even a government post in Rawalpindi. So, in America, it is astonishing to see the academic Mandarins willfully spurning the great native literatures of this continent in the name of an arguably great but dubiously pertinent European import.

snobbery that equates high culture with flawless Tuscan—*la padro-*
nanza della lingua), the dialects have begun to disappear just as the
incredible regional diversity of old Italy has almost vanished beneath
the inroads of civilization and the asphalt imperialism of the
Autostrada del sole.

Bilingualism and biculturalism are clearly the *cultural answer.*
There is simply nothing to be said for a society which effectively
condemns a child—Spanish-speaking, say, which means, too often, a
substandard, skeleton, ghetto Spanish—to be illiterate in *two* languages
at once. There is no conceivable reason—and every imaginable advantage—in a citizenry which can pass with ease and without embarrassment, shame, or penalty, from a language like Navaho or
Choctaw to a functional *koinē* English and, beyond that, to the
language of Shakespeare and Milton. We cannot culturally preserve
genuine openness, unless we are prepared to honor otherness. In this
sense the fate of minority dialects and languages is symbolic of our
fate as an open and pluralistic culture. Nowhere else does the civilization reveal its inherently mindless mission of reducing the entire
habitable world, from old Oraibi to Peshawar to "Akenfield" to
Zakynthos, to the needs of advertisers, computer programmers, and
economic imperatives behind these things, than in this relentless
emphasis on assimilation, and the standardization—which is to say,
the extinction—of all otherness. If otherness is, as I believe, the heart
of all education and the only possible sanction of morality and compassion, then here, in the apparatus of the civilization is the most anti-
educational, the most immoral force the world has yet encountered—
a shadow culture which projects, as its final product, a stunted and
miserable humanity.

3. *A Cultural Bill of Rights.* For obvious reasons, minorities
need protection, especially if the minority in question has a language
in which its culture is still, though perhaps precariously, embedded.
The advocacy of civil rights is, I sometimes think, a direct consequence
of American assimilationism, not always of the passion for justice.
Minorities obviously could not be *assimilated* except in terms of
rights. Civil rights legislation was thus only the ultimate step in an
essentially egalitarian process. But egalitarianism is, in human or
cultural terms, simply another form of standardization. And what
perhaps began as a cultural imperative—justice and equal opportunity
for all—has in fact ended up as simply an imperative of the civilization,

a bureaucratic and technocratic imperative. Anomalies *must* be erased, differences annulled. Indeed, the civilization nowhere is more nakedly revealed as the usurper of culture than in the mindless ruthlessness with which bureaucratic and standardizing imperatives (Affirmative Action, etc.) have now replaced an older ethical imperative. The reformers do their work in the name of values—but the values they actually serve are the dynamics of their own self-perpetuating routines. Cultures, no less than individuals—and perhaps much more so—need protection from this mindless suboptimization. Which means, or suggests, a cultural Bill of Rights—a Bill designed to protect cultures from damage by other imperatives, by policies of bureaucratic standardization.

The American Constitution was the product of a coherent culture—coherent at least by the standards of the English Enlightenment. It could therefore afford to leave to family and church, the other institutions of culture (which, among themselves, constituted a real colonial *paideia*) the effective safeguarding of morality and what was once called "the spirit." Civil rights needed legal definition; the defense of *human* rights, implied in the arrangements for civil rights, were the province of church and family. The Founding Fathers could not have foreseen the fearful eclipse in our time of church and family, any more than they could have predicted the ominous syndicates of power and privilege stronger than almost any state or the eclipse of culture and its replacement by its own means. Successive judicial interpretations have in small part repaired the damage of obsolescence. But it is undeniable that we confront a world which, in 1776, could not have been imagined. And there is a piety, both noble and pitiful, that prevents us from rewriting the patents of our freedoms, rights, and responsibilities. Yet the fact is that we confront a civilization with a constitution composed by a true culture—a culture which is no longer itself, or no longer ours.

Hence, no national project seems to be more urgent than a cultural Bill of Rights which will put an end to the long nightmare of assimilation and melting-pot ideology. Minorities need protection from economic infringements of their cultural identities, and soon, for those identities are in desperate peril. The Endowments, for instance, might reasonably be explicitly charged to save Indian (and other) literatures and art-forms on the point of perishing, just as they now attempt to salvage the crafts-tradition of the Appalachians. Even more useful would be the effort to salvage disappearing languages by training the young—still embarrassed by tribal heritage—to speak the language spoken still among the old. The chief disability of illiterate or uneducated minorities in the world of commercial English *koinē* is the ease with which they can be exploited; hence the need for an effective tribunate to which minorities might appeal, just as a Roman of the Republic might claim the tribune's protection against consular abuse. Such institutions could be the effective consequence of a formal preamble to a constitutional document committing the nation— as the first step in protecting cultures from wanton or mindless destruction—to the belief that any reduction in the variety and range of cultural responses is as detrimental to the species as a reduction in the genetic pool.

I do not discount the difficulty of composing such a document or of legislating it. How, for instance, do we assess the right to self-determination of an Indian tribe as opposed to the right of the citizenry of Albany, Georgia to protect themselves and what they regard as their way of life from the invasions of erotic high art or hard pornography? The problems are both moral and political, and their resolution will require no less genius—and probably much more— than originally went into the making of the Bill of Rights. But the architectonics of a great pluralistic society, an American Baalbek, whose supporting arches would be the great international structures of law, science, a common language, etc.—this is to ask no more of moderns than the Mediterranean received from the men of genius who built the *pax Romana* and its enabling institutions. If it is idle and visionary to imagine that such positive talent should come from universities, given their present economic misery, their torpor, and professional bad faith, it is surely not beyond human ingenuity that we should charter new institutions designed and empowered to diffuse their findings, to advocate and teach those findings. So far as culture, an American *paideia,* is concerned, no value is so much needed as the undeniable evidence of responsibilities assumed and met, in the service of an agenda in which our lost culture can be recreated or made anew.

And there is the crucial, but also incredibly difficult task of framing a tenable theory of human rights in a society so liberal or secular, so devoid of a consensus, that no traditional sanction can conceivably command assent. The problem could not be more acute or pressing. We confront an increasingly inhuman world with a doctrine of human rights—man's putative resemblance to God—which is no longer valid, no longer generally, or even widely, accepted. The problem of establishing philosophically—or rather, persuasively, in the hearts of men—a new rationale of human rights is the great priority; the issue is our own unprotected humanity, our own aggressive and destructive humanity. Despite strong religious stirrings, the only prospect is for a long secular interregnum. And in this difficult interim, our best prospects lie with those whose defense of human rights, however imperfect, does not lie with the idea of a transcendent God. We must look elsewhere, in time and place. Neither American Indians generally, nor the ancient Greeks, so far as I know, founded their theory and practice of human rights on any fancied resemblance to their gods. The central, governing idea was rather a solidarity of fate, a *con-sortium* in death and life, which made it possible to feel identity as mutuality: my fate—the fact that I am mortal, that I suffer and die—exacts from you the same compassion, the same dignity of treatment, that your fate requires from me. This, for instance, is surely what Sophocles is saying through the mouth of Odysseus as he looks at the misery of his fallen enemy, Ajax:

> ...I pity
> his wretchedness, though he is my enemy
> for the terrible yoke of blindness that is on him.
> I think of him, but also of myself,
> for I see the true state of all of us that live—
> we are dim shapes, no more, and weightless shadow.

Similarly, the Blackfoot cosmogony stresses the way in which death enables compassion—enables it as nothing else could. Thus when First Grandmother and First Grandfather were making man, they disagreed as to whether man should die. First Grandmother, however, insisted on death, for, given death, she said, "men would pity each other. There is no other way."

I repeat: the great fact of human conduct in the present, in the face of this coercive civilization and its almost autonomous life, is bad faith, *mauvaise foi.* We characteristically pretend that we are not free, and the aim of our pretence is to deny our freedom and therefore our moral responsibility to think and act. As Sartre knew (and as the Greeks knew long before Sartre), men are *condemned to freedom.* The human project itself is the openness imposed by the fact that every man is condemned to freedom, his own as it confronts, openly, that of others. That freedom cannot be burked except at the cost of one's own humanity. The more turbulent the times, the greater the temptation to bad faith. Bad faith now covers the country, and Western civilization, as John Jay Chapman said, like the grease on a Strasbourg paté. It is everywhere, in politics, business, education, and ordinary life; in all of us. You cannot find a man who is not tainted by it. "Even the critic of culture is unhappy with civilization, to which alone he owes his discontent. He speaks as if he represented either pure Nature or a higher historical stage. Yet he is necessarily of the same nature as that to which he imagines himself superior" (Adorno). Who are we, here at Southampton, we happy (or unhappy) few?

The complicating mechanisms, the range, power, and complexity of civilization, the paralyzing apparatus of suboptimization, are enough to "make cowards of us all." This collective cowardice is itself coercive. To be Lear cursing the world, or Oedipus with bloody eyeballs demanding more responsibility than the gods ever gave him, is one thing, quite appealingly and appallingly noble. To be Don Quixote, amiably tetched but lonely, or Chicken Little, is something else again.

What then, dearly beloved? Earlier I mentioned "an enterprise that might liberate, in the very effort to create a common culture, a responsible community, the values without which such a community could not cohere, act, or endure." The enterprise I have in mind, however, is not the direct, doomed frontal effort to create a culture in opposition to our botched but triumphant civilization, nor even the sane, modest, and perhaps useful efforts to create community schools, or little pockets of cultural resistance, or radical Edens, or secular monasteries. The effort I have in mind is the effort to reform the civilization, to make the civilization what, in a better world, it might be—the responsive instrument and enabling device of the culture it now threatens. A Quixotic task perhaps, but less Quixotic in the long run, it seems to me, than the effort to mount rearguard actions, guerilla campaigns, or all-out war; certainly less Quixotic than the effort to save intellectually bankrupt universities from merely fiscal disaster. We meet, I hardly need to say, in the shuddering slack of a bad time; there are no Messiahs in the room or on the cultural and political horizon, and none visibly looming. We are what we are, a group of largely discouraged, decently frightened intellectuals, bureaucrats, administrators, functionaries, modest has-beens and modest will-bes. But the spectacle of modest men and women immodest enough to assert responsibility in a world of bad faith may be the only human show in town. My example is the bureaucrat Watanabe in Kurosawa's great film *Ikiru*. Dying of cancer, a cancer which is inside him but also in his contextual world, his society, he succeeds in breaking the chains of his own professional and personal bad faith by claiming the one freedom he has—the freedom to act in the modest parish his bureaucratic post permits. His freedom apparently liberates at least one other and, temporarily, exhilarates all the rest; for, as Kurosawa knows, freedom, like bad faith, is transmitted by example and contagion, not by formal instruction. In the long wake which concludes the film, we see the director's deepest concern: a meditation on freedom through a confrontation with death, freedom enabled by dying; the possibility, however muted, of a new *paideia,* a new ethos founded on a true myth of freedom.

Brave hopes, an existential art. Examples gross as earth exhort us. Can the civilization be reformed? Perhaps not. Perhaps only by a cultural revolution. But such revolutions can only be provoked by the effort—moral, organizational, political, hortatory, exemplary—to reform and revalue this invasive and suboptimal fraud, this intolerable zero-culture in which we live. Formal education cannot be wholly discounted, but its present seizure by the civilization has rendered it nearly altogether useless for any large or generous human purposes; even if redeemed and reinvigorated by intelligent leadership and new goals, it is all too vulnerable to countervailing national forces, professional inertia or stupidity, the intolerance of those whose taxes support it and who, because they have not themselves been educated, perceive anything which does not simply replicate the civilization they confound with culture as threatening.

I realize that this must sound apocalyptic, but I have no apology. The experience of being "thrown into mere fragmentary life" is nothing if not apocalyptic. We are by now prepared to leave Paradise perhaps, but there is little to be said for a world in which we expel both ourselves and others from our common humanity. At the University of Texas where I spent twelve years, I knew the only genuine community—the only true intellectual community—I have ever known. And I saw it utterly and accurately destroyed by the oligarchy of Cro-Magnon thugs who now rule that unhappy state. I have spent more time and energy than I care to contemplate in efforts to reform institutions, from the University of California to M.I.T., from high school humanities programs to national professional guilds to paraprofessional training. And I cannot recall a single success, even a partial one, that endured. In every case either local resistance or torpor defeated the reform; or the national grid reasserted itself locally, and quietly but effectively reversed the changes. A decade of ferment in education has in fact produced immense changes in colleges and universities, but very little substantive educational reform. Ten years ago I attacked what I chose to call the "shame of the graduate schools"; ten years later, their shame strikes me as even more scandalous than before.

Some of you may have been luckier. But it is not easy to be sanguine unless reform is undertaken with a full sense of the general crisis in culture, and the difficulty of sustaining successful local reform against the gridded pressure of the civilization. Byzantium, after all, was not reformed from within, but without; and the reformers were not young Turks, but old and terrible Turks. The internal effort is of course indispensable; nothing worth doing will be done unless we can locate the potential fifth-column in the ranks of the civilization. But there must be someone at the gates. An army seems unlikely, but Homeric legend tells of a beleaguered town on a windy plain, and a wooden horse. . . .

The civilization is not of course unique in its claim to be the culture it once served to mediate and diffuse. The country is chock-a-block full of *soi-disant* "cultures" which are in no sense cultures at all but rather makeshift shelters designed to protect refugees from, or rebels against, the civilization. Ethnic communities in name only, they are too often marginal, desperate, and deeply unsure of themselves. Suffering and oppression make for solidarity, it is true, but the solidarity of oppression simulates the warm embrace of culture without the substance; and once the oppression ends, the old fragmentation reappears. True, a few Indian tribes have with some degree of success (usually modest and temporary) resisted the civilization, and even the old European ethnic minorities have retained a vestige of their heritage. But these minorities are in no sense "unmeltable";

the melting-pot claims them even in their frantic efforts to avoid it, in their struggles to retain symbolic and often token differentiation. As for youth cultures and countercultures, they are transparently middle-class inversions of the civilization, and they are dying daily. Still, it is impossible not to feel sympathy for their efforts to resist; and I wish them well. What they cannot command are precisely the cultural skills they tend to dismiss as irrelevant—applied intelligence; moral understanding; the expertises of the learned professions; in sum, the skills still deployed, aimlessly, in the civilization. And while it is certainly important that minorities and cultural refugees should feel, in contrast to consenting adherents of the civilization, that they control their own destinies, it is doubtful that cultural identity is so easily achieved; expelled by the front door, the civilization returns by the window. To take the most casual example, it is, I think, worth asking whether the Navaho Community College is not in fact simply a more subtle—because Navaho-controlled—instrument of assimilation, designed to produce a Navaho who can transfer without penalty to the universities of Arizona and New Mexico and then, presumably, return to the reservation as an unconscious agent of the civilization which has educated him largely against his own culture. Which is not, of course, to claim that civilization is a white conspiracy or anything of the kind. Minorities, I fear, all too rarely understand that white culture, Wasp culture, genteel middle-class or mainstream culture are all, like minority cultures, the prisoners of a civilization which is too vast, too autonomous and bureaucratically impersonal in its dynamic, to be actively, intelligently, racist or sexist (which requires some degree of discrimination), or anything but indiscriminately, universally, omnivorous in their assimilation.

Civilization in this dimension is a vast, self-perpetuating, self-diffusing mechanism, our own contemporary version of Shakespeare's "appetite, an universal wolf" which devours everything and, finally, itself; the same wolf which the Greeks knew as the pith and spirit of imperialism and called *pleonexia*, and which Nietzsche splendidly translated as *Mehr-haben-und-mehr-haben-wollen*. "If a man's desires are boundless," wrote the Renaissance theologian Alberico Gentili, "and there is not sufficient glory and power to satisfy them, that is not a law of nature, but a defect." A defect in man, one hastens to add; or, rather, a defect in culture, in *paideia*, synonymous with universal license in our late civilization.

For the foreseeable future, the residue of true culture will tend to inhabit these isolated efforts by groups and individuals to resist, in their different ways, the emptiness and pain and life-in-death of of mere fragmentary existence. And it is surely the task of any elite that aims at something more than status and power to identify these groups, to help them articulate in thought and action an integrated and harmonious culture, and assist them in resisting the civilization. Concerted, responsible, intelligent action—the very action which might create or liberate the values of a culture in the act of resisting the shams that have taken on the claims of authentic culture. Such action necessarily supposes an elite, a new elite—an elite which derives its title to lead from its accurate sense of the crisis, its outrageous and unheard-of assertion of responsibility, and its ability to elicit assent in those it would lead.

Praise of elites in these days of participatory democracy is of course unfashionable and perhaps dangerous. And for obvious reasons. The old governing elite, which once identified itself and Wasp culture with the civilization, has disgraced itself as surely as the Italian bourgeoisie disgraced itself in Mussolini's shoddy *Roma rinnovata*. But we cannot do without elites; no great society or true culture has ever come into being without the active maieutic work of elites; and the greatest human cultures have been the creation of elites which actively accepted competitive excellence—Greek *arete*—as their cardinal value. Now, the most formidable obstacle to the appearance of an American elite is the synthetic elitism fostered by the civilization—the elitism of what is sometimes called the Establishment or, more deceptively but not more honorably, the meritocracy. It is this elite which now manages the civilization, which has effectively imposed on the university and society its own meritocratic goals. Ultimately, advocates of meritocracy rest their case upon the argument that a managerial elite can be *educated* by professional skills which, in their random juxtaposition or sequence, are supposed to confer a collective impress dubbed, for no apparent reason, education. And in support of this theory which rationalizes actual practice (one of the commoner forms of bad faith), candidates for meritocratic consideration are screened by testing procedures which test only their professional aptitudes. The bad faith involved could hardly be greater. But upon these proceedings rests the whole superstructure of meritocratic machinery—the monstrous statistical apparatus of the Cartter Report, the Welch Report, the G.R.E., college boards, and other quantified caricatures of quality. Behind the scientistic front of "objective measurement" lies the sorry, shabby-genteel reality: an old-boy network in disrepute and disrepair but still functioning, the wreckage of an old privileged elite, still established in the universities, foundations, and corporate boards, desperately attempting to rationalize the whole vast suboptimal system as an emergent social reality and also to suggest the noble aura—in fact, quite appallingly absent—of old *arete,* professional service and compassion, human wisdom, long views, the risk of freedom, and high imaginative enterprise.

Of *noblesse oblige* you will not hear a word. The inventors of meritocracy, like Ortega y Gasset's spoiled and childish mass-man, are eager to inherit the privileges, but not the responsibilities, of the hereditary elite they claim to replace. That this tawdry but cagey Establishment—which stands to a true elite as civilization stands to culture—should lead to distrust of all elites is not surprising; but the disenchantment is costly, since it works to the general disrepute of genuine leadership. Obviously leaders are unlikely to appear when leadership itself is in question, and high abilities are grounds, not for admiration, but envy and distrust. Any true leader must of course have real rapport with those he leads; he must know their minds, in Machiavelli's sense, and elicit their assent by anticipation of their noblest aspiration.

Their noblest aspiration: Machiavelli's prince can lead not because he is democratically affable or expert-certified, but because he literally crystallizes, like Stendhal's lover, the best aspirations of those he leads, those who love him; his power is precisely this power to crystallize aspiration, the kind of *charisma* or grace that Plato saw as the divinity of those we love, those teachers who crystallize our highest love, who teach us how to approach the god to whom we are indentured, and whom we hope, on tiptoes, to touch and *be*.

Leadership is in bad odor because it is disgraced by its own bad faith. Yet the prevalent popular distrust of all leadership and authority is, I think, a symptom of equally bad faith in the led. Commitment is refused because it spares us the terror of responsibility and risk. It is all the more important, then, that fraudulent leadership and synthetic elitism should be exposed for the shams they are. In education, I have argued, as in every other field of organized intellect, there is an effective national grid of restraints and attitudes which reinforce the general suboptimization. But this grid is vulnerable, morally and intellectually. The Archimedean point therefore at which all our energies should be directed is the bad faith on which the civilization is built; unless attention is directed there, the fifth column of culture is doomed to useless sacrifice inside the walls, like a child's sand castle threatened by the incoming tide. But the tide is the thing; whatever the folly of Canute, what is called for is the capacity, by courage and skill, to turn that tide.

It was that tide I had in mind a few years ago when I seriously proposed what I then called a "university of the public interest." I was almost certainly wrong in supposing that a university conceivably could or should become a true custodian of the culture or act as a true tribunate of the public interest. But I believed then, as I still do, that liberal learning—reformed, lively, humane, and intelligent—is indispensable to any form of cultural or social action that is not simply suboptimal. True learning *liberates;* it also suggests the significant, the best, use of freedom. Even in its present form, the university is the only available shelter for liberal learning. It is the university that now trains, and that might educate, professionals. The tasks I once proposed for my tribune-university are, after all, professional, requiring knowledge; those tasks are still undone, unrecognized, unclaimed. Sternly revised, sparingly planned (there must be no illusions about federal benevolence or foundation courage), the idea is still practicable. More practicable, I think, than the piecemeal effort to reform intellectually and morally crippled universities—in the teeth of financial bankruptcy or insolvency—against the ruthlessly suboptimal assault of Affirmative Action, the Cartter Report, and the Buckley Amendment; against the wishes of a timid and apprehensive professoriate supported nationally by the shabby-genteel syndicalism of the new, somewhat shabby A.A.U.P.; against all the instruments of the nationally gridded civilization.

The name of the reform hardly matters; but enterprises of such aim and nature are one of the few institutional reforms, short of revolution, by which those who possess knowledge can apply it to correct our common ills, and perhaps, by so doing, reform the institutions themselves or the disciplines themselves, now so obviously in such bad faith with the culture they are meant to mediate in the work of education. Only by using what we know in tasks whose complexity mocks even our pooled skills, let alone our conventional specialisms, can we create a true intellectual community, which is to say a model of the common culture we no longer have. If we are to achieve a *paideia*, then we shall have to improvise an energizing *arete*, and a new elite whose principle is service, not privilege or a meritocratic surrogate.

The elite would ideally be composed of those who assume responsibility for the disastrous state of the culture. To accept such responsibility is, in itself, bold, even arrogant; at the least it requires unusual confidence combined with an even more unusual humility. All true culture begins with the individual; only he can terminate his own bad faith—in company with others. But in a society of institutions, in the teeth of a gridded civilization, individual courage must also be, as best it can be, organized too; good faith requires a community, since the individual needs others to be effective, to keep him honest, humble, human, open. Implicit in my argument is of course the conviction that culture, like freedom, like *arete*, is only to be had by striving for it. Such *arete* is, of course, only another name for heroism. Heroes do not become heroes because they clean the Augean Stables or kill the Lernean hydra. The hero engages the values of a culture, energizes them, galvanizes them, just as a great teacher galvanizes the texts he teaches. The tasks they perform are presumably tasks that symbolize the ordeals and difficulties of creating a great society. Tasks like cleaning the stables and killing the hydra—these too are "examples gross as earth," they too exhort us. Herakles is the name of the *arete*, individual and collective, that is equal to the task. Responsible action—which is now, in our condition, equivalent to heroic action—galvanizes freedom. No sooner is it exhibited than everyone recognizes it. It had merely to be exhibited in action, assume credible human form. Once exhibited, it may not be loved or even admired, but it is rarely disbelieved. The true measure of our loss of culture is that we no longer believe in responsible action, nor in the values which heroic action enables and embodies.

Improvised *arete*—the institutionalization of the excellence that must, when culture fails, be reinvented and reenergized, in significant striving and purpose. The age is wretched and noisily desperate; it suffers from knowledge which has been deformed and barbarized or, in many cases, cancerous, an explosion of invasive and alien excess. And though the traditional custodians may suppose the problem is the barbarians outside, howling down all merit and standards, the real danger is bad faith at the top and everywhere else, the absence of leadership and responsibility, and, concurrently, among the learned themselves—in a knowledge-society—the terrible degradation of the professions. Those who have knowledge in a world controlled by deformities of knowledge cannot morally evade the responsibility for humane and concerted action, for any action that is less than optimal. In one of the classics of human openness and active freedom, a great writer declared:

I cannot praise a fugitive and cloistered virtue, unexercised and unbreathed, that never sallies out and sees her adversary, but slinks out of the race, where that immortal garland is to be run for, not without dust and heat. Assuredly we bring not innocence into the world; we bring impurity much rather; that which purifies us is trial, and trial is by what is contrary. That virtue, therefore, which is but a youngling in the contemplation of evil, and knows not the utmost that vice promises to her followers, and rejects it, is but a blank virtue, not a pure; her whiteness is but an excremental whiteness. . . .

References

Sapir, Edward. "Culture, Genuine and Spurious." *Culture, Language, and Personality: Selected Essays.* Berkeley: University of California Press, 1970.

Sagan, Eli. *Cannibalism: Human Aggression and Cultural Form.* New York: Harper & Row, 1974.

11

An Overview of Southampton

Henry Steele Commager

We acknowledge—give lip service, is the phrase—the distinction between education and schooling, and then forget it in our discussions and our plans. It remains, however, fundamental. A great part of the confusion that has attended the various conferences here (at Southampton) springs from failing to recognize that distinction. We persist in calling on schools (half the time for "education" read "schools") to do all the things that society should do: to face and solve all the ailments, and to program all the improvements in our society. We do this, as Peter Brooks observed, even in and perhaps especially in, the realm of higher education, though we are not always clear what it is higher than. We lay so many responsibilities on colleges and on universities to be "relevant" (that most irrelevant of cant words) that they become relevant to everything but their special function which is to pass on the heritage of the past to the future, to train for technical and professional expertise, and to carry on research which may solve problems.

If we persist in calling on schools to do everything—set all priorities, solve our social problems, inculcate virtues, open up vistas, release all talents, we are bound to be disappointed and defeated. Our task as spokesmen for more than schools—for education—is to make clear, if we can, what are social and what are academic responsibilities: if we fail to do this, we place too heavy a burden on schools, and we shall end up distracting and enervating them.

I return to a point which has been made again and again but which we seem to persist in ignoring when we come to our conclusions: that education is not something apart from society but an integral part of it and inevitably reflects the dominant traits of that society.

How often we have heard that education—schooling—in America is unjust, that facilities are inequitably distributed, that there is discrimination and elitism. Alas all true enough. For ours is an unjust society. Our housing is unjust; our job situation is unjust; the distribution of health and hospital facilities, the treatment of prisoners, the application of the law to rich and to poor all are unjust. We are not going to reform one part of society without reforming the others. The way to get justice in education is to get a more just society.

That is not out of our reach. Think how unjust were the societies of the old world in all of these matters only fifty or 100 years ago; how, we should ask ourselves, have England, Germany, the Scandinavian countries lifted themselves by their bootstraps and created more just societies? We made great progress toward this goal in the 1930s; why have we made so little since? Inevitably the question arises, do we really want a just society? We think that we do, but there the evidence is far from persuasive.

I do not despair of progress here, anymore than Jane Addams despaired of progress in dealing with the slums of Chicago and the delinquency of juveniles. Things can be changed, but they can be changed only if the people are ready for it and if they are prepared to pay the price for it. Society can be changed; but only if there is leadership—the kind of leadership that a Horace Mann, an Elizabeth Peabody, a Charles Eliot, a Jane Addams, a John Dewey, an Eleanore Roosevelt provided. Here is where the heart and the head must form an alliance, but that is something you cannot bring about by resolutions either.

There are historical reasons for this phenomenon, but that does not mean that these reasons are still valid. After all there are historical reasons for racial discrimination in America, too, but that does not validate such malpractices. More to the point is to compare the situation in our country with that in similar countries in Western

Europe. The papers and discussions in this conference have been so parochial that we have no illumination of this subject at all. To the best of my knowledge no European school system expects or requires that schools bear the whole burden of education: that schools inculcate racial tolerance, teach morals, virtues, internationalism, peace, the military arts, cosmopolitanism and national patriotism, encourage both public service and private enterprise, etc. Why should *we* lay everything on our schools? The suspicion will not down that one reason is that as educators we rather fancy the idea that everything depends on us, that the nation cannot develop well without us and that therefore it is right and proper that society should depend on us to do everything.

There is a parallel, needless to say, in the way colleges and universities act. Their theory is that nobody can possibly learn anything unless somebody gives a course in it, so we pretend that the printing press has never been invented and that we have to give courses on everything. Even those who have said all they have to say in books on the American Revolution or the Bill of Rights or Milton are expected to give courses on these subjects. Most of what the young learn they learn outside the schoolroom or the classroom, or even in spite of these; most of what they learn in college, they learn from each other, or from "life," not from teachers.

I find emphasis on emotion, on the heart, on the "affective"— to use the jargon term—largely irrelevant to education, not because the thing itself is not of utmost importance but because nobody is going to be argued into being generous, kind, sympathetic, etc., by an organization or a series of recommendations; nor can generosity and sympathy be "taught." We should all love one another: so every preacher in every western country has been telling us every Sunday for centuries, and we end up hating each other more than ever before. Clearly persuasion is not going to open the doors of heaven. It is all very much like the spectacle of preaching the necessity of honor and peace (did we not combine the two?) while we provide a public display of dishonor and war. What do you think the young are going to believe? They are going to conclude that we are hypocrites— which indeed we are.

After all, it is a bit late in the day to discover with cries of joy what was the essence of Rousseau, and the life work of Pestalozzi; what animated Oberlin and Grundtvig and Froebel; what Bronson

Alcott preached and practiced; what triumphed in Jane Addams, almost a century ago.

And, note, too, that the way these educators championed the role of the heart, or of love, was not by formal preaching or by passing resolutions: it was by providing examples in practice (which every American teacher is quite prepared to do, I am sure) and by putting some of their philosophy into things that everybody read, such as *How Gertrude Teaches Her Children,* or perhaps *Little Women,* or even *The Spirit of Youth in the City Streets.* Where are the novelists, the poets, the social workers who dramatize to children the role of love?

The *cri de coeur* of every group such as this is, how do we bring about change? It is customary to invoke psychology or sociology, and I leave that approach to those who know how to use it and who have confidence in it. I suggest that one thing we might do, one thing the Office of Education might do—if it is indeed interested in change— is to conduct a series of case studies on how changes in American education (or in modern education) have indeed been brought about. I have in mind something like Paul de Kruif's studies of *Microbe Hunters* and *Hunger Fighters*—or case studies a bit more scholarly than de Kruif's, just to make our colleagues happy.

For as we consider the history of education, not in America alone, we cannot but be impressed with the number and character of changes that have been brought about by the ardent efforts of one or a few dedicated leaders rather than by government. I have spoken before of the role of Abraham Flexner and his report on medical education in the United States, a report which revolutionized medical education: from that report we can date modern medical education in this country. To this dramatic example we can add some of the following:

1. The creation of the Normal School in America, a borrowing from Germany and France, Americanized by Horace Mann.

2. The creation of the Kindergarten in America, borrowed, if you will, by Bronson Alcott and Elizabeth Peabody and Susan Blow, but in the end so thoroughly Americanized that Froebel could say that only in America would the kindergarten achieve its final character.

3. The creation of the modern university in America, the

achievement of Philip Tappan at Michigan, of White at Cornell, Eliot at Harvard, Gilman at the Hopkins.

4. The creation of the modern law school by Langdell of Harvard, an achievement which influenced not only legal education but all education, in the United States and in much of the western world.

5. The achievement of independence of the school from religious control, a story which starts with Thomas Jefferson and his plans for the University of Virginia, embraces the schools which Girard set up in Philadelphia, and the struggle of Horace Mann for emancipation from religion in Massachusetts, and reaches a climax in the Everson and the McCullom cases of our own time.

6. The establishment of women's colleges and of the principle of co-education, now everywhere triumphant: the work of Catherine Beecher, May Lyons, Emma Willard, and other crusaders in this field which the United States all but pre-empted.

All of these achievements are part of American history, but there is no reason why we should confine ourselves to our own experience: indeed the history of American education has always suffered from parochialism. One of the weaknesses of this conference has been its parochialism. It assumed, so far as the papers and the discussions can be trusted, that nothing was to be learned from English or European experience, and this in face of the palpable evidence that education has been a good deal more successful in Britain and Scandinavia and perhaps Germany than it has been in the United States; this in face of the palpable fact that most of our own educational ideas—the normal school, the kindergarten, the university—came from Europe. We could do worse than to concentrate on the history of German and English education, or on the history of the Danish Folk High School—on the whole the most successful program of adult education that has ever been devised. We could do worse than to study how Europe lifted itself by its bootstraps after World War II and managed to create a democratic educational program without sacrificing standards. We could do worse than study the experiences of the Soviet Union; instead of concentrating on the impact of Sputnik, we should concentrate on the conquest of illiteracy.

These far-reaching changes were rooted, in every case, in

philosophical considerations. They did not, generally, start with the announcement of some broad philosophical program, nor were they launched on a national or global scale. They started, for the most part, with one man or woman agitating an idea or inaugurating an experiment. Rousseau wrote one book, and was content with that, but *Emile* is probably the most revolutionary book in the whole history of education. Pestalozzi set up his little schools at Stanz and Neuhof, and wrote his revolutionary books without support or even encouragement—but he conquered the western world. Grundtvig and Kold funded the Danish Folk High School without any aid from government, and the High School revitalized Denmark and spread from there to every Scandinavian country—where it still flourishes. Froebel got the idea of kindergartens from Pestalozzi, and established them in Germany: he was put out of business by the Minister of Education, who regarded kindergarten as subversive, but it spread throughout the world. Bronson Alcott taught at the Temple School which an outraged public closed; but in the end it was Alcott who triumphed over Boston. Jefferson worked for half a century to create a university which was, in the end, the lengthened shadow of one man, but what a man! It was the first real university in America, and it was all his making, from the charter and the professors and the students and the curriculum to the buildings and the gardens. Eliot was content to use Harvard for his experiments in modern education and Gilman to use the Hopkins, but between them they revolutionized the university in America. Jane Addams lobbied at Hull House for her reforms, and in the end the rest of the nation followed; was that not where John Dewey first saw the light? Was that not the origin of *The School and Society*?

This is, needless to say, a plea for reliance on individual initiative: a call for philosophical leadership which has almost always been individual rather than governmental. Not one of the great innovators I have mentioned relied on government to do the job. Not one of them, except for Flexner, had Foundation support. All of them deserve the wonderful lines of O'Shaunessey, that

> One man with a dream at pleasure
> Shall go forth and conquer a crown,
> And three with a new song's measure
> Can trample a kingdom down.

The group of scholars and educators gathered here tended, I think, to avoid the concrete problem: they brought up injustice time and time again but had little to say about how to remedy injustice. I was struck with the paper (not included in this volume) on Blacks and the Supreme Court. A paper which argued that the Court had not really dealt very well with Blacks; not a very surprising conclusion. The paper ended with *Brown v. Topeka*; a curious place to end. Why not Serrano, why not Rodriguez? To the best of my—admittedly fallible—recollections, nobody here has brought up either Serrano or Rodriguez, or if they have, none has done so with a view to canvassing the possibility of effective action to (a) win support to Justice Marshall's position, (b) devise strategy to circumvent the Powell decision, (c) get congressional legislation to declare education a matter of fundamental importance in the eyes of the 14th Amendment. Here is potentially the most powerful gesture towards equalization of rights in education in our time—just what a great many members of our conferences have been concerned with. But none has pushed the matter, none has turned to practical programs that might get results.

Let me conclude with a plea that we make the Office of Education what Henry Barnard originally wanted it to be:

1. To engage in research in education, as the Smithsonian, the U.S. Geological Survey, the Surgeon General's Office, etc., engaged in research.

2. To respond to needs and requests of the Congress; to prepare material for its use; *to help in the drafting of legislation.*

3. To provide analytical and statistical studies of education throughout the world, cooperating here with analagous organizations in UNESCO, thus helping to overcome the parochialism of our current discussion of American education.

4. To sponsor publications comparable to those sponsored by, for example, the National Portrait Gallery, dealing with history of education in America, in particular states, in special areas. This was one of the major contributions of the Office in the 1880 to 1900 period.

5. To create a network of alliances with professional and other organizations with interest in education—with the American Bar, the American Medical, the American Historical, etc., societies; with

all organizations engaged in work on or with children, with the underprivileged, with special education and, most urgently, with American and international organizations concerned with world problems. Education is clearly not a national but a world problem.

PART V

Voices at the Table

12

Participation at Southampton
(Excerpts and Commentary)

R. W. Lid

Malcolm Shaw: *In response to some of the comments about Project Open,*
I think, you know, there will be questions as to whether Project Open is or was,
or what it will become or—
Michael Rossman:—*or whether it was a last ditch or a first ditch stand.*
—Sequence II

The weather shifted from cool to warm, and then to hot, at the
end of the third of the four Southampton Summer Sequences. The
rain, which had been incessant and chilling, finally turned traditional
and seasonal—quick summer showers which brought respite from the
heat. On Main Street, in downtown Southampton, the hardware
stores began to sell the electric fans already featured at discount
prices because of the cool summer. At Southampton College, the ice
maker located in the connecting building between Montauk 300 and
400 broke down.

The morning winds blew from the south. At noon they became
box-like and confused the compass, before settling on an afternoon
course, southwest off the ocean (the prevailing wind), or north and
west across the Island. Down at the beach the north wind brought
greenbottle flies which stung. In the cinderblock dormitory "suites"
at Southampton College, the air did not move, whatever direction

the wind blew. Towels and soap ran in short supply. The morning delivery to the suites of continental breakfast and *The New York Times* was sporadic. The morning walk from the cafeteria to the meeting rooms left the participants sweaty.

The measure of the Southampton Summer Sequences surely includes Southampton College and the weather, just as it includes Ridge House (actually the Punnett house on Ridge Road, some ten minutes by car from the campus), where the get-acquainted parties were held, and later, when the weather changed, the barbecues took place. It was at Ridge House that the VIPs stayed. Identification with Ridge House bespoke a certain air of exclusivity, less than full camaraderie with the egalitarian dormitory crowd. Several of the staff living there moved back to the college, feeling cut off from the action.

Southampton meant moving—arrivals and departures, planes to be met, schedules to be kept. Logistics. It meant fifteen papers prepared by participants, some of whom never arrived. It meant five major addresses. It meant the Kohon String Quartet on Sunday evening, June 30, in the Fine Arts Theater. It meant the appearances of a U.S. senator and two congressmen. It meant meal tickets for the cafeteria. But above all, Southampton meant the recipients of all this planning and preparation: the participants.

By and large the participants had been selected because they represented distinct and different constituencies, and hence they stood for divergent points of view which would be funneled into the vortex of talk that was to be Southampton. More men than women (the staff was oblivious to its chauvinism), more age than youth, more anglos than minorities, more academics than businessmen or labor figures, more public school types than any other type. They all tended to share one characteristic: they had made their name, acquired their reputation, developed their expertise in the 1960s. By and large, their personal myths and lifestyles had been devised and revised during socially troubled times, and their defenses, which matched these myths and styles, were expressive of those times. In the more tranquil 1970s, the participants gave the appearance of being powerful, self-willed people used to doing and achieving. Even the academics were doers, and only the lack of familiarity with the type by the other participants made possible the misjudgment rendered them. All over, the participants tended to be significant managers of public properties, institutions, agencies; of enterprises with social goals; of organizations with a public conscience. Few represented merely themselves.

In the 1960s Southampton would have been a "happening"—except that Southampton could not have happened in the 1960s. Many of the participants would not have spoken to each other, or would have addressed each other with derision and contempt. Yet only their participation in the events of the 1960s made their participation at Southampton possible. The participants were civic-wise and public-wise. The many interfaces of encounter and confrontation were familiar to them, as were the concepts of hidden agendas, emerging identities, and psycho- and socio-drama. They had learned tolerance over the years. Content as style had been the "bag" of the 1960s, their bag. And so they came genuinely prepared to meet, engage, encounter—even while they were openly skeptical of the announced intentions and goals of the program. Psychically they were ready to love the unloved, and even the unlovable, but mentally they were prepared to be querulous. They were sure of themselves but unsure of the future. The Age of Aquarius had ended—and no new dawning was in sight.

Participation at Southampton centered around the lives of small groups. Inventions of the Steering Committee, they became instant congeries of interests created out of lists of people. Set on their course, they were expected, like Bunyan's Christian, to make their way through a Vanity Fair of special interests to broadly defined social goals. Much was expected of the small groups at Southampton, and with good reason. They embodied the beliefs of the Steering Committee about what could and could not be known about American society, as well as the degree of certainty and specificity with which things could be known. Content as process in one vocabulary; content as form in an older language.

At times the small groups staggered under the weight of the Steering Committee's epistemological beliefs. They turned inward on themselves, and then outward toward the Committee, questioning the meaning of process—of the various senses of participation embedded in what they were trying to do and the way they were trying to do it. "Participation" was the key to the door of the 1970s as represented by Southampton: the center of all that happened and all that was said. Sometimes the small groups failed to find that key. Sometimes they tried to force the door. As often as not, they first tried a skeleton key from the 1960s. The past was not easily shucked off, though gradually a new sense of participation did emerge amidst old cliches and new shibboleths. It became one of the entitlement and enablement of a citizenry in its broadest sense. At once visionary and rooted in the American past, an echo of the "vibes" of the 1960s, the concept took on a grand dimension at Southampton—one that Southampton itself could not fulfill. At Southampton the participants, the small groups, the plenary sessions could talk about it. They could not enact it. But, oh, how they could talk!

Southampton means some 2,000 pages of transcript recorded by a young court stenographer—a seemingly endless flow of language. Yet all told, the transcripts represent perhaps one-fifth of the words spoken in public during the four sequences. In general, only the large group meetings were recorded, and, in the first two sessions, not all of these. The Steering Committee was for some time unsure about what it wanted recorded, what was worth recording in the deliberations, and only midway did it decide that all the large sessions should be transcribed. From the outset, then, the transcripts were not complete, though they were always remarkably good reproductions, considering the number of people who often spoke out with near simultaneity and who had to be identified by name by the reporter.

The pages which follow are taken from the transcripts. They are intended to be representative and informative. They are not intended to be a catalog of all (or even most) of the topics covered during the four sessions, nor do they provide a complete record of even one working meeting of the conference. They do not constitute a collection of "highlights," or high points, of the conference. Rather they are intended to suggest the kind of talk that went on during the four sessions, its texture and quality, and the context in which the talk took place: usually meetings at which small groups were being asked to report back to the participants-as-a-whole. Each of the four sequences maintained basically the same pattern, which included commencing with an evening meal in a banquet setting. This was followed by a major address in the Fine Arts Theater. The participants then adjourned for drinks to Ridge House, where they had an opportunity to mingle and meet each other.

The next morning, at the first general session of the sequence, participants were divided into three or four small groups. The groups were assigned general areas of concern and sent off to work at their tasks, reporting back in general session three times—very early on, as they were just getting underway; midway (the point at which feelings frequently erupted); and on the last day of the sequence. Additional general sessions were held to listen to guest speakers and panel discussions. At least one night session of small group work occurred in each sequence.

The transcripts that follow begin with the first evening and first morning session of the fourth sequence. They then move backward in time to the first two sequences, showing initial and mid-point group reports, as well as, with the inclusion of the third sequence, some of the problems the participants felt in reporting out and also some of the interchanges that occurred between participants and staff, particularly those that deal with participation and "process." Both the initial and final reports of the groups in Sequence IV are included in shortened form, as is the controversy that ensued. Finally, some of the interchanges of the staff, after the participants in Sequence IV had left, are presented for the light they throw on that sequence, and on the staff and the conference as a whole. Ellipses indicate where there has been an omission within a single response or within sequences of dialogue. Beyond that, the editing includes only the omission of repetitive words and phrases, the regularizing of punctuation, and the division into paragraphs.

Donald Bigelow: I will be very brief on this very hot night. . . . American democracy rests in part upon what we used to call the Town Hall and what in the world of tomorrow we might find other terms for. Here let me just speak of it as the ability to get along with people not of one profession—with people whose language, whose ideas, hopes, and beliefs you and I have not been intimately involved with; with people who come from quite different backgrounds with quite different outlooks and who look for quite different outcomes. This, it seems to me, is the basis, the purpose, the original thought behind these four sequences. We have indeed, as you will see by looking at your neighbor, brought a diverse, disparate group of people together in the totality of what is known as the American democracy. What we are trying to do is to learn how to deal with segments of that totality that don't often, if ever, come together. It is—I said this in my first introduction on a similar occasion a month ago—a noble experiment. It is not necessarily doomed to failure. It will only be a failure if we don't come to understand what we learn here.

I want to say something about how you might know in the future what we have learned here. A young man in the audience is taking down every word I am saying; he will also take down most of what you say in the next few days. You would be surprised, when you put together what all of us say, how something emerges that does not seem to have been intended. You all remember the story of Noah, the original story, when he was counting the animals as they came off the ark at Mount Ararat. The two animals came roughly one by one, the big ones slowly, the small ones rapidly. He looked up in astonishment at nine cats following two big cats. The father cat said to Noah, "and all the time you thought we were fighting." Historians have a way of looking at the pairings that go in and the pairings that come out. The events in between have to be covered in other ways. In our case, some will be on steno tape, some on audio tape, and some on video tape—which is why we are in this hot room tonight. Still, we always seem to miss important parts. Historians are used to that. They have been inventing long before Charles Beard and will continue long after you have left Southampton.

May I welcome you here. Thank you very much.

Malcolm Shaw: Good morning. I think we will start. Let's begin. You may want to move your chairs around so that you will be more comfortable. We will talk this way, in a large group, for a little bit, and then we will be moving into other settings. Someone said at the last session that we should have had an environmental psychologist present. You may want to work in rooms other than those assigned to you—whatever feels comfortable.

One major purpose this morning is to provide a general framework and then to focus pretty quickly on where this group might go, both in terms of what has happened in the past sequences and also in terms of our sense of what should be happening. I think it might be useful if I took a minute to review some of the broader purposes and strategies of Project Open as it relates to what we are trying to do in the three and a half days we will be here.

Without giving a long history, let me just say that Project Open is, as some of you know, an extension of a federal program called

TTT—the Trainers of Teacher Trainers program. It initially took the point of view that educational change and social change require a flow of information between and among the various components of the educational system and the various components of the society. It was our view that in many areas there were walled-off enclaves of activity, and that in many cases communication among and between those concerned about educational, about social change was limited. Our view was that in the process of social change it is necessary for the components involved in that change to take part in something that one might wish to call "learning," as Don Schon defined it last night: something involving feedback, processing of information, and the possibility of some observable behavioral change.

There is a direct analogy between genetic evolution and social evolution. In one way or another, institutions have to draw from the variety pool surrounding them, have to draw upon the diversities existing within their own environment, within their own walls, in order to emerge with a new form and new way of working. Project Open takes the view that the locus of change, the locus of development, lies in the interactions—in the nature and quality of the interactions among the parts of the system we are concerned with. Therefore the thrust of Project Open over the last two and a half years has been to try to bring diverse and varied individuals, groups, and institutions into new kinds of communication processes.

In some cases, these processes have been localized and pragmatic, dealing with problems involving public schools and community representation and local government; in other cases, they have been rather broad, involving educators, deans of education, peer groups in the educational area—but always, I think, coming back to the notion that the focus of our attention has to be on the interaction between and among the components rather than upon changing the components from within. Another way of putting it, probably, is that the schools can't reform themselves—whatever that might mean—and hence the question really is one of how to open them up to some kind of new involvement, some kind of new transaction, making it possible for them to modify their own processes. It is with that kind of general framework and within that framework that we are asking you to work together this week.

Malcolm Shaw: I think we will begin. Our purpose in the next thirty minutes or so is simply to get a kind of quick feedback—not to reach broad conclusions or consensus, but to give people a chance to get some sense of where the groups are and what kinds of issues they are beginning to struggle with. Our view is that the process of coming to conclusions and reaching closure will extend probably until the last morning. We would like to get some individual and group reactions to where you are, the kind of issues you are dealing with, and some sense of what is happening. Let us explore where each group is so that we have some common experience.

David Florio: Identity, access, and interconnection are the underlying themes of our group. We thought identity was necessary so individuals could participate in society; access, to give entry and also skills, knowledge, and resources so they could not only enter but sustain participation in various aspects of society. Interconnection we saw as trying to avoid the parochialism and chauvinism and narcissism that develops in a total, community-pocket kind of isolation. We were constantly aware of the need to raise to public consciousness a recognition of the interdependency of people. We want to do that through a variety of ways. . . .

We need to give resources and aid for entry, underwriting entry not only in terms of educational institutions but in terms of employment. We also talked in terms of experiencing temporary careers or of multiple careers in a lifetime, opening up educational systems to this process, working with emerging youth or adults experiencing mid-career change. We want to promote, and this is a radical change in the structure of society, the moving in and out of institutions as far as careers are concerned. People ought to have that kind of access. This is where we picked up Senator Pell's comments about sixteen years of education. We would like to maybe push it farther than sixteen years, spreading it over a lifetime, so that if an adult wants to retrain or retool, he can demand that right and get supported for it. We want to make it economically feasible for people that have families and other responsibilities.

Max Dixon: I have been asked about some of the conclusions of our small group. Yesterday we pointed to the divisive issue of democracy versus meritocracy—for education, the issue of whether our egalitarian emphasis is more just than an emphasis on achievement and excellence. This issue is divisive ideologically. It is reflected specifically in two other issues we talked about. One is fairly broad—

the issue of unity versus diversity, cultural assimilation versus cultural pluralism. Here we concluded that there should be frank recognition of the virtues of both unity and diversity, particularly in a country with many minorities. There should be a recognition of the national need for the former—that is, for unity—and of the inevitability and the need involved in the latter. Whatever the emphasis on national unity, we concluded that legal protection of cultural autonomy should be guaranteed; recent court decisions in this direction should be applauded.

A second issue involved the patronizing of public versus private schools. Here, alas, there is no nice solution we can point to. We say the same kind of thing: there should be a frank recognition of the dilemma confronting a parent who feels he has a responsibility to support public education and yet has the private aspiration that his children secure a quality education—an education which at a given time and place may be found best in a private school. The parent's choice must certainly be free in this matter, and in our system this is guaranteed—but it is a real public dilemma, apart from the private choice that parents have involving sacrifice. It is a real public dilemma as to whether the wholesale desertion of the public schools should be therefore somewhat discouraged or in the name of efficiency encouraged—with, for example, a voucher system promoting competition among schools.

Richard Ford: I think we came to only one conclusion in our deliberations—that the purpose of education in its ideal sense should be to keep options open, or to make options open not previously open; also, to make people aware of options that are open that they might not have known about.

Beyond that, I don't know that we came to any consensus. Instead I think we talked about a number of contradictions. One contradiction, for example, is that there is a myth of openness as contrasted with the reality of American life. Does the myth of openness in American society, does the myth of rags to riches, the myth of success, create problems when individuals discover what the real society is all about? Is there such a divorce between the imaginary or mythical world, perpetuated in schools or other institutions that young people come in contact with, and the real world that we create alienation and anxiety?

Paul Olson: Some of the most serious divisiveness in our society has to do with the sort of Oedipal antagonism that exists between people in middle life, who are in control of the professions and in control of the occupations, and the young people, who are kept in school for twenty years without being initiated in some meaningful way into the world of responsibility. I think that education which is meaningful must be cross-generational and must accomplish some kind of vocation. Through the vocations existing in small towns and rural areas which were available to young people after school, there was a kind of acculturation to the adult vocation that took place spontaneously. In urban societies, by virture of the child labor laws and factories and the way working space is laid out, there is no way of doing this. I think it creates a whole different sense of the perception of reality in the young as contrasted with the old.

Joel Henning: The best of the new education would include not just clinical experiences, not just visits to the zoo, so to speak, but meaningful critical experiences that go beyond the four walls of the classroom as well as occur within the four walls of the classroom—experiences in dealing with the real problems of the school community, rule making and rule enforcing in school, and experiences within the community which allow students, as part of their educational fulfillment, new and desperately needed roles, service roles in the community, engaging with society and having an impact on society in ways meaningful to them, even if it means no more than moving the community to pass bond issues for tennis courts. That was the sort of thing we talked about yesterday.

One last point, going beyond what we are talking about. It requires repeating. Two things I have said this morning: there is no institution, there is no profession which any longer in this country ought to be left to the insiders. Yesterday I talked a lot about courts and how the courts have for too long been designed to serve the insiders—judges and lawyers. I think education, to a large extent, has been designed, and still is, to serve the insiders, the bureaucrats and the teachers, but not the students and not the parents. There is a demand, a constructive and useful demand, in this country for consumerism, and consumerism ought to affect the school, as it ought to affect the medical profession and legal profession.

Page Smith: It seems to me that ideally, from my point of view, I don't want to do away with teachers, but I do want to develop the notion that everybody teaches and has a teaching function to perform at a stage in his life where it is appropriate to perform it. This has to do with the professionalization of teaching; one of the things that professionalization does is to exclude a great many people with enormous teaching talents from teaching, and that simply has to be overcome somehow. That is a professional snobbery—certification and those things that enter into it. The result is an enormous loss of available teaching intelligence and energy.

Benjamin DeMott: Page, can we add to that? This speaks directly to it. My way of seeing this in the good society is to say that every human being has it within him and her to be at some point in his or her life not only a teacher but a healer and a defender of the weak; that is to say, a teacher is like a doctor is like a lawyer. These roles are now hived off in such a way that you cannot get to them. Access to the role of healer, access to the role of defender of the weak, these are closed off and you live a life in which you never function that way as a healer, as a defender.

You do not have to have an M.D. in order to heal; first aid helps a lot. By the same token, you don't have to have a Harvard law degree to know something about the way to maneuver legally and in order to provide that information to someone who doesn't know it when he is in the court system.

Samuel Nash: I have the same feeling I got when I read this year that there are going to be surplus people; you know, surplus people. It sounded funny, and then I felt that we already have surplus people: those to whom we give the nice title of "senior citizen." They are already surplus. They get in cheap to the movies; they get a bus ride cheaper—we like to keep them out of our way. In a sense, youth are surplus people. They have a lot of energy we don't want them to use; it doesn't fit in. We don't want them to think because they are not at the age yet; only adults do real thinking. Youth are in a sense surplus, and that gets to powerlessness and power and so forth. But the whole notion that people in their lives can become surplus is an affront to being human.

Michael Rossman: That is a point that is getting overlooked and is really important. What I hear you saying is that we all have in us, training or not, the capacity to fill all basic human roles, and that

good process brings—it brings each of our faces out in turn when the
time is right. You may never actually be the healer in this group, but
because someone else happens to be filling that role, not because you
are denied—

Robert Benton: Access to basic human roles.

John Wideman: I have been both in and out of this process.
There are so many reservations which I have been trying to make
concrete to myself. What I am feeling now, and what I have felt for
the last couple of meetings, is that there are some really contradictory
demands being made on the groups and on individuals. I think the
groups are being asked to do the kind of thinking that individuals do
best. That is because I don't think that as a group, no matter how
well the individuals are working together and no matter how intelligent
and experienced they are, they can in a short time like this, and
without previously having prepared themselves to focus on specific
issues, come up with anything much better than platitudes. *Platitudes*
is rather—well, yes, platitudes, in terms of problem locating and ideas
for solving problems. I think there is going to be a lot of generality.
I think that when one reads the group statements they are going to
be pretty disappointing to everybody. . . .

Will Smith: Yesterday you were asked to formulate your
thoughts about what good education is and what a good educational
process is, and to attempt to relate or to express how you saw good
educational process relating to a good society. What we would like
to do from now until the time that we break is have you articulate
where you are right now in responding to these concepts. I phrase it
that way to avoid saying that I want you to summarize what your
thinking is.

Bernard Kaplan: I have a little reservation. I think I mentioned
it to you and want to suggest it to everybody: we had some people
coming in from other groups into our group—Page Smith was one of
them—and one of the things we tried to do for them was to summarize what had been going on. There was a kind of triviality in
trying to summarize in a few statements what was going on. I don't
know if you had the same experience, but I think you did respond
that way. There is something lost for me in trying to summarize what
I did or did not learn. I feel that summarizing is somewhat deadening.

Michael Rossman: Yesterday I felt at least part of it was not stultifying but invigorating. I felt a body of ideas was coming together through one group, and others were relating to it. That is a process I am interested in, and I would like to separate the wheat from the chaff.

Robert Benton: When I write your ideas up on the board, I am a little embarrassed about the simplicity of the things we come up with, like "freedom to fail" and love and truth and motherhood.

Richard Foster: I really want the group to take, from the nine or ten items that it sees as major concerns, the three or four that you think are of the highest priority. I want you to commit yourselves to these and to work out strategies. I want the other groups to do something similar, so that we can have a general session tomorrow in which we collectively try to see whether we can agree on four or five items and put together some strategies of a collective intelligence. That doesn't mean you have to do that, but that tells you where my head is. I really want you to go back to work, and from your nine or ten fight it out—take two or three or four and be able to say, if we could bring these about, we would move America. Then, you should lay out whatever it is that might do it. That is what I want you do to.

John Macrae: We don't believe that is going to move America.

Mary Murphy: We have to smile at that.

Richard Foster: I understand your comment. But we need something to place in front of Senator Pell, and people like Senator Pell, as being the commitment we think we would like to work with.

Wilcomb Washburn: What you need here is an environmental psychologist. Here you are in this beautiful spot, about a mile from the sea, and all of the meetings have been in these ill-designed rooms for the general sessions. In the smaller session, you sit in classrooms that could be anywhere in the country or world, with the windows shut and no air coming in, and outside you have this marvelous air and trees. No one seemed to have thought to schedule a meeting on the beach. It seems that someone was totally blind as to the effects of the physical environment on the educational process. This doesn't surprise me because I don't have much confidence in educators anyway.

William Arrowsmith: One other point: maybe, again, the dynamics of this kind of concentrated process makes it impossible, but it seems to me awfully important to note not merely the "geography," which I feel is important, but a kind of compulsive groupiness. There is no moment at which you can skip the group and go off and think by yourself. After all, we are individuals whose destiny is to be lonely. Humanity is tragic and lonely—

Salvador Luria: I was wondering, with some horror in a sense, about picturing a society in which a man who likes to be many hours in a room without windows—whether this person would not have certain emotional pressure put on him in our current environment. I am one such person, needing four hours, and possibly eight, of solitude every day and not to see the environment, because the environment to me is very threatening. Because I have been a failure at every sport, every time I see a beautiful environment, this is to me a symbol of failure. Maybe a supporting community would make failure tolerable.

Thomas Fletcher: I have not only a sense of being uncomfortable and frustrated, but I am getting angrier than hell right now. This discussion is interesting, but I want to go back into the group and continue what we are doing. I have an enormous hunger to start tying knots in what we are doing. I have this great sense of progress that we made, and now it is being frittered away. I am going to get more angry if we don't start getting some resolutions around this damned thing and get back into groups and do some productive work.

Malcolm Shaw: It does seem to me—it came up last night—that there are quite a few people in the group who, in different ways, want to work. Quite a few people in the group are frustrated with the amount of time we take to decide what to do.

Richard Foster: I want us to go back in groups, but first I want to pick up something that Mike talked about. We said that in our *paideia* power would flow from people to people, and everybody would feel that sense of power. As I realized myself yesterday, and for everyone else living in the present, the power seems to flow among about half a dozen people. Either we—you and me, Mike— well, in doing something to try to extend power, we take power away. In small groups or large groups, we have done the same thing.

Is there a way we can extend power to people who don't have it? Maybe the small group ought to talk about how we are performing rather than talking about it in the large group. I get the report the next morning that people who behaved powerlessly in this group are very powerful in cocktail parties and other kinds of things, and I—anyhow, I am concerned with that.

Phillip Runkel: What you have built is a structure that we can't really get acquainted with. We sit around these damned tables and don't really get to know each other. We have built a structure that we—we have structured the damn thing for failure in terms of what we might want to do from this point. Right now there are a lot of people that really don't want to participate in this damned kind of discussion because they think it is bullshit. That is really where it is at. I think it is a bunch of bullshit. I would rather have gone to mass this morning and heard the priest talk. . . .

Joseph Duggan: To continue this battle, I think, is a destructive thing. I don't want to go back to my group; I think it has gone— I don't feel a part of that group at all. Somehow I sense you have a good group. There was also another group, part of which came into my group and into your group. I think those groups are dead. Yours isn't dead, but that is how I feel about mine.

Will Smith: Might it be interesting to just suspend the large group session and not to prescribe any method or product for anything but let people come together as a group if they choose to? We can then agree to come back together at 11:00 or 11:30 to see what the outcome or product is.

Michael Rossman: If you suspend the process and leave it open, maybe we can agree on a meeting time.

Will Smith: Michael, that is what I said. I said to come back at 11:30 and see then what happened.

Salvador Luria: You realize there is a certain tyrannical quality in all forms of democracy. Why should there be agreement?

Bernard Kaplan: Let's not talk about it any more.

Malcolm Shaw: All right. We will break.

(Whereupon, at 10:20 a.m., the session concluded.)

Malcolm Shaw: There is a fault in blaming what happened this morning on form—and I am not defending form. Several people last night said, "we want to work and we are tired of talking about process." Those words flowed from there to the group over here, who said, "process is really important and these people who want to work had better hang in and learn about process because we know that process is important." That to me is not a matter of form but a matter of interpersonal communication—sensitivity, perception. . . .

Page Smith: This assumes that something happened this morning that was wrong—and that might be. But at this stage I don't know whether that is right or not. I just hate post-mortems, even though I know that evaluation is part of this business. I think that the real post-mortem is a year from now, or five years from now. It is overloading the situation constantly to scrutinize it. And I have to say that the staff rushing off after every meeting gave the participants a spooky sense that you were deciding whether what we were doing was what you hoped we would do or whether—well, the next step.

Malcolm Shaw: The alternative is a group of people in a room. They talk, and when we return two hours later—well, would it then be fair for us, in our roles, to say, "the Committee hasn't talked about anything that has gone on, and we have no responsibility," or—

Michael Rossman: That was a sharp critique, and I don't think you ought to pose a false alternative.

Malcolm Shaw: I am not posing a false alternative, but at every conference I have attended—as a convener or staff participant—the people in some way who are organizing go off somewhere and talk, and that creates tension, I think.

Page Smith: That is all right as long as they come back and say, "we had a discussion after the meeting about how things went and we had a feeling that"—I mean, people might or might not like that.

Michael Rossman: You know that people feel manipulated and paranoid. Handling your ongoing process conferences that way is a form of theater, sort of maximally pitched to make people feel manipulated and paranoid. It is true. There are two ways to deal with that: at least don't rush off so soon, at least hang out with the the people. If you don't hang out with people, it destroys the possibility of establishing the web of interaction that makes you members of the group as well as its tenders. What happens later on, if you begin to demystify the whole process of process, if you hold your conferences about the thing in the open—not have formal conferences but just sit as another subject group of people in the entire ensemble—

Malcolm Shaw: I have to respond to your presumption of magnificent expertise and experience. . . .

Malcolm Shaw: Good morning. Our purpose this morning is clear, and that is to ask each group, in whatever fashion they wish, to summarize what they did or have done since last evening, and anything prior to that you think would be useful.

Richard Ford: I felt that what we achieved not just last night but in the course of the last two or three days was really to organize ourselves and to have some much deeper feelings for attitudes, values, notions. We spent most of our time last night talking through the viability of—well, our perception of a just society, ways in which political endeavors do or do not change attitudes and values within the society. From my perspective, that is an important event during a short life of three or four days. As a group of people who didn't know each other before, and who come from different professional or vocational backgrounds, we have bridged a very important—I was going to say "gap." We have come to know each other in a series of very different ways.

David Dennison: The topic that our group was supposed to deal with is "public learning." It took us a while—because most of us rebelled against that topic—to decide to attempt to try to define what it meant. We moved to disagreement—we moved to a point that public education and public learning had to be totally separated and that we needed to get a clear understanding that what we were about is the development of public policy, public education policy. We had to be concerned with the techniques of learning, whether they related to the health field or the educational field or to somebody on the corner. . . . At the end of the session or near the end of the session, we wrote out four questions, and we began to attack them: (1) Does present public education policy reflect constituencies, values, and goals? (2) If not, what changes in education policy are necessary? (3) How does the public learn and who teaches? (4) How does public learning get transformed into public policy, or vice versa? That is where we are. That is our beginning. Our beginning states that we are in a total state of confusion, that there is a lot of conflict at the table, that there is a lot of disagreement, and that we are trying to zero in or focus on a manageable procedure to deal with it. We are going to do that.

Jonathan Messerli: We are particularly focusing on elementary and secondary schools but we spent the first part of yesterday afternoon talking to each other about each other. I suspect what we were doing is saying, "I'm okay and you're okay." By and large, we seem to think that that was the case. It took a larger time than we expected, not because it was difficult to do, but because we enjoyed it so much.

This morning we talked around some global issues. I think we came to a general conclusion that anybody born within our society moves within it with a heritage of a great deal of culture, whether he likes it or not, chooses to accept it or not. Anyone coming into our society is going to need skills and attitudes and abilities to broker with this cultural heritage. Maybe until you have a number of those things you can't begin to make more independent choices as you wish. . . .

The group at this point is divided, I suspect, between the overarching premise of this conference, which is focused on a delimiting of the role of the school, and the idea that the schools can become even more effective by interacting more with the other kinds of community agencies. I do not think we have emancipated ourselves from the assumption of schools as social panaceas. I think someone watching could tell the drift of our discussion. Although on the one hand we recognized the inadequacies of the schools, as we continued to confront certain kinds of social issues, there was almost this reflective assumption: that *there* is an institution that can do something. We have moved forward to assume that, whether you delimit the school or expect it to assume a greater burden, it must be set in a more interacting relationship with the total ecology or community.

Frank Wuest: I was just named by two people to do this report. It comes down to two questions which we got to by spending most of yesterday laying out eleven agenda items which were all over the lot, though all were on higher education.

Today we began to break up that pattern, bringing in more of the societal context within which we were debating our issues. I think the focus was a nice one in that Will Smith role-played Congressman Brademas and Jim Hall was a state legislator for a while. They kept coming at us with—well, what Brademas stated: I keep coming to you people and I keep telling you to tell me something, and you are not telling me, and I need your help.

We ended up with two questions. The first is: What is the

substance of the enrichment function of higher education? We have not defined "enrichment" yet, by the way. It has several different meanings, ranging from what I think Joe Katz talked about, psychological development, to a sort of introduction to what culture has transmitted down to our point in time. Anyway, what is the substance of the enrichment function of higher education? How can it be expressed most effectively? What are the chief linkages to the functions of institutions of higher education? We worked with six or seven, I think. Does somebody have them written down?

Peter Brooks: The first is training for jobs and professions. The second is production of knowledge or discovery of truth. The third is what we put down as the core function, the enrichment of people's lives: helping them understand the world around them. The fourth was known as indoctrination or socialization. The fifth was—Joe Katz' term—the holding tank function: keeping students out of trouble for four years when there are no jobs. The sixth was producing social change. The seventh was service to the community.

Frank Wuest: The linkage we have focused on is the third one, the enrichment function: How do we take that function and link it in to the others? The second question: What are the internal reforms in the educational system that can best achieve this enrichment function, given these linkages? Is it a kind of consciousness-raising—training or retraining—of faculty and administrators? We intend to pursue these two questions as though we were talking to a Congressman, dealing with substance. If Will keeps playing Congressman Brademas, we will make it.

Malcolm Shaw: Comments? We will meet back here at 1:15 this afternoon.

(Whereupon, at 12:00 noon, the session concluded.)

David Seeley: What's bugging you?

Lillian Hellman: What's bugging me?

David Seeley: You seem to be bugged since you have come here. What is bugging you?

Lillian Hellman: Something bugs me all the time; it is not just here. It's too slick to say the state of society we are in. It wouldn't be a truthful answer because I don't think anybody is that bugged. Certainly it is a contributing bug. But then I have always been bugged with the state of society we are in or we were in. Do you think I am extra nervous, is that what you are saying?

David Seeley: No, you seem to be annoyed, and I don't know whether it was about the state of the world or this conference or. . . .

Lillian Hellman: I really shouldn't come to conferences; I haven't a nature for conferences. That is what you are saying. I don't think I have a collaborative nature. Like most writers, I have worked alone all my life, and the idea of working in collaboration is very difficult for me.

Nat Hentoff: Could it also be the way language is used in conferences like this?

Lillian Hellman: Partly. I genuinely don't understand the English talked at most conferences. I don't understand sociological English, and I have to say snobbishly that I don't wish to understand it. It is a corruption of the English language to me. I think we have come in my lifetime to turn out what is to me sociological English. I am all for the murder of all sociologists, the immediate murder, without any trial, without any democracy, without any. . . . I think the ideas have been so corrupting and I think the enjoyment of language has been so corrupted by it—I don't think the contribution has been much good for any of us. I don't mean only the language of sociology—it is silly to pick on it. I think the language of academics in general is a very low-class language, disrupting to ideas. It has taken the place, for some reason, of philosophy in America, which is puzzling. It is often jabber substituted for a real look at things. It has never seemed to me that it could attack any real problem in our society. It theorizes and uses long words and comes to conclusions, none of which seems to me to face the hard troubles of the world.

David Dennison: In our group we were concerned with, whether we labeled it or not, a cycle that deals with *inputs* (open education, continuous education—values), *thruputs* (the different kinds of funding that are necessary), and *outputs* (turning out a product that can compete in our national economy with communications skills and mathematical skills, or whatever kind of other skills that are necessary to survive in this environment). Then we went on to talk about the feedback in the cycle and the levers in the community to move whatever it is you say is necessary to move to lead to public learning.

Henry Taft: Some of us in Group I devoted a lot of our

thinking specifically to what we do next. One of the frustrating aspects of it was that we had a list of things that interested us very much and which we thought the ideal educational system should include, but we hadn't really pinned anything down in detail. It is fine to say "choices" and "options"—these are the code words. But what do they mean? You ought to argue that through and say exactly what they mean. We knew the things we were interested in, but we were not quite there yet.

So, looking at these items, there is one around which you could collect most of our other concepts, and that is what we have been calling *the umbrella-supermarket concept*. The thought is that of a learning supermarket which addresses different age groups. It has continuing education; it has undergraduate and graduate. It has cross-connections between all these groups, perhaps teacher apprentices teaching the continuing education; perhaps older people coming in and teaching younger people. It has disciplines outside of the teaching profession. We want the health people in the community to come in and be part of the educational system. We want the legal people in town to come in, and maybe housing groups coming in and taking part in the learning process—all those social agencies coming in from the community and being part of the learning process. The community would be involved in the learning center, and various groups would modify each other. It would be a very deep involvement. Choices and options can be grafted on to that kind of a system; pluralism can be part of that system; affective, cognitive—all of those things we say are desirable can be part of such a system. . . .

Peter Brooks: The choice of "umbrella-supermarket" as your model bothered me in what I thought was an exciting report. The "supermarket" image has been around for a long time and implies to me rows and rows of goods where a fairly undiscriminating shopper picks up a little of this and a little of that. If you don't know what to choose, you get ripped off in a supermarket, and that happens every day, literally. How are you going to direct the shopper?

Malcolm Provus: I would like to respond with a diagram. If you take a school, existing or not, and the community context— probably the attendance area—what we had in mind as a focal point was the identification of community problems which make teachers of learners. In trying to deal with these problems, there is a whole array of options in the school and outside of the school, in the larger society, that they draw upon, and that is where the super-market comes in.

David Seeley: How do you keep the kids from getting ripped off?

Malcolm Provus: They stay honestly task oriented.

Anne Dosher: Do you mean a "learning exchange"? That still has the marketing idea.

Malcolm Shaw: The implication I got from Mal and Dave's comments is that—obviously it needs more deliberation—what is being created is a two-way influence process, and not simply a ripoff.

Eugene Slaughter: Peter is a literary man. This is bad poetry. He is objecting to the poetry. The country general store would be a much better poetic image.

Henry Taft: I don't agree with that because I think the super-market is exactly what we meant, in this sense: supermarkets are places where there is a great variety of things, and varieties of new things are offered in the market place and accepted and rejected. Secondly, it is something that is not imposed on you; the clientele has a method of choice. We are talking about not only young people, but old people who know exactly what they want.

Will Smith: I think Peter is making a good point. We talk about information overload, idea overload, and choice overload, and a supermarket literally presents that. It can immobilize a potential learner to have so many options available and no viable way to connect those options.

Robert Benton: I think the metaphor doesn't beat me, and I like the idea.

James Hall: I think "supermarket" typifies all the things wrong in American society—the fact that it is laid out and the fact that it is designed to manipulate people to choose. What I have heard at this meeting is a testimony in the nature of a revival meeting, leading one to come forward to the bench. I am frankly excited by that idea, but I really do not understand what the substance and core of what has been said is, other than a very overloaded rhetoric which I doubt would be clearly understood.

Malcolm Shaw: I suggest that we come back to Jim's concern about what the testimony and the rhetoric is, as we develop the other two groups' notions, so that we can jell out of that something that feels sound to you and everybody in the room. Group II?

David Dennison: Our group had a load of paper to put up but when we looked at the wall, there wasn't any more room, so we have decided to save time by just going on. I think Group I monopolized too much of the time because I think there are other people who have some things to say.

Before I came to the conference, I looked at what was on the agenda and to me it seemed as though it was going to be dealing with public policy, so I wrote a little something to myself. I am going to read part of it because I think it is related to everything we have been discussing here. The title is "The Making of Public Policy."

(Whereupon, Mr. Dennison read his paper.)

Anne Dosher: Group II decided that models for citizenship participation which have heretofore always been termed "failures" do provide important learning, but the existing structures are really dysfunctional now and the people in them are very tired. There is also a feeling on the part of political and bureaucratic policy makers that they are cut off from spheres of information and spheres of research, from informal networks, and that informed policy is not working in the country.

We are recommending that a clearly articulated network of public policy and public learning development centers—in essence a network of networks—be developed in the country. Now, the model that you have been talking about here is a network in which the product is learning for the individual, who then will be able to function in the society. The model, I think, that we in our group are proposing to you is a model in which the product would be the way in which the citizen—the consumer, the producer, the teacher, the policy maker—learns how to develop public policy, so that public learning becomes conscious and can inform policy, which is always a consensus position.

How do we do that? We could have a network of networks in which, in the local areas and communities, an arena was created in which the goal would be to develop a clear voice or voices which would express the ideas of that pluralistic, mosaic-patterned constituency. It would have as its goal to educate and assist the local communities in the processes of public policy development and the strategies for public policy change. We have citizens who are highly intelligent, who might all have these kinds of ideas in mind, but who do not see or understand the processes by which public policy is affected. What the work of the centers or the work of the networks would do would be to make those processes apparent—to show the routes which will empower the local communities. We would come together where we live to begin to learn how to be public policy decision makers, how to create public policy.

We would want these centers to do a lot of consumer education: to educate and assist consumers and providers in community-need assessment, resource acquisition, idea diffusion, and action research data collection as a guide to near future planning. This country always plans reactively on the basis of crisis: we seldom plan pro-actively on the available images of the future. We would want in our network to assist consumers and providers in articulating those formal and informal organizations involved now in subterranean ways in policy development—articulate those organizations and tie them in at local, state, and federal levels. . . .

We also think it might be necessary to introduce the concept of making available, through our network of centers for public policy and public learning, opportunities for national service to education. At a time when unemployment is rampant among young persons and others, if the opportunity for meaningful national service could be supplied as one of the sub-goals through this network of networks in this center, we would begin to have moving a group that I don't see here: namely, our clients, who are the children and adolescents and youth of this nation.

Joseph Katz: Excuse me for interrupting. Our group is in a dilemma. It is 11:30, and buses are leaving, and we are finishing up a statement that will go in the general record of the conference. Perhaps we can make a presentation that—perhaps we can make a meaningful contribution if we complete our work. I suggest you tell me what to do.

Malcolm Shaw: Let's go off the record for a short time.

Donald Bigelow: Could I ask a question? I would just like to know—well, I'll put it this way: it is clear that Group III is not obstructionist, nor are you lazy, but is there something else hidden behind why you are not ready to talk now and just want to get it in the record later? I need to know before we disband. What is the holdup?

Peter Brooks: Our holdup is that we came into this room

prepared in an informal way to present our thinking and our conclusions to you, but we have been interrupted in the preparation of what we considered our final report. We had understood originally that we would have to 10:30 in order to put it together. So we are just faced with a choice of whether it is more important to report to you or to finish drafting a document that no doubt no one will read but has become important to us.

Malcolm Shaw: I can only suggest, then, that, as these two groups continue their deliberations, you will get in writing the collection of your generalizations so that we can have them. I suggest we take a break at this point.

(Whereupon, a short recess was taken from 11:45 a.m. to 11:50 a.m.)

David Seeley: Just the issue of public funding—I am suggesting that there can be public funding. The processes of public funding, open access—you can have public money for a program.

Malcolm Shaw: Well, since our time is just about up, I suggest we wrap up. Thank you.

(Whereupon, at 12:10 p.m., the last general session of Sequence IV was concluded.)

Malcolm Shaw: My notion would be that we still didn't come up with the optimum method. The optimization would have required more interchange among the three groups of a positive nature.

Richard Foster: Our real problem came today because higher education was not ready.

Peter Brooks: Not that we weren't ready to make a report, but just that we were so concerned about writing down another kind of report that when we ran out of time—we were blaming it partly on the other two groups. The first group took so damned long reporting—

Richard Foster: That is not fair. You held us up by forty-five minutes by not being in the meeting on time.

Peter Brooks: When we broke yesterday afternoon, we were under the impression that the plenary session was only meeting at 10:30 or 11:00.

Will Smith: I was going to negotiate that.

Peter Brooks: When we got in there at 9:00 this morning, we had at least an hour and a half before us.

Malcolm Shaw: For whatever value it has, and I don't want to overstate it, there was the potential—and I don't think it is top priority—for a social action committee to have come from thirty people. We are not clear on what we want to do, but we do want to network and intercommunicate, get things happening after we leave.

Will Smith: I think that is a desirable goal, but we really hadn't talked about structuring that meeting for it to come out to that end.

Richard Foster: From my point of view, if somebody is not ready—well, we ought to make sure everybody knows the next time what is going to be expected. I would have felt better if our group hadn't given the report. We wouldn't have gotten into that kind of crazy relationship. I don't feel good about making a report and knowing that another group or a member of another group must attempt in some subtle way to destroy it or the experience of it, which has nothing to do with the report.

Malcolm Shaw: My last comment, from my point of view, would be that there was a lot of excitement and social momentum coming out of Group I, and even though it was only nine people, I believe those people might have moved out further in their own lives and in supporting some X. You need not define the X. The second group would have joined in that X. I don't think that is an attack on the third group. All we are describing is the dynamics. There would have been a lot of tension between Groups I and II, if you hadn't been there.

Peter Brooks: Dick, what was your word, that the attack was destructive, that criticism of the first group was destructive? I didn't feel that at all.

Richard Foster: I was sitting in the group and could feel it. The group was saying: "Rather than grabbing the big ideas, they are grabbing a word." I can use the word "umbrella" and describe the word "umbrella." Somebody else was using the word "supermarket," and it really didn't matter.

Malcolm Shaw: I see that Ben has joined us.

Benjamin DeMott: Hello, gents.

Peter Brooks: I was really excited, Ben, by the way you presented your outline. You are talking about the profile of a desire—the sense of being "empowered," of fulfillment, of control; of mastery over one's life, of not being impotent. I am struck by the consensus you have pulled out of the sequences, and to me it corresponds precisely to the deepest desires that were being expressed and not expressed but present in my group, and to everything heard about the other groups. I think it was a very good way of putting it.

R. W. Lid: It sounds like good DeMott to me.

Benjamin DeMott: I think you are putting me down.

R. W. Lid: No, no! I do have a question, though. In what you've said, do you feel that you have told the story of the conference?

Benjamin DeMott: No, I have told the story of what kind of appetite overwhelmed us as we watched. That is the story I think I will tell.

Donald Bigelow: How do we officially disband this thing?

Eugene Slaughter: I think we die a natural death.

Donald Bigelow: Participants have to be written "thank you" for coming, and there will be a report on October first. Somebody has to say that and do that. Does anybody have any thoughts, suggestions, expectations?

Eugene Slaughter: I think timeliness is worth something, like a newspaper. Right now it is important to say, "we are glad you came, and you will hear some more from us."

13

Evasion at the Border:
Notes on the Summer Sequences

Benjamin DeMott

Item: Jonathan Kozol writes asking for "any printed, Xeroxed, or just casual summary of the end-results: i.e., *what it* (Southampton) *led to*." When I invited him to come, Jonathan declined, predicting the project would be wasteful, but his letter says he's writing "in a friendly spirit," "with old and continuing respect." I've had his note for six weeks now; it's still not answered.

Item: In New York the other day I had a minute, by happenstance, with Ms. Lillian Hellman, whom I'd pressed particularly hard to accept an invitation to Southampton, and who I subsequently learned was displeased if not angered by her experiences at the meetings. Neither of us brought up the sessions during our chat.

Item: In Washington, D.C., for three days during Thanksgiving week, and then another three days in Arizona, Bill Arrowsmith and I, friends for years who quarreled in plenary at Southampton Session II, ate, drank, and worked together through twelve separate committee sessions, with but one allusion to Southampton, this an agreement—settled in a phrase—not to discuss it.

The inventory of my post-Southampton silences with Southampton participants could be extended: two editors, a classmate, a former student, a foundation person. But the point is obvious: I am hiding out. I "learned a lot" at these sessions—from Christopher Lasch, Peter Brooks, Elizabeth Janeway, Harold Cruse, Victor Alicea, Rene Cardenas, June Wilson, Ralph Fasanella, Charles Kelso, several others. None of the jobs I did as a Steering Committee member—letter and brochure writing, site inspecting, paper editing—was done perfunctorily.

Yet I've been evading questions, turning my back on the enterprise. "I will be grateful," Jonathan Kozol says in his letter, "for whatever answers you can give me without feeling that you are infringing on the privacy of others." He is an effectively committed man. Is it not chicken to pretend I don't owe him an answer? "Nor, knowing you . . . do I think that you will feel harassed by my questions." Would it not be altogether proper for him to harass? But why do I think I deserve harassment?

Looked at historically the Southampton Summer Sequences constituted a sort of last hurrah of the participatory ethos. The immediate background was a congressionally authorized Training of Teacher Trainers program—Triple T as it was called, a $40 million scheme for interinstitutional cooperation aimed at producing better schools. Under TTT auspices teams were formed consisting of discipline-oriented professors in graduate liberal arts departments, professors of education (a break with the past, because these two parties hitherto seldom spoke), high school teachers, graduate students, school superintendents, and community representatives. The arenas for teamwork included in-service seminars, community meetings, teacher exchanges; the goal was to bring new forces to bear on teacher-trainers—the best current academic understandings of subject matters, for one, and, for another, the convictions of parents and working teachers about students' real needs.

As TTT money ran out—Congress had never intended to bankroll the operation forever—attempts were made to set up informal agencies or networks composed of people who had worked together in the cooperative endeavors and "action training programs"; the assumption was that experiences and "strategies" might continue to be shared, and that spheres of influence might widen, if the good news of "broad-based communication" could be passed on. Three or four training films were made, showing stages in the development of relationships between the education community proper and "outsiders." A network of school superintendents incorporated itself as a nonprofit group offering communications and other services to communities interested in developing interinstitutional cooperation in setting local educational aims.

At length—coming closer to the present—OE program officers decided to try out a Triple T model for community interaction on school issues in a national framework; in effect, a form of national town meeting. Existing educational agencies seemed to have reached a condition of disarray or demoralization; no movement toward clarification of goals was in progress, the new governmental research agency (NIE) was unfunded, and drift and disillusionment were pervasive: why not attempt to fill in the vacuum? Step one would be to commission a group of first rate intellectuals and academics to produce working papers on unresolved educational issues, which could be circulated to a cross section of citizens, as a preliminary to a national meeting. Step two would be to invite the chosen citizens to a site at which a consensus about these issues, as well as about broad goals and means of achieving them, could be sought, with the aid of experts, relevant TTT experience, and other resources. Step three would be to bring the consensus, if achieved, to the attention of Congress, state legislatures, and other public and private agencies with policy-making powers.

The idea bloomed. Logistics were settled quickly—120 participants divided into four groups, each concentrating on a single area of problem solving for three or four days, with a small Steering Committee to provide continuity. The Committee, after consultation, concluded that, instead of waiting till the end for a report to be forwarded to the appropriate Congressional committees, liaison should be established during the sessions themselves with the committees' ranking members. They also concluded (more of this shortly) that the theme to be stressed from the start was that educational reform is the business not of educators alone but of the whole society: "schools are not the major educative influence on this society; they are only a reflection of the larger forces controlling all our institutions." To conduct this business well, educators and non-educators alike need, so ran the reasoning, firsthand knowledge of how (in a vital society) each part relates to every other part; they cannot come by such knowledge except by leaving their own professional or other enclave, by talking with people ordinarily understood as totally "other," by tasting The Life of the Whole.

Thus the objective framework. Was it natural beamishness that made me think well of it? (Is it a mark of the times—the sense of an ending—that I take stern self-examination about this not to be absurd egomania?) I had no role in Triple T, never worked for the Education Office until last summer—and yet from one point of view I could argue that my last dozen years of life were all, in a metaphorical and perhaps not unloony way, Southampton-bound. In the long-gone 1950s I made a start as a "sound professional"—an English teacher-essayist—but shortly thereafter I joined the dropouts, spending much of my time on projects that had nothing to do with the profession I trained for, and that reflected a longing to believe that escaping from the woodwork, learning to function outside the enclave, was the surest way to improve both yourself and Them.

We were legion, to be sure—teachers, bureaucrats, businessmen, whites and blacks alike—characters who in this period lost their way, went public, what you will: I lodge no claim to uniqueness. People of my professional stripe were propelled into our befuddlement by conventional American redbloodedness (palefaces alone can build a full life in a library study), by the new political activism (civil rights movement, war protest), by standard American authors who were enthusiastic about what Dewey called "conjoint communication" (in addition to Dewey the voices I heard included William James, G. H. Mead, Charles Cooley, Jane Addams, and the Randolph Bourne who argued that irony—the rhetorical trope—could itself become an instrument of democratization), and by post-Marxist culture criticism that inveighed ceaselessly against fragmentation, polarization, segmentation, and specialization. I expect most marchers in the legion had special living heroes of commitment or intellect, people who had demonstrated the social uses and outreach of particular humanistic abilities. (Richard Hoggart, of *The Uses of Literacy*, was the heartening example of the late 1950s.) But idealism was not the sole stimulant. The liberated humanist flew his warren for love, chic, politics, or peace more often than for loot: but sometimes the whole consort, piety, pocketbook, and intellect, danced together: history won't allow me to pretend otherwise.

What exactly were we up to, the academic (and other) day-trippers of the 1960s, what exactly did we do? Where did we go? How did it feel thus to trip? The temptation is strong to speak in deprecation of what one was and what one did, picking up on Tom Wolfe's accents, seeing the period as an extended Panther Party at the Bernsteins. I wince remembering some of the old sillinesses of that time past—my joy, for instance, in being taught by Herb Kohl, in his West Side apartment, how to read the graffiti and Harlem gang taunts on subway cards and posters, my joy in exploiting this "material" in staff meetings and in classes at an elite college—sliding it in as evidence of my unique experiential range. I wince also at my gutlessness when mau-maued. Think how much time I put in as an unpaid, unofficial flakecatcher—"Whitey," "The Man," etc! It was in June 1964, at a planners' session (the Huntting Inn, East Hampton) for the Teachers and Writers Collaborative (it still exists, head-quarters in Brooklyn), that I took my first punches, hearing for the first time, incidentally, mystified yet gratified, the word *rap*. ("I ain't gonna rap with you," said one black teacher, "you don't stop interruptin'." "What's coming down?" said another. "What kind of crazy rap session is this?") And afterward a current of sardonic mockery at black-white sessions flowed steadily in "my" legion's direction. Often the note was exacerbated or ferocious. "You honky racist," said Charles Hurst of Malcolm X College to me at a Palm Beach Holiday Inn one winter morning in 1971, "I don't have to ex-plain anything to you and I won't." But no less often the note was pure innocence and charm, as one morning in the late 1960s in a Wash-ington, D.C. classroom—the Madison elementary school—in an ex-change with an eight-year-old black pupil. I'd been "working with" this lad, tutoring him in how to act the part of the king. Would he talk to his serf, I asked, the same way he talked to his friend? He looked up at me with an impatient, get-lost expression—and then suddenly, surprisingly, softened. Curiosity came into his glance, seriousness too, because a thought had dawned, a conceit about this huge blonde monster bearing down from above with his sillyass storytalk question about a picture book. "Hey man," the kid said to me, eyes asquint. "You Daniel Boone?"

Always, though, amid whatever discomfiture or surprise, there was a frisson of relish, a tendency to regard flakecatching as a learning experience. More important (maybe), never did I see myself then as fool or fraud. I remember the exhilaration with which I and others answered Marion Edelman's summons to go south and "work with the kids" in the Mississippi Delta counties who were about to enter integrated schools for the first time—children who needed help with their new textbooks. I wrote about that venture in a magazine, and thereafter I was off and running. The Central Atlantic Regional Education Lab was looking for a resource person for kindergarten through third grade English teachers in the District of Columbia—run a seminar, develop new methods of teaching reading (helping "the disadvantaged"), visit classrooms for demonstration work. I held the job for a year part time. The Northeast Association of Teachers of English in Two Year Colleges sought an unpaid counselor from an elite four-year college—somebody with ideas about bettering relationships between community colleges and traditional institutions. I did an extended hitch for them. NET proposed that I help with a series of on-location TV shows about heroes of American culture—I went on the road for six months. A Carnegie Commission wanted some "input" about serial dramatic production in the TV sausage factories— Universal City and all that. I was their man on the Coast for a spell, the Hollywood Hawaiian motel, corner Yucca and Vine. A state-based foundation for the humanities in public affairs wanted help setting up town and gown chautauquas. I signed on and drummed up academic interest in the scheme. And—cynics will credit this instantly—I worked the other side of the street with (virtually) the self-same zeal, taking the occasional job as "consultant" to big business, explaining Youth to top leadership at Bell, insurance conglomerates, the U.S. Foreign Service, the Post Office, any who claimed to want to listen.

Had a question of pertinence to teaching been raised, I'd have answered confidently that there was a local base and rationale for these activities: I was a member and chairman for long terms of my college's independent and field study committees, and I considered that every off-campus project—from teachers' workshops for the MLA Association of Department Chairmen to brainstorming sessions for a Children's TV Workshop—put me in touch with material of use to students chasing off-campus opportunity. But no questions were asked, and I myself felt no need to apologize. I had promised myself (and the world) a half-dozen long stories, a Dryden essay, a book-length survey of Amlit in the third quarter of the twentieth century, and these items had sunk without trace. But did it matter? I had at least made a commitment. I had experienced the upsurge of the will to spring myself forth from the appointed slot in the culture of slots, to triumph over reductionism and inhibition.

And, as a result, when the voice on the phone began talking

about (putative) Southampton, I was in almost before the deck was cut. He had helped, this caller said, to run an educational reform venture drawing together academics, students, protest leaders, executives, mayors, and school superintendents in a concerted effort at improving instruction in the schools. Our money is gone, he said, almost gone, but we want to try once more, now on a national scale, to see whether the beginnings of inter-enclave communication that we've worked out locally can be moved out onto a national stage. We need your help, he said, on our Steering Committee—choosing paper writers, developing a framework, writing brochures, inspecting sites, editing papers, defining small group tasks. It has to be, the man said, a *working* group.

The call went to others besides myself—to the superintendent of the Berkeley, California, school district, Richard Foster; to a Connecticut specialist in human relations training programs, Malcolm Shaw; to Gene Slaughter, an Oklahoma English teacher who had been active in Triple T from its inception; and to Will Smith, a former University of San Diego dean and pro-football player, experienced in minority-majority group relationships. (The caller was an OE project officer named Donald Bigelow.) I know more now about the past that each Steering Committee member brought to the venture, and about the differences amongst us. But I knew from the start that we had at least one point of union: not only were we experientialists and optimists, we were co-religionists. The doctrines and disciplines of the participatory denomination were our dogmas; we were brethren in a faith.

As my tone has implied, I keep this faith in its purity, its strictness no longer. And the reasons why—the connections between the Southampton Sequences and my apostasy—are less mysterious than might appear. The case is that the Steering Committee venture served to crystallize the id-like murk wherein I'd been wandering, obliged me to confront my miscellaneous grab-bag of opinions—my sentimentalities?—as ideology. Among the stuff in the bag was the following: (1) certainty that the health of the social whole depends increasingly on the frequency and quality of communication among the social parts; (2) inklings that "new, improved" procedures and techniques for overcoming suspicion, hostility and other barriers to communication between groups might shortly produce major advances in social understanding; (3) the theory that no work of art, no conceptual model in science, is so complex or subtle that some of its essence can't be made available to all; (4) a categorical imperative: those who are most highly skilled and best educated will have, tomorrow, a particularized obligation to engage a portion of their energies in extending general human learning—through popularization, *haute vulgarisation*; (5) an expectation that the inevitable consequence of such engagement will be to enlarge understanding to a point at which Everyman himself, through intelligent participation, modifies the meaning inherent in, and created by, great works of art and science; (6) an assumption that people experienced in interchange, accustomed to working for a sense of what and how The Other feels and thinks, are likely to be citizens well qualified to propose changes in educational systems; and (7) the hope that by pressing for such changes, these citizens will succeed in effecting a transformation of the land which restores fraternity and sorority to their place as prime values—without doing dirt on equalitarianism.

In a manner not wholly accidental, since I had a role in the planning, Southampton organized these and a few other wisps and fragments into an order—actually into a program, a series of steps directed toward particular public policy ends. Participants were chosen with an eye toward ensuring that each small group would be composed of representatives of sectors of society usually cut off from each other; resources were set aside for experienced facilitators, specialists in group dynamics, so that whatever could be done to clear a path toward openness would be done; authors of twenty or so commissioned papers were alerted to their responsibilities as communicators beyond their own disciplinary confines, seekers-out of means by which the most pertinent resources within their special bodies of knowledge could become available to nonspecialists and could be subjected to their critical scrutiny, however tentative and diffident; nonspecialist participants were alerted to their obligation to resist intimidation by expertise and to draw on lessons of their working life and on their experience as parents, neighbors, taxpayers, and citizens at large, in assessing proposals and arguments; reasonably detailed agendas were provided, subject to amendment by the individual task forces and working parties once assembled, so that recommendations in all the key areas (patterns of schooling in relation to age, sex, and ethnicity, articulation of school and community, vocational and career education, certification of nonprofessional faculty, and so on) could achieve maximum specificity.

In sum, the fit was tight between my old, half-verbalized beliefs and fancies and the design of the Southampton meetings. And, in the sequel, reality didn't scorn the design: the events and situations called for in the scenario of the Southampton meetings did in fact take place. Twelve small groups assembling widely disparate interests and expertise—one group included a college president, a labor organizer, a black historian, the mayor of a middle-sized Eastern city, a mother and housewife, a blue collar worker, and a Congress-man—worked together, each over a period of seventy-two hours, formulating, in college seminar rooms, their versions of ideal school-ing arrangements, occasionally interrupting themselves to participate in plenary sessions or to hear panels and formal presentations, but returning quickly to their own deliberations. Each of the groups in question numbered among its members a "process expert" free to intervene when forward progress slowed. Several first-rate papers clarifying knotty conceptual schemes currently exciting historians, economists, or systems analysts were delivered and discussed. (The most interesting paper in this line was delivered by MIT's Donald Schon, on the theme of "public learning"—modes of education occurring in nonacademic settings in American society. Suggestions for revisions came from nonspecialist corners of the room, and several groups subsequently drew on Schon's analysis of "dynamic conservatism" in laying out their own tactics for securing systemic change.)

Most important, positions and persons unaccustomed to dealing at close quarters with each other did indeed come face to face, to be mutually trained in negotiation. Sometimes the encounters were of a familiar sort: a man of public power spoke up strongly for a bill aimed at "doing something for the people" and heard from the people he meant to help that his sort of help was unwelcome. (Senator Claiborne Pell was told by minority representatives in plenary session that, for their people, the expanded vocational educa-tion he found exciting looked like a ripoff.) Sometimes the encounters marked the beginnings of talk between two parties of equal power passionately mistrustful of each other or suffering from "image" anxiety. (The far right and far left of the school board of a great Southwestern city, factions that, by their own words, could never be seen together back home without each at once losing its political power base, dined together and worked together in a small group at Southampton.) More than a few who participated in the sessions became so attached both to co-workers and to the concept of the meeting itself that they shed tears at departure time. And at no moment was there an air of emptiness or cutoff—a feeling that talk between opposites and tangents, thinkers and doers, tories and rads, had completely broken off.

Yet none of this alters the fact: Southampton, far from energizing a faith, dramatized its limits, errors, and fatuities. If the meetings had a value, it consisted in the compelling demonstration of the need for understandings socially and morally deeper than any envisaged by the religion in whose name we assembled. To some who glance over these words, the errors I have to enumerate will seem altogether unastonishing. But, since I made them and lived with them, I can't easily dismiss them as trivial; each warrants (to my mind) a minute's scrutiny.

Not the least embarrassing of them—descending to particulars—is the error of believing that The Mix in and of itself will invariably generate fresh thought. Southampton established for me that, while heterogeneous groups meeting together engender admirable fellow feeling, they do not produce an idea: the presence of widely divergent perspectives and interests within relatively small groups lowers intellectual pressure, encourages the reinvention of the wheel and the reenactment of stale arguments, shifts the focus from issues to conflicts of personality, creates an audience for numbers, routines, and cardtricks. Time and again plenary session raveled out into cliche. Consider, for one example, the afternoon session that "pitted" Michael Rossman, West Coast alternative school theorist, against Representative John Brademas, chairman of the Select Subcommittee on Education. Rossman had a point of substance to make, namely that a problem-solving approach to racism by legislative or judicial authority tends to oversimplify the behavior and feeling with which it means to cope. But the route to utterance of this point was itself paved with oversimplifications, each of which shivered before us like a 1960s ghost.

A thin dark wary-eyed mid-thirtyish man, Rossman seemed driven by a compulsion to *penetrate*, to shatter Establishment invulnerability, "technological rationality"; each of his movements and gestures brought back the open air meetings, moratoriums, Days of Concern of yesteryear, when moral intensity flogged itself to seethe,

when Everyman cried Bullshit! and good manners were shamed as
bad lies. Trembling as he spoke, Rossman went at the public official
for being inhibited, repressed, out of touch with the roots of his
being, and afflicted with a facial tic. He noted that the previous
evening, during the Congressman's talk, he, Rossman, had scrutinized
the condition of the talker's inner being: "I saw that your body
English is careful," he said, "the really balanced emotions of a man
who is sort of prepared to answer anything coming from any side. I
saw you inside the form of that body motion, twitching uncom-
fortably because there was too much vitality and emotion to be expressed in those gestures, and with those gestures you jerked. Here is
a man that was torn. . . ." He went on to describe his own inner
confusion and humiliation as he listened to congressional competence
speaking its confident piece: "I am feeling, listening to you, it was
crazy, just crazy, quite crazy. . . . Jesus I am feeling, I have nothing,
I have rhetoric, passion without substance. My stuff—it's not re-
searched, not realistic, pragmatic, it's simply empty."

But then, Rossman continued, by good fortune he was lifted
out of his despair. A man of the people, a working-class participant
at Southampton with whom he went to a bar following Brademas's
original talk, showed him a way out. "This old dinky man pissing
and cussing in a dark corner . . . and his language was so foul—it was
choked, it was turbulent—that I couldn't make sense [at first] of
what he said." But soon enough the sense appeared; Rossman began
to hear a truth in his friend's speech, the truth that "starts in the
stomach, the working man's stomach," and it recovered for him a
perception of his own value. He knew better now than to let
himself be put down. He knew what was right about himself and
wrong about the Congressman. "My language gets it up in ways
yours can't. . . . In [your] detail there falls away the sense of
the whole." Brademas didn't understand that "to advise the legislator
you have to advise him as a poet." Brademas was a failure for not
"recognizing Tao," and for not being "a Moses," for "not finding
some focus for the spirit."

Outside a small breeze stirred the piney shadows and worn grass.
(Southampton College isn't a posh setting for a lark.) For a moment
the room was quiet—but quite quickly another set of trad sounds
began, each as familiar as those that preceded them. Professor

Commager berated the counterculturalist for new Romanticism. ("It is astonishing . . . for one connected with the university to celebrate the stomach rather than the mind.") A Yale psychologist damned Rossman for pride. ("Something . . . strikes me as holier than thou.") Off on the left came a shout that the problem wasn't too little religion but too much. ("It's all parochial education, . . . the White House is the Pope. . . . American history is [an] icon. Progress is an icon.") The middle too was heard from, seeking (as ever) peace, offering assurances that flutes and triangles must also be heard, no vice wholly lost. ("We don't fully appreciate that there are different kinds of consciousness, different ways of looking at things, different ways of constructing the world. I think we frequently get caught up in the belief that one belief is more right than the other.") And at length from the Congressman himself came the predictable, bare, bleak, pridefully unself-indulgent statements of religious faith ("I am a Greek Methodist, that is my background"), political faith ("everybody doesn't have to be working within the system; I happen to think that someone has to be working within the system"), faith in the System itself:

I think the whole secret in the American system is that you have some power, I have some power, and everybody has some power. I broker it off, you do the same, we bargain with each other and we hope that it is so worked out in the end that all of us, together, as I said, advance justice in the society.

Amen, says a voice.
Bullshit, says another.
Men differ—but the afternoon had passed and no forward step had been taken. Michael Rossman, according to the testimony of his latest book, is extremely knowledgeable about the function and formation and nourishment of alternative teaching networks; John Brademas, according to the testimony of his legislative record, knows a good deal about the kinds of educational initiatives that might at this hour stand a chance of interesting a congressional majority; the mystique of The Mix somehow defeated their best selves. Many persons in that room knew the day's tunes by heart, hits of the 1960s—now a touch of Dostoyevsky, now the mucker pose, now a macho flourish, now the pastoral-Tolstoyan strain—now the Gibbonian skeptic, now the practical doer of good, now a soft-shoe turn by Mr. and Mrs. Apologetically Liberal Nice. But, given the heterogeneity of

the assemblage, the possibility existed that some in the room did not, that some in the room had never heard "Stardust" before, never tuned in to rationalism v. romanticism; for their benefit the old favorites would be rerun, worlds of discourse already over-explored would be scratched at as virgin soil. Repeated, the incident became predictable and at length took on the character of a stock pattern, confirming, then reconfirming, that professional selves operating in their segmented specialist contexts are not necessarily inferior, in the quality of their intellectual contribution, to "My Credo" selves. Also: contrary to my assumption, professional selves are enormously difficult to position effectively in the environment of The Mix. Fantasists, we had assumed that the presence of difference near at hand couldn't fail to entice men and women of mind forward from themselves, forward toward their unwritten chapters. Error one.

A second error was that the doers of the world, the improvers, the nonprovincial, the well-traveled, the experienced, cannot but introduce into a mixed assemblage qualities of flexibility and multi-perspectivity that teach and refine by example. For every expert at Southampton silencing his best self for a chance at the My Credo organ, there was another expert clinging to what he knew with a holy fury and dealing damnation round the land at those who knew something else. For a month, in truth, the Southampton campus was fairly littered with hobbyhorse riders, figures whose unique past had given them the answer. Here was President John Silber of Boston University, angrily denouncing the Steering Committee at a special lunch meeting held for him in "the windmill"—how could we be so stupid as to consider any recommendation for federal action other than a massive new Head Start program? It was never *tried*, insisted Silber. Pump every penny into prenatal nutrition, health care, early learning opportunities, birth to kindergarten. There is no other way, anything different is rot and sentiment. . . . Here was Henry Commager again, announcing that the answer was Europe. Why don't you simply follow the lead of the Danish Folk Schools? The Danes know how to provide education in values to farmers and mechanics. Or why don't you simply follow the lead of the English National Trust? They know how to make direct grants to communities. . . . Here was Ms. Anne Dosher, community worker from San Diego, contending that the only kind of effort that could possibly bring about real educational change was that of the old

OEO Community Action Programs. It was never *tried*, there is no other way, the only idea we ever had. . . .

Men and women on hobbyhorses are not much interested in interdependency, contradiction, complication. You say minority problems don't exist in Denmark? You say vitamins won't heal the disease of self-contempt? You say conquering self-contempt requires a (dangerous) mobilization of the resources of hatred? . . . Ah, replies Dr. Hobbyhorse witheringly, but you don't *understand*, you are an outsider. And as the ego-undertone becomes insistent, a blade of contempt begins swishing from side to side: I *am* Head Start, you see, it was my idea, I *am* a philosopher king. . . . I have been to Denmark, my man, I am a fellow of a Cambridge college. . . . I am of the people, I am *streetwise*, do not question this knowledge so remote from your own.

Faith—my old faith, my old flame—held that, once out of the woodwork, expertise, previously rigid in its view of the right move and the genius stroke, would be released into wider, more comprehensive understanding of its own ideas. My old flame held that tories and counterculturalists alike, once toned by the general air, would be relieved not to have to repeat their numbers. Not so, all of it not so.

Not so either—proceeding to yet another error or lesson—not so that the specialist in group relationships can set society on a new cooperative course. It is true, as just stated, that man-with-the-answer types are bad for "group process" (they never negotiate, merely condescend), and that our "process persons" occasionally did succeed in mussing their hair, checking the hobbyhorse rock for a beat. It's also true that the Process Person, this character who divides you into small groups and tells you it is time for you to break up, time to work at your task, time to report to plenary, this magician of the flip charts who listens to your reports, scribbles the points down with the magic marker, never weighs, never rejects, never ceases to speak foreign idioms such as "I think I hear you saying" . . . "that's where my head is at" . . . "little more feedback and then we'll go"—this figure is seldom without charm. At once vaguely furtive, vaguely reassuring, vaguely vague, he possesses a store of soothing words attesting that he encompasses both positions in conflict, carries them within himself. (Sometimes his protestations in this vein are hilarious: "The affective domain and the cognitive domain," said one process person sincerely, cooling a heated place in plenary, "are running through me all the time, and I am feeling them and trying to act upon them simultaneously.") Bearded, sad-eyed, small-boned, with the delicately marbled white skin that Chinese grandees once ate ground pearls to secure, easy in movement, inclined on occasion (like a character in a Chekhov play) to break restlessly into a fragment of rhythmic gesture or song (one bar of "Sugar," accompanied by a sudden whirl or dance step), secretly lofty with a novelist's confidence that he can "read the feeling," the individual insides of each person on the scene—the process person is no negligible being. But he is the incarnation of detachment: his pride lies in his perception of himself as process person in life, a man in the middle distance entangled but momentarily in the bustle of here and now, dealer in good feeling, in cadences that never close. "Resolution is not my thing."

And partly because resolution isn't, his ultimate influence is pernicious. Subtly, deviously, Dr. Process teases me out of my awareness of social life as it is; persistently, unflaggingly, he insinuates the notion that learning to abhor substance could be my most negotiable path to grace. In the front row Dr. Process is all smiles as Group I, Sequence II, launches its report in plenary, sharing a list of policy recommendations concerning high school and community relationships in tones of high exhilaration. June Wilson is spokesperson; she's a beautiful and articulate Manhattan matron keen on cradle-to-grave educational rights and on experiential teaching (history in the courthouse, science in the clinic). Her examples multiply, her eyes glisten, excitement is communicated—but suddenly comes an interruption, a male voice calling out sharply: "I don't believe in this. I don't believe in any of this."

What? You—what? All turn, the room stares. The speaker shakes his head, seemingly embarrassed at his own response. It's the novelist Lennie Michaels, an intelligent man. He shakes his head again but knows he's obliged to go on. "I'm sorry," he says. "It feels wrong to me. We haven't changed any fundamentals in the society. So much hope is impossible."

The reversal is jarring. We're stunned. June frowns, tongue on the sill of her lower lip. No hesitation, though, for Dr. Process. He is smiling no longer. "That's what you do, isn't it," he says, ready with ad hominem thrust. "That's what you always do, you academics, isn't that right? Literary people." Dr. Process's expression mixes pugnacity and knowingness. There's a faintly discordant half-smile on his face as he speaks. "The minute there's a good feeling among a group of people working together, you knife the feeling, isn't that so? Why do you have to do this?"

Lennie turns up his hands. June's poise returns. In the hall a half-hour later Dr. Process grinningly remarks to me: "That was something. That was my best intervention of the conference so far."

Best or worst, it was a typical "intervention," reflecting bottom-line beliefs of the process tribe. First among the beliefs is that there's no reason for hesitating to banish discord from a group even if the price is banishing substance from problems. Troubled by some abstractness in his group's excited reconception of school patterns, Lennie Michaels was attempting to speak out on the need for critical recognition of limits—and was responded to as spoil-sport, one whose reservations could properly be dealt with as neurotic hostility, a chorister complaining petulantly, mid-song, about the key. And that response to his criticism transformed the "situation" into a show, a performance, an experimental-improvisational-psychodramatic spot of time, not an earnest grappling with intractables.

And again we are speaking of a recurring scene. Rapt in process magic, united as a congregation of good feeling, men and women were continually discovering at Southampton their capacity for harmony, cooperative creativity, reconciliation. But, having come together for the stated reason of thinking through educational problems in the context of society as it is, the discovery became an invitation to shed the sense of reality itself—all feeling for the conditioned nature of existence vanishing in a puff. Woo me, woo me, wonder-world, I yearn for the universal happy hour, the womb of loving consensus: Camaraderie is All.

As would be guessed, we are approaching the error of faith that's most troubling, the mistaken assumption which, studied after the fact, opens the most merciless view of dimness. It would be comfortable to attribute our troubles at the meetings to the finaglings of process persons, hobbyhorse types, people obsessed with 1960s tunes. But the root cause lies elsewhere, in a misconception of the importance of educational forms, in a false assumption that changes in educational arrangements can profoundly alter the moral tone and quality of life, in obliviousness to the enemy within.

Southampton had no trouble "coming up with schemes." People "knew what they wanted" or what they thought they wanted (their proposals have been or will be dutifully transmitted to congressional authorities). If only, people told each other, if only education could be a lifelong proposition, like social security, medicare, etc. (You dig into the bank when you're ready, you can take some of your twelve or sixteen free years at forty or sixty or when you will.) If only education could be intermittent. If only schools could be linked up with other institutions—a community center thing. If only there were an alternative credentialing scheme, so that adults with skills or arts or crafts could enter and leave the system without all this fuss. If only the school could be linked up with a local, community-based, public policy study center with media access, so that local problems and local desires really could become shaping influences. . . .

Dozens of specific proposals, patches of genuine ingenuity. At the end of the fourth day of Sequence IV, as group after group laid out new versions of lower schools, higher schools, colleges, professional schools, school boards, trustee roles, you name it, the air was buoyantly alive. What were we doing if not improving ourselves? Together in these actions as purified beings, as children reciting poems, pasting sunlit dreams on blackboards for authority to look at, praise, grade, we were surely launched at last, were we not? We were doing the good work, connecting the school with the general society, connecting educational with "real world" issues, putting an end, in and through ourselves, to the artificial separation of children from adults. Imagine what'll happen when these proposals are enacted: we'll begin to see the amelioration of all social ills, will we not? Slowly these ever-more enlightened modes of teaching and learning will become the norm, slowly we'll begin to move toward the just and humane society for which every decent soul has so long yearned— and then will come the real surprise. We'll see that these odd little sessions of ours, these schoolroom meetings, were themselves the new start, a crusade for conjoint communication, an alternative to the culture of slots, a community in which the key verb is *flow* not *hypostatize*. History is choices, nothing but choices, our choices. History begins here and now.

You couldn't enter the rooms, once the participants were gone, could not look round the walls at the results so neatly taped—proposals, proposals, proposals!—like children's first haiku or Halloween cutouts or Christmas collages, without feeling the poignance of the fantasy. PRICK THE CONSCIENCE OF ALL OVER WHOM YOU

HAVE ANY INFLUENCE, cried Blue Magic Marker. PROBLEMS TODAY IN AMERICAN EDUCATION, said Green, ARE CLASS-LESS-RACELESS AND SHOULD BE SEEN AS SUCH! Red asked a question: HOW CAN WE BRING OUR VALUES ABOUT WHERE EDUCATION SHOULD GO INTO "GOOD CURRENCY"—BRING OTHERS INTO THE DIALOGUE? And answered with page on page of instructions and proposals concerning networks and alliances. HELP CREATE A MOVEMENT! shouted Green. BASED ON: 1. NEED (kids not getting what they need and society needs them to get) 2. HOPE (it *can* be done!). WE WANT CULTURAL PLURAL-ISM WITH LESS ABRASIVE INTERFACES, said Black Marker. *We want, we want, we want . . .*

The center of the fantasy was the assumption that all one needs to do, if one wants to think about goodness in education—educational goodness "in the context of the whole society"—is simply sit down and do the job. This was the belief that we could not, would not lay aside: goodness is here within us, in the grain of our feeling. Having announced our determination to cross the border—to re-imagine the school in relation to what lies beyond it—we found nothing out there save ourselves, and nothing in ourselves but love. One symptom of the self-deception was the ease with which men and women from various minorities, classes, and interest groups were seduced—by the will to happy process?—into obliterating their consciousness of differences of privilege, imbalances of power, wars about equality of results versus equality of opportunity, unresolved arguments about the hierarchy of values appropriate to democratic society (equality below fraternity? above love? above aesthetic creativity? below self-lessness?). Whenever power surfaced as a subject we turned to it in irritation, as though a bad smell had been released in the room: the polite among us would rise and leave gracefully, or otherwise protest the impropriety. PRICK THE CONSCIENCES . . . REACH THE OTHERS . . . RACELESS-CLASSLESS . . . Even those discussions that treated power balances in terms of existing political structures seemed somehow vulgar. (When restructuring was mentioned in his hearing, Representative Brademas instantly referred it to party status: "I earned my power legitimately," he asserted. "I went out and asked for it and fought for it and I am not about to resign and allow the person running against me in the fall to have the job on the ground that I have some sort of responsibility to give away the power." Appeal denied.)

In theory we knew—having been told so by Coleman and others—that much if not all reformist bustle about education in the recent past had been without consequence. Open classroom? closed? . . . oral? aural? oral-aural? . . . disciplinary? interdisciplinary? . . . school? deschool? . . . field? stream? Increasingly these battles seemed weightless. Increasingly, too, workers in other fields were speaking up more directly against those who give themselves forth as hopeful while barring serious entry to "problem areas," and allowing no probes of the marrow. A voice in revolt on the Op-Ed page, angry at ecological urgings to peel labels from jars to facilitate recycling: why should I do this? the woman cries, why can we not arrive at a more forceful and more comprehensive address to our needs than label-stripping? A voice in a liberal weekly, a physician commenting on research on the "problem" of Pica—children in the ghetto suffering lead poisoning from eating "too much" paint off the wall. Is this disease to be regarded, he asks, as an epidemiological challenge? What is the connection between "responsible health care" and research into how to unlead a ghetto baby? The "cure" for pollution is not label stripping. The "cure" for Pica is not a course of drugs. Knowing these things, we therefore also knew—did we not? how could we not?—that the "cure" for, say, corruption in high legal circles is not a project in moral education for law schools.

But this was among our proposals—and it could soundly be said that all the Southampton proposals were identical with this one, in that all flowed from the conviction that we are ready (the others need pricking), all betrayed ignorance of the true grain of common feeling. When I am not being "handled" by a process person, cosseted in conference, from whence does my sense of human solidarity derive, my sense that we—fellow citizens—are part of each other? Not from need of, or joy in my neighbor, not from intimations of shared mortality. My sense of human solidarity is grounded in a recognition that ruthlessness is the common necessity: scarcely anyone, after all, escapes the obligation to be mean. The banner above me, above the cabbie, above the orthodontist, states the unity of mankind in the imperative dog eat dog: you must, I must, he must, all must beat each other to the light. And we cannot run this race unless wary, unless skilled in the arts of denial and doubt. ENABLE ALL SEGMENTS OF SOCIETY TO EXPERIENCE THE FEELING OF BEING IN A COMMUNITY OF HOPE. Is it not "a problem for schooling" that parent and child in the present culture are closest when together they see through the lie? Together my daughter and I before the box see that the happy fellow singing "I smell good" is a deceit. We see that America the Beautiful isn't, we see that Jefferson owned slaves, we see that cynical disbelief is, like the shared bitterness at the unremittingness of competition, among the firmest of the blessed ties that bind.

And it follows, given this grain of feeling, that while a voice or face in a classroom or flip chart may hold that fairness is good, that the weak and the strong must know and value each other, that those who pollute the mind with falsehood deserve and will receive punishment, that life-meaning and enhancement flow from the mastery of the powers of discrimination, the refining of sensitivity, the development of love for beauty and for truth and for each other—while a voice may "stand for" these "verities," I know, we know, all know that this voice is producing at best only a theater of hypocrisy: the school in its organization, its form, its essential interior life, is no more supportive of such truths than the friendly Exxon station at the corner, or than I myself am, once the party has ended and I am back on the road.

Who can believe that thought about education in the context of the whole society can begin elsewhere than with existing structures of feeling and value? Who will contend that cradle-to-grave educational entitlement, ethnic programs, intermittency, public learning community centers, supermarket learning centers . . . that any of this touches us where we live? As long as we're bemused with "alternative devices," and with visions of our own inner selves as instinctively embracing and unguarded, we hide out from the essential continuity of school values and community values; as long as we say Pica is a problem for the preventive medicine department or hold that the "conscience of the others must be pricked," we cannot hope to know our secret opposing selves, the enemies of true learning within. Dear Jonathan, Dear Lillian, many people my age, or a bit older or younger would not have needed a Southampton party to get themselves straight on these matters. But you must understand that we are treating now of a farm-town Methodist with no Europe close in his past. I can see that, as a god that failed, my 1960s flame had nothing like the style, radiance, or intellectual force of 1930s gods. I should have seen the tinsel—*is* it tinsel?—earlier. Certainly some who were there with me knew what was wrong long ago; for them Southampton was a personal waste or a federal waste or both. But I needed this special occasion for staring boldly and coldly at—the 1960s. Can you believe this? Do you see that it's only after good will and intelligence have levitated themselves in a determined, sustained, cooperative endeavor for the public good, only after somebody with my past stands in an empty classroom looking at dreams, images of self-conceived selflessness, fluttering in the draft, only then that he can grasp the terms of his own evasions? Can you see that the use of Southampton might have been to help virtuous free citizens, virtuous choice-makers, grasp that, really, *they* are in prison, that they must reach deeper into themselves.

But I am defending, justifying—and in any event the point at stake matters far more than the worth of a month of federally-sponsored talk. It is that, whether troubleshooting, exhorting the conscienceless, or touting Tao, men and women of good will, innovators and reformers of *my* 1960s stripe rarely confronted their own will not to confront, rarely mapped the borders of their own evasions. The worn phrases float back: We did not know who we were. We did not know what we truly wanted to be. And I claim I know more now.

"The longer I live, citizen"—this is the way the great passage in Péguy begins, words I once loved to say (I had them almost memorized) in the dark backward, at Mary Holmes Junior College in West Point, Miss., in the "seminar room" on K and 17th Streets, with the ghetto kindergarten teachers, elsewhere. . . .

> The longer I live, citizen, the less I believe in the efficiency of sudden illuminations that are not accompanied or supported by serious work, the less I believe in the efficiency of conversion, extraordinary, sudden and marvelous, in the efficiency of sudden passions, and the more I believe in the efficiency of modest, slow, molecular, definitive work. The longer I live the less I believe in the efficiency of an extraordinary sudden social revolution, improvised, marvelous, with or without guns and impersonal dictatorship—and the more I believe in the efficiency of modest, slow, molecular, definitive work.

I had these words by heart, as I say, and I held them close, taking them in a special way. What the great man meant, as I understood it, was that this is the way you make the revolution—only this way, only by discrete efforts, small earnest movements, new adjacencies, work commitments. I blush for myself, shake my head: I *leaned* on these words, secretly, as proof that I—tenured in tennis clothes, owner of a house on a hill with a pool—was some kind of revolutionary . . . a serious doer of molecular deeds.

I wake up a little now. I see that molecular deeds are nothing unless the doer feels, registers, publicly insists on the difference between the frail impulses from which the deeds spring and the infinitely more powerful habitual understandings within himself—the unexamined feelings, the numberless unregistered acceptances of things as they are—that are forever obliterating true imaginings of change, forever insinuating that the true arena of change lies out there, not within, out there in the arrangements. My problem, simply stated, is that I need to know why I don't want what I say I want, why I can't yet want what I say I have always wanted. My problem is that I catch sight of one or another of the ironies multiplying roundabout me—children continuing to die at an early age while tens of thousands of dollars are spent to clarify to me at fifty the fantasies of my liberalism—but the sight invariably goes blurry. It is as though for this out-of-the-woodwork man there is an invisible sealer, a restraint. Amidst ecstasies, great gusts and choruses of hope, I notice hitherto unnoticed bars on my windows, padlocks on doors. I see that I'm waiting, have been waiting, will doubtless go on waiting for some indeterminate stretch for "things to open up"—and I grasp that this is both odd and wrong, since in fact I alone have the key—and I go on waiting.

Postscript

Scheme for a Further Step

Benjamin DeMott

Central in the congressional charge to the participants at Southampton were three demands—for aid in achieving a more rational kind of educational planning, for clarification of the proper tasks of schools, and for guidance concerning federal intervention in education in the next decade. The response from the authors of papers, discussants and work groups, while not unanimous, gathered overwhelmingly in support of the following points:

1. Federally funded efforts by existing institutions to perform special educational services for any designated segment of the relatively powerless in American society—the handicapped, the disadvantaged, the minorities—have had poor records of achievement for their clienteles, and have had small impact as prods to inner institutional reorganization and reform. Where, on the other hand, existing educational institutions have been called upon to serve the interests of the largest definable citizens' groups—union memberships, the aged, working women, others—the sequel has often been a series of helpful alterations in institutional structures and processes.

2. Educational reform which has concentrated its energies and resources "within the gates"—on The Curriculum or The Course

(interdisciplinary or otherwise), for instance, or upon revisions of balance among academic subject matters, or on revised disposition of existing faculty time—has usually failed to engage widespread support either inside or outside the school or academy itself. But educational reform which has concentrated on developing relationships between students and teachers and the work and leisure life of the community beyond the schoolyard or campus has drawn enthusiastic response both inside and outside, and has often achieved results beyond those predictable on the basis of size of original investment.

3. Attempts to create, by federal funds and programs, new relationships and collaborations between formerly separate, self-contained, noncommunicating sectors have had poor records of success. Attempts to extend or deepen relationships and collaborations between institutional divisions or enterprises separate but lately engaged, on their own initiative, in a cooperative project, have had clear records of achievement.

On this last point concerning collaborative enterprises, the most telling evidence presented at Southampton came in Dean Messerli's paper, which detailed the demise of hope for effective relationships between graduate education and liberal arts faculties. That hope had been a foundation stone of the Training of Teacher Trainers Project, which in turn was pivotal in the history from which the Southampton meetings sprang. In TTT the federal government sought to make a major teaching and learning event happen *ex nihilo*, that is, sought to open lines of communication and collaboration between graduate professors of education and graduate professors of the disciplines. The effort failed: prior to the federal initiative a will to collaborate had not been demonstrated, and federal funds could not in themselves bring it to birth.

Testimony on the first conclusion, that which counseled against special educational services for categorized minorities, came from a variety of voices at Southampton—most powerfully, perhaps, from a university president, John Silber, and a black novelist and teacher, John Edgar Wideman. A wealth of unhappy evidence, including Government Accounting Office evaluations, lay ready to hand to justify their positions. But while one dimension of the failure of well-intentioned efforts like the Title I programs in compensatory education had previously been widely publicized—namely the inability of academic remediation to overcome nutritional and other nonacademic deficiencies—other dimensions of failure were less familiar. At least three separate work groups at Southampton were at pains to stress the inability of special-services-to-special-populations programs to produce pedagogies appropriate to their task. Wherever a school is placed in a missionary position, dealing with a group perceived as "lesser" or "subsidiary," the school becomes invulnerable—incapable of remaking itself, of adapting its structures to the realities of the world outside. The claim was repeatedly made at Southampton that in engagements with the empowered, the school and college find it easier to shed their self-importance and to consider seriously questions about the worth and pertinence of their ways to the broader public.

Regarding the participants' conclusion about educational reform concentrated inside the gates, it is sufficient to note that no single theme sounded as often or as forcefully at Southampton as that concerning the remoteness of the school from the general life of the community. The point lay at the heart of one of the more stimulating papers presented during the sessions—Page Smith's proposals for a "universal curriculum." It provided the energy that charged one of the most remarkable public sessions, wherein Professor Henry Steele Commager, speaking for the clear majority, declared that:

> The most promising enterprise in the realm of education would seem to be to make education once again the business of the whole of society, to close the gap—nay, the chasm—between school and society; to enlist all available energies of society in the task of *paideia*.
>
> The most practical way to go about this is to create a new network or recreate an old network of educational institutions, "new" only because we have forgotten how old it is; a new network of the school and the innumerable voluntary organizations whose functions are educational but whose activities have not for long or ever been educational. We need to construct alliances—when I say "we," I do not mean schools alone but all those interested in education—with the churches, which used to be the major educational institution and were indeed for almost 1500 years.
>
> We need to construct alliances with fraternal orders like the Masons and Elks and the Woodmen of the World and the Eastern Stars; the great veterans' organizations, the American Legion and the Veterans of Foreign Wars; the Boy Scouts and Girl Scouts.
>
> We need to construct alliances with labor unions which have grossly and scandalously neglected their responsibility of an educational character and whom the schools have forgotten or neglected.
>
> We need to construct alliances with the YMCA and the YWCA, the

Hadassah, the Knights of Columbus, local Chambers of Commerce, the Bar Associations and the other professional organizations—there are hundreds of these names you can add—all those organizations whose function is not profit-making but society-making, and whose role should not be limited to the current scene but should be fiduciary.

The participants appeared well aware that The School as presently housed and financed cannot soon become a disposable item. Regardless of the amount of enthusiasm among the thoughtful for programs of outreach, or for the notion of school as community center, PS 67 to the number of tens of thousands is assured of survival. But it is equally certain, given Southampton as a guide, that the warmth of public support for the "system" as it is, will increasingly be dependent upon the school's degree of success in linking itself with skills, occupations, problems, challenges, and aspirations that exist beyond its walls.

What follows? Legislators who read the Southampton record accurately will conclude that:

1. The center of any new federal intervention in the field of education must be schooling for grownups—worker education and retraining, programs designed to meet women's educational needs, programs answerable to the situations of the retired and the reduced time worker generally;

2. The focus of such federal intervention should be those existing programs wherein teachers, administrators, and others have succeeded *without federal support* in developing lines of communication between institutions not engaged in education as conventionally conceived—agencies of government, businesses, unions, youth organizations, arts institutions, professional associations;

3. One overarching goal of such intervention should be the creation, within the emergent school-nonschool network, of alternative secondary school tracks—alternative settings, in short, in which, by self- and other modes of selection, students and teachers can work at opening the stance of the school vis à vis society in the large.

Clearly this is not the place for an in-depth survey of current undertakings in lifelong learning that might serve as centers for the kind of educational development toward which Southampton pointed.

It is worth noting in passing, however, that the range of existing programs is sufficiently wide even at present to provide excellent foundations and growing points. There are, to begin with, a number of cooperative arrangements between professional associations (in medicine, law, and engineering) and university faculties, the purpose of which is to provide postgraduate training in recent developments in the field to mature professionals. Such programs exist at Nebraska, Michigan State, Oklahoma, Georgia and many other state universities. Seed money and planning grants, reconceived, could enable institutions to extend their activities, looking toward a widening of scope— programs of general public education in issues in law and medicine, one year internships for high school students, the building of adjunct faculties composed of professionals and of others with extensive problem-solving experience. An extraordinarily suggestive program in "adult education" involving professional associations, university faculty, and lay personnel is currently in progress in Grand Rapids, Michigan, where the students are patrolmen on the city police force. The subject of study is advanced level emergency medical care—how to diagnose and effectively treat a wide variety of ailments—up to and including cardiac arrest, that a cop on a beat is likely to encounter in his career. The length of the course is six months, and the settings and devices in and by means of which it is conducted are both conventional (classroom and lab) and unconventional (the street, the beat, the two-way radio, policeman at one end, hospital technician at the other). The faculty consists of MD residents at a local hospital and staff from the state university medical school.

Other institutions have experimented with linkups, within continuing education institutes, between city officialdom, political leaders, academic social scientists, urban planning specialists, and lay citizens. These resources have been combined with local media in efforts at identifying crucial urban problems, appropriate areas for research and voter decision. (See, for example, the programs of the Center for Urban Studies at Rutgers.) A number of arts institutions have successfully developed new arrangements between museum personnel, university scientists, and private industry for the purpose of interpreting new scientific developments to the lay public, and of building courses suitable for local educational TV stations. And a dozen other kinds of collaboration could be mentioned—programs with notable achievements to their credit in shaping working relationships between those formally accredited as representatives of the learned disciplines and those with day-to-day experience of the way in which knowledge functions in nonschool worlds. Ideally the programs of limited federal grants that would enable these places to enlarge their effect would define some long-term objectives—goals lying beyond the mere strengthening of existing arrangements. And, as already implied, the goal would be the development, ultimately, of nonresidential field study centers of continuing education staffed by academic and nonacademic professionals, including as integral parts laboratory secondary schools.

The aim should not be to dictate a single modality or value as supreme. Neither should it be to underwrite further domination of the educational process by the universities and the schools. Included as essential to the life of the network concept was a wide range of organizations and agencies responsible, in various ways, for "community involvement curriculums"—the American Bar Association's Special Committee on Youth Education for Citizenship, which works to further the expansion of law-related studies in the lower schools; ACTION, the National Student Volunteer Program, which encourages volunteer programs in the lower schools through teacher and coordinator training sessions; Executive High School Internships of America, which enrolls 2,000 students annually as unpaid special assistants to senior officials of organizations and institutions within local communities; the National Commission on Resources for Youth, Inc., which collects and disseminates information on community involvement programs for youth; Students Work with the Handicapped, a California organization sponsoring high school students as resource recreational and instructional persons for the handicapped and aged; Adopt a Grandparent, a similar organization in Connecticut; the Black Liberation School at Ann Arbor, which runs an educational enrichment project using high school students as tutors in elementary schools; the Children's Art Bazaar Art Gallery in St. Louis, a joint high school student-professional artist gallery exhibiting art works from the community; Students Concerned with Public Health, a Philadelphia organization which employs young people to make presentations on public health to elementary school children . . . scores if not hundreds of other groups and agencies.

The aim, as it came into view during the Southampton sessions, should be to foster the kind of "mix" evident in these already existing, wholly unpretentious initiatives in "educational reform"—initiatives that link schools and society, youth and grownups, professionals and nonprofessionals, recreating schoolworlds as cross-sections of the powerful and potentially powerful within the society as a whole. Would it not be feasible to extend the range and influence of such initiatives? If it were feasible, would it not be a mistake to despair about the possibility of significant change in contemporary American patterns of schooling?

For the present writer to pose such questions is to hint at a recantation; in fact none is imminent. The words set down in previous chapters by myself and others, in deprecation of faith in the school as an agent of social change, need not be taken back. The same holds for those statements critical of the pretense that the chief barrier to change is other people's fear or cowardice (as distinguished from one's own). The question—why despair?—amounts only to an admission that moral immodesty isn't a necessary or inevitable component of educational innovation and that even at this late date, after much disillusionment, acquaintance with even a single, well-conceived enterprise uncursed by immodesty can renew a sense of educational and social possibility. For many at Southampton it seemed plain that clearer, sharper definitions of "well-conceived innovations" than those hitherto available could be framed, and that the immediate educational past could be made to yield some lessons about how to temper immodesty in this field—lessons capable of being worked up into principles and made available to legislators, program managers, program initiators. But in order for this to happen the audience would have to be prepared for a new measure of complexity in the definitions—a focus not limited to discrete entities but embracing the variety of interrelated parts.

And implicit in this view is that the "learning society" can only truly come to exist when it is conscious that this indeed is what it is. The consciousness is bound to carry with it, so the Southampton participants appeared to believe, a conviction that learning is too important and too universal an activity to be left to the schools and the "professionals," that learning is all-pervasive, that each of us, in the pursuit of his and her development, must necessarily be both lifelong learner and teacher, and that institutional structures need to be reordered in ways that enable us to function comfortably in these roles at every stage of our growth. While such a reordering cannot guarantee moral transformation or broad social justice, it could contribute to the refining of a steadier balance between modesty and pride—a state of mind in which believers in educational possibility could acknowledge the general human condition and the universal human limits, and still continue to breathe and shape and create. And it could provide, in addition, a basis for sounder federal initiatives in the fields of schooling than any hitherto known—programs which, instead of hiding out from the past, whether in ignorance or in shame, face up to its lessons, and generate from them a philosophy of intervention rooted in realism as well as in good hope.

Contributors

Contributors

William Arrowsmith is University Professor and professor of classics at Boston University. His translations include works from the ancient Greek, Latin, Italian, French, and German.

John Brademas is a United States Congressman from Indiana and chairman of the Select Subcommittee on Education of the House of Representatives.

Peter Brooks teaches in The Literature Major at Yale University. He is the author of *The Novel of Worldliness* and other literary and cultural studies.

Henry Steele Commager is professor of history at Amherst College. He is the author of numerous books in American history.

Benjamin DeMott is professor of English at Amherst College. He has written two novels and four collections of essays.

Martin Green is professor of English at Tufts University. His latest book is *Children of the Sun: A Narrative of "Decadence" in England After 1918.*

Elizabeth Janeway is a novelist, social historian, critic, and lecturer. Her latest book is *Between Myth and Morning, Women Awakening.*

R. W. Lid is professor of English at California State University,

Northridge, and the author of *Ford Madox Ford: The Essence of His Art.*

Jonathan Messerli is Dean of Education at Fordham University. He is the author of a biography of Horace Mann and has written widely on educational reform.

Claiborne Pell is United States Senator from Rhode Island and chairman of the Subcommittee on Education of the United States Senate.

Albert Quie is a United States Congressman from Minnesota and the ranking minority member of the House Committee on Education and Labor.

Michael Rossman is a free-lance writer and political activist. He is the author of *On Learning and Social Change* and the forthcoming *The Politics of Psychic Power.*

Kirkpatrick Sale is a writer and editor. He is the author of *SDS,* a history of the Students for a Democratic Society, and *Power Shift: The Rise of the Southern Rim and Its Challenge to the Eastern Establishment.*

Marian Simpson is director of the Center for Academic Assistance at Smith College.

Theodore Sizer has been Dean of Education at Harvard University and is currently headmaster at Andover Phillips Academy. His latest book is *Places for Learning, Places for Joy.*

Page Smith is an American historian and former Provost at the University of California, Santa Cruz. His latest work is the two-volume *A New Age Now Begins: A People's History of the American Revolution.* .

Appendices

Appendix A

The Call: Statement of Purpose and Procedure at Southampton

The Southampton Summer Program of Project Open

Purpose: The objective of the summer program is to engage a broad range of citizens—from inside and outside the formal education establishments of this country—in shaping recommendations for the development of educational policy for all societal agencies engaged in the teaching and learning process.

Key Assumption: As stated in earlier papers, we believe that neither educators nor the schools they staff can reform society; we also believe that "reforming the schools"—by whatever means—will not greatly improve the education of our people. The reason is that the schools are not the major educative influence in this society; they are only a reflection of the larger forces controlling all our institutions. Nobody can change his appearance by daubing at his reflection in a mirror.

Participants: Public officials, community and media people, businessmen, industrialists, labor union executives, teachers and administrators from secondary and higher education, foundation representatives and artists are among those who have accepted invitations to these meetings.

Procedures

The program is divided into four sequences, each with a different group of participants, a special theme, and an action-oriented agenda; yet we see them as connected, even interdependent, and we are looking toward a cumulative redefinition of recommendations and policy statements. To facilitate this, each session will be transcribed by stenographers or recorded for use as appropriate in subsequent sessions. Thus, a presentation by Congressman John Brademas or professor Henry Steele Commager or Dr. Salvador Luria, or a dialogue between business executives and university presidents, will have significance for the session in which it occurs but can also serve as a resource for later sessions.

One focus of each sequence will be upon conclusions reached in a set of paper commissioned and written beforehand by social critics of some reputation; these papers will be employed in various ways to define basic issues and maintain continuity.

A core staff and resource group will be present throughout, together with a team of writers assigned the task of summing up and integrating the results of the session.

As a participant, you may meet in a group composed of individuals whose positions or concerns are similar to your own (i.e., university presidents meeting with university presidents). You may also meet in rather more diverse groups—e.g., with representatives from the communities, the arts, or from labor and the public schools.

Themes of the Sequences

Sequence I (June 14-18) will attempt to study and clarify forces of unity and divisiveness now operating in American society, and to assess the extent to which the people of this country still participate in a common social reality. (Some relevant issues: Pluralism and Social Control, Equality and Elitism.)

Some specific problems to be set under examination include distrust of leadership and of the "responsible element," explosions of rage at the rich, alienation among blue collar workers, busing, protests against busing, black separatism, prospects for democratic or "non-partisan" citizens' coalitions.

Sequence II (June 21-25) will attempt to study and clarify the respects in which education in the U.S. presently works to strengthen or weaken the social fabric. (Critical issues here: Social Roles of Education, School Culture, Slot Culture, Mid-Life Career Change.)

Specific problems to be examined include changing conditions of work, classroom versus real world, restrictions against entry and exit from the crafts and professions; the roles of local institutions and administrative authorities in opening up closed systems of schooling and career pursuit; moral obligations of professionals; prospects for inter-institutional cooperation in developing career mobility.

Sequence III (June 27-July 1) moves forward to consideration of a blueprint for the future. In an ideal society what would be the social role of education? Where and how, for instance, would "moral education" take place? What measure of social unity, how much sense of common purpose is desirable or necessary for the health of a citizenry?

This series of meetings is prompted, as is perhaps obvious, by the increasing national awareness of the gap between what we say we believe and how we behave. Public schools have a mandate of a sort to see that young people are humanistically oriented and prepared to function as effective citizens in a democratic society. Professional schools have a mandate of a sort to concern themselves with professional ethics within the framework of a democratic society. What can be done to assure that these mandates are heeded? More specifically:

What kinds of intra- and inter-institutional arrangements, if any, could help to define (or even to develop) behavior appropriate to a democratic society?

How and where should teaching and learning occur in the future?

Sequence IV (July 7-11) takes as its focus the question of whether alterations of public policy can bring us nearer to our goals, and, if so, what changes are most necessary now. How can the interdependencies of educational and other socio-economic policies be made visible and acted upon? What steps can be taken to insure that decisions at the national level about, say, welfare policies or national self-sufficiency are not shaped in isolation from decisions about the goals and financing of education?

Participants in this session will include many with specific experience and background in the processes whereby society and its institutions change: legislators, behavioral scientists, creators of new styles and interests in the media. The chief problem will be: How in practical terms do we reach the desired goals developed in earlier sessions, for teaching and learning in the good society?

Just Another Conference?

The past two decades haven't lacked for conferences on education and on The Issues Facing Our Rapidly Changing Society. Inevitably these Southampton sequences will resemble many earlier assemblages. We hope, however, to create an atmosphere in which meaningful talk leads to results far different from those of conventional conferences. We conceive the period in question as a series of working/training sessions in which peers—in course of examining their own institutions and their potential roles in developing a decent social and economic harmony—develop concrete recommendations for action and public policy. As we've repeated more than once, we believe that the development of norms, standards, and values for a democratic society is everybody's business. We also believe that the important outcome of these meetings may well not be a conventional summary report. (The recommendations that emerge during the Southampton training program will be carefully documented and disseminated to local, state and federal officials, and to the entire range of institutions concerned with educational process.) Our hope is that the "outcomes" will be determined by the participants' own commitments and convictions, as they return to their original bases. With luck, in some sessions, industrial, educational, and public leaders from one or another geographical or community setting will succeed in working together not only on broad agendas, but on specific proposals related to their own localities. The latter labor may—again, with luck—provide ongoing case studies for other participants. As the city manager, school superintendent, mayor and community representatives of a given city, such as Dallas or Cincinnati, examine their problems and press jointly for solutions, they will be interacting with federal officials, business leaders, and educators from other parts of the country who may be able to relate those problems and solutions to their own locales.

Appendix B
Comments by Congressional Leaders

Senator Claiborne Pell

The theme, as I understand it, of this first sequence of Project Open—in fact, the whole rationale of this project—is one in which I struggle in my own work as Chairman of the Senate Subcommittee on Education. Your assumption makes a clear, simple statement, one only now being recognized by the majority of the people in our nation, the fact that neither education nor the schools working in a vacuum can reform the defects in our society.

Unfortunately, we in Washington must take a great deal of the responsibility for setting up a set of circumstances and a situation by which we force the schools to become the blunt edge of social reform. I think the schools are being forced to take on the responsibility of many of the nation's ills, and we have sometimes lost sight of the true objectives of schools, which is an improvement in the quality of education.

My paper today touches upon the purely practical considerations of your key assumption as it affects legislation in Washington, legislation which is a product of a democratically elected House and Senate.

We should remember that when people criticize the President for the war in Vietnam—and I was one of the early doves in that—we should still not condemn the President too much because the Congress bore along with it for many, many years. When we condemn policies, let us keep in mind that the Congress, as a rule, is pretty much responsible for them, the reason in my mind being that the Congress is usually a year or two or three years behind public opinion.

To me, one of the most inaccurate facets of foreign commentary on our society is the assumption that there is a sort of master plan in operation, that we plan our future and the outcome as being foreseen and expected. When viewed from Washington, it is clear that such is not the case. We seem to abhor any instance of planning that tends to cause socialism and we avoid it, and nowhere is this more apparent than in education, where federal programs have grown and developed in fits and starts with no long-term overall planning and particularly with too little commitment and too little direction.

In the 1950s and 1960s, we turned to the schools as vehicles for social reform in an instinctive reaction for a need for a method to deal with social and racial problems, and the attendant disadvantages in education. The decision was instinctive rather than the result of a long study culminating in a rational decision in terms of the schools, coming from the success in education resultant upon the upward mobility of immigrants who came to our nation during the period of time between the Civil War and World War I. This immigrant group was one that became involved with education and quickly seemed to become economically sufficient and able to participate in the mainstream of American life, with their children and grand-children becoming leaders of our nation.

We interpreted the success of the immigrant as proof that the universal system of education had made their integration possible. When we faced the problem of the 1950s involving two nations, one black and one white, it was natural to try to use the methodology that had proven so successful.

I don't have to tell you what the result of that selection has been. Many public schools in the nation are in disarray; many middle-income and upper-income white parents now view tuition as a sixteen-year obligation rather than a four-year one. The parent paying $2,000 yearly for elementary and secondary education is less willing to pay $5,000 in higher education costs.

The schools have been urged to take on the responsibility of segregation, whereas you find segregation by the pattern of living and employment is not faced up to in the same way and is not handled by law in the same way. You can't force people who live in one place to live in another. You can have an effect on the schools by law, and this is why the schools have had to take the brunt of achieving integrated society.

The federal role has not been one of leadership, nor did Congress take a leadership role in the 1950s. It was all too easy to let the courts bear the burden and sit back and disagree with those decisions which were not pleasant. During consideration of the three major omnibus education bills in the Senate in the past five years, 90 percent of the debate has been concerned not with education but with busing. Here again, a democratically elected legislature wouldn't face the real issue but continued to pass and tie in busing legislation which only exacerbated the situation.

The Congress is loathe to face the hard, real issue of today. I must admit that in our discussions on the present $25 billion ESEA bill, we hardly talked about the serious problem of quality in our public schools, but rather we treated all our school problems as ones of financing. The theory was that perhaps with a little more money you could make the schools better. We have enacted a large compensatory education program, Title I and others, which will certainly make some improvement in our youngsters' education and help more disadvantaged ones to read. I do not believe it will change the real issue facing our public schools today.

The attempt to generate discussions on educational issues has not been easy; the democratically elected Congress does not seek to discuss those issues which are inherently problematic. In 1965, together with Senator Cooper, I introduced legislation establishing a national test as a means to identify those school districts doing a good job from those not performing as they should have been. It was called the Quality in Education Bill, and it sought to improve the quality in schools on a voluntary basis; nobody would be forced to take the test, it would be optional and somewhat like the Regents test in New York. Those youngsters applying to take it could take it. We thought it would apply gradual pressure on some of the school districts to raise the quality of the education in those districts and in those schools. Needless to say, the NEA—the National Education Association—and all the professional people in the field opposed my idea very strongly, and it was never able to get off the ground. We also succeeded in getting into law the provision for the National Council on the Quality of Education to again try to improve the quality in the schools so that when you graduated from school you either had a good grounding in a vocation or a good grounding in education, rather than, as so often happens now, no real competence in any single field. However, we are not able to get this council set up. Like some edicts of the Congress, it was ignored by the administration, and not only not funded but the people not appointed. The Council on the Quality of Education was one of those groups which, while legally set up has never in fact been set up, and in part accounts for the present impasse between the Congress and the administration.

I occasionally questioned witnesses on the highly controversial question of Jensen's thesis, not whether it is right or wrong, serious or mischievous, but in search of witnesses' views, which are not usually forthcoming. Instead, I get opinions colored by the politics or the ideological bias of the witness. If there were ever a bit of truth in Jensen, one smidgen of it, shouldn't our education reflect it? If there is no truth, shouldn't our educational system be rewritten to take into account the diversity of people and cultures that make our nation? Further, shouldn't our I.Q. tests be named "achievement tests"? Youngsters from deprived backgrounds are automatically at a disadvantage when it comes to scoring well on I.Q. tests. In raising the discussion on Jensen informally with my staff and friends, it became vituperatively hot, and when raising it formally, I am usually given a stony stare, with people very much wishing the subject would go away, wondering whether it has to be raised at all.

Any politician raising an issue with respect to quality in education is charged with elitism. There seems to be nothing wrong with enacting hundreds of programs for the disadvantaged; nobody minds being called disadvantaged, perhaps, but when individuals try to establish programs for gifted and talented children, they are called elitists who want to destroy the public school system and set up a dual system, one for the bright and one for the others. I am afraid the snobbish attitude of high I.Q. groups adopted towards the rest of us having a more average I.Q. does not help either.

A politician wishing to remain in office and accomplish some good must be very careful of charges of elitism; the simple sponsoring of legislation for the talented and gifted is enough to bring down the wrath of many groups. Yet, we must face these issues if we are to have any coherent approach to education.

We seem unwilling to recognize that the changes, the great changes and advancements in knowledge, are usually the result of the efforts not of the retarded, not of the people of normal I.Q., but really the efforts of the gifted and talented. Accordingly, should we not concentrate more on them and put less effort on schools as vehicles for social reform and more on the whole question of the quality of education and raising it? There is much too much talk of newness and breakthrough and reform as ends in themselves. Ten years ago what was spoken of was innovation; it seemed every week there was a story about some major new educational program going to teach all youngsters everything. Unfortunately, Americans want instant success, and yet we must realize that this is not going to happen. Education takes time. We can't enact a Title I program for compensatory education which is underfunded for five years and then get mad because it did not do the job.

At the other end of the scale, I am thinking of the G.I. Bill, which worked after World War II because it was an adequate amount, adequately funded, and the public was behind it. The present Veterans' program is puny; there is not enough to help the man really seriously complete his education, and that is the main reason for its lack of use.

We must be able to commit our national treasury to a national goal, a plan for a setting up of a program, and then we must sit back for ten years or so and see if it works. It is good to note that the Congress has, although not by design, recognized that the so-called melting pot theory has fallen by the wayside, albeit that recognition is somewhat late. We have programs of bilingual education; we have set up programs of ethnic studies. These programs reinforce the desires of those not in the so-called establishment to have their own stories told and be able to learn about their own backgrounds in school.

Here again, however, these programs were not adopted out of a rational plan but, honestly, the result of pure political expediency. Perhaps nowhere is the disillusionment of the so-called blue collar worker more evident than in his regard for public education. Blue collar people saw education, and the attainment of security it brings, as the be-all and end-all of American life. The 1950s and 1960s helped destroy their impressions and, besides, they are told by the New Left and even by their own children that many of their aims and goals are worthless and that material desires are shameful. They were also made to bear the brunt of the integration of the races, and it is their children whose schools became the battleground for ideological and physical warfare. One cannot blame the blue collar person for becoming embittered and for seeing in this situation a plot to keep him and his people in their place.

This individual is susceptible to the impassioned rhetoric of any politician who talks about "pointy-headed liberals" and social planners. There is the paradox. As I said, there really is nobody at the federal level doing social planning in connection with the interests of the disadvantaged and the minorities, but can there be any greater example of a federal policy adopted in a hit or miss manner which has created such animosity and had very real effects on national politics and the outcome of national elections?

What I have laid out is a litany filled with shortcomings, as viewed from the perspective of a Senator who does believe the federal government can be a real factor in bringing about the improvement of the education of our nation's citizenry, and ancillary to that an improvement of the social and economic conditions of the nation.

I think education should be the goal and always perceived as the main emphasis. We are constantly confronted with a problem of how to translate this laudable aim into reality, how to write programs that will benefit and not have adverse side effects that we never considered possible. I will admit the need in Washington for an awareness that overall planning must be considered when adopting any federal policy.

I go back to the beginning of my talk, and I state that we must have more long-term planning and we must accept long-term planning and see that it is adhered to once decided upon. We can no longer manufacture social programs without relating them to each other and the whole spectrum of current government activity. We must be aware that implementation of government policies can be aided by an awareness of and study of the types of planning and predicting being done. I am not advocating all-out social planning, but the Senate and whoever is running the Executive Branch must be aware of the interrelationships between disciplines, between goals and certainly must recognize that the means to do so are at hand. This is where the academic world must become involved in the legislative and administrative processes. We must be able to take the style of the planner—both substantive and procedural—and bring it to the everyday world in English that is comprehensible rather than educational gobbledygook. We can't live with political scientists trying to quantify all political theory so they can relate to their peers, on the campus and in think tanks, dealing with mathematics and physics. We must also realize that social problems have an unquantifiable factor, the human being. If we don't humanize planning and programs, we will re-experience most of the disruption and ultimate despair we have gone through in the last ten years.

Finally, and most importantly, we must recognize that only a portion—maybe a third or fourth—of a child's character is formed by school; the remaining two-thirds or three-fourths is the direct result of his home environment and of his genes. There is an analogy here to cholesterol and how diet affects it: the bulk of cholesterol is produced by our temperament and the stresses we undergo; nevertheless, we know diet does have an effect on it. So, perhaps as something of a crutch or stick, those of us with high cholesterol—of which I am one—follow a diet to try to lower it, but that only affects a portion of the total production of cholesterol.

This is what education is all about: only a portion of the child's development comes in the school. We must do this, and this is a program I look forward to working on hard in the next few years in the Senate, to try to relate schools and education with the home environment. If you change the home environment—and if there is no home environment somehow bring the children further into the schools—then we are going to have an impact not on a quarter or a third of the development of our children, but maybe on a half or two-thirds, and then we can see much more real and quick effects.

It is my hope that we should not expect schools to carry out the major responsibility for a child's development; I think the load to be placed on schools today is almost an intolerable one. If there is any problem, we put it on the school and hope the schools will solve it for future generations. I think that this is beyond many schools and we would do better to wake up a little bit and try to be sure that the education the youngsters receive is in the highest possible order. I am not saying here that we should increase the academic standards. I think we should increase the vocational standards, the career standards.

I am proud to state that I was able, a couple of years ago, to make sure that career training was given the same federal recognition as the theoretical liberal arts training. We must recognize that some children want to work with their hands or with material things, and that these children have as much ability as those interested in the liberal arts.

I hope, in conclusion, that conferences, such as the one you are having, make the needs of the academic community clear to the people in Washington, and we in the legislative field become aware of your needs and are able to help. With the mixture of disciplines here will come perhaps a greater recognition of what education can do and also what it can't do.

Representative Albert Quie

Here is something that I see as a deep concern, at the elementary and secondary school level as well as in institutions of higher learning: how do we transmit the values of the older generation to the younger generation?

We are not, I believe, developing in our school system the values necessary to our society. I believe that the young people today are handicapped by being involved for such a large percentage of their time with their peer group and not enough of their time with other age groups in the population. Our whole lifestyle has brought this about. We no longer, even in the rural areas, have the grandparents, parents, and children all living in the same household. Children don't have the opportunity of watching their parents work, because their parents usually work far away from home. Children often can't understand what their parents are doing anyway. It is difficult for today's children to feel related to the work of their parents; and it was this relationship, which existed from the beginning of time until recently, that allowed them to interact with other age groups. For the first time, they are involved primarily with their peers.

Therefore, I think our schools must be viewed as a means whereby values can be transmitted from one generation to another.

Now, this immediately brings up fears in people's minds: "Is there going to be a stereotyped set of values that will be promulgated?"

If we are going to provide an adequate education, I think that development of values would be forthcoming if the community is involved more in the educational system.

Now, as I have watched public education, it seems we are moving to larger and larger school districts and larger and larger attendance areas for the schools being constructed. Although these large groups of children may be offered a great deal, the sense of community around the school is nevertheless lost. It takes a great deal of effort for teachers to be involved in the work of the community, with all the various interests and frictions that exist there. However, it seems to me that if education is really to relate to and provide what the young person needs, then the young person's community must be involved in it.

Now, as the young person becomes older, the community can expand: the vision of the adult expands; the community of the young person can expand. Those of you who are over fifty probably remember—well, I lived in a community where everybody was Norwegian, and we talked Norwegian at the recess. I have forgotten all the Norwegian I ever knew, which indicates how we have had the melting pot in operation. We knew where the Germans were and the Czechoslovakians were, and those horrible Swedes—we stayed away from there. Yet we had a sense of community that gave us a pride in our culture and heritage. I think it is still important to the development of the individual.

John Brademas indicated that he and I were involved, probably more than any other two individuals in Congress, in writing the Education Amendments of 1972. At that time, we were asking questions about the direction we ought to go in higher education and could not find those answers from people in higher education.

We both had been recipients of substantial studies by groups, and I mention especially the Chamber of Commerce and AFL-CIO. If you want an economic study to support the AFL-CIO position, they will get it for you and they have hired a good researcher from a college or university to do it for them. You can ask the same things on an economic study from the Chamber of Commerce. Either they have it available, or they can get it before very long.

We asked the same questions of institutions of higher education or the American Council on Education, and we weren't able to secure any of that. They felt their role was to compromise the differences between the individuals and their members, and then to hand us the compromise. We were supposed to pick it up and run with it, and we were ready to do that. All we wanted to know were the reasons.

Some people look at Congress as about the equivalent of a sixth grade education, and it may be many people's view of the Congress, but there are some individuals in the Congress who are doing some extensive work now. Still, I feel that there is not adequate information being made available to them. We had hoped that through the National Institute on Education, through the Executive Branch, we could then have a series of studies available to us. The Office of Education was conducting research for a long period of time, but it never seemed to be the kind of research that we were looking for.

We ran into the same problem, or at least I did, in working on the Elementary and Secondary Education Act this year. Back in 1965, we assumed that if you were poor you were educationally disadvantaged; if you were educationally disadvantaged, you were poor. So, you count all the poor kids and you channel all the money into that. Nobody seemed to be challenging that assumption.

I found two studies indicating that there were no educationally disadvantaged children from families—in numbers, in our school system—with incomes above $6,500. Nobody was talking about that as a bench mark. There were 60 percent of the children coming from families of that income, and about 40 percent who were educationally disadvantaged—in reading and math—from below.

Ingrained in the Congress' mind was the feeling that poverty means disadvantaged and disadvantaged means poverty, so we continued that. In the House we attempted to at least give some option to a local school district to use other means of determining the educationally disadvantaged. In conference all we could retain was that there could be a trial in twenty school districts in the nation of using other criteria than just poverty.

There are not the kind of studies available to the Congress that the Congress needs. This is our greatest shortcoming, not being able to point to independent studies that are made available to us.

Therefore, we are legislating in the dark, and I think it is unfortunate that the Congress continues to legislate in the dark. We will continue to legislate on our biases.

Representative John Brademas

I am honored to have been invited to speak to so distinguished a group of persons—brought together by a common concern about education. Clearly, Don Bigelow and Bill Arrowsmith and their associates have a talent for rounding up a remarkable cross section of thoughtful people.

And I want to talk to you tonight on a subject Bill Arrowsmith raised in his original letter to me about this conference: "opening up lines of communication between groups usually sealed off from each other." In fact, that is what I spend a good deal of my own time doing as a member of Congress. Indeed, I must warn you that my contribution to this discussion will be from the perspective of a practicing politician, a legislator, a member of that Committee of the House of Representatives with chief responsibility for education and a number of related areas. So I hope you will forgive me if I refer to some of my own experiences and observations in working on education legislation in Congress. But I take it that is one of the reasons you invited me here!

In the House, I sit on the Committees on Education and Labor and on House Administration, and on the Joint House-Senate Committees on the Library of Congress and the Government Printing

Office. On House Administration, I chair the Printing Subcommittee and sit on several others and every morning these last few weeks I have been working on the bill to reform campaign financing. On Education and Labor, I sit on the higher education subcommittee, labor subcommittee and chair a third. Every afternoon in recent days, I've been in House-Senate conference sessions on the bill extending the Elementary and Secondary Education Act. The subcommittee I chair has jurisdiction over several areas, including educational research, early childhood, older Americans, environmental education, vocational rehabilitation, education of the handicapped, libraries, museums, drug abuse education, international education, and the arts and humanities.

I shall not take time to recite the other nonlegislative aspects of my job as a Congressman.

I give you this rapid litany of part of my responsibility as a legislator so that, as the students say, you know where I'm coming from and, more to the point, so that you will understand why I, as a legislator working on education, feel so strongly about the importance of "opening up lines of communication between groups usually sealed off from each other."

To Know What Is Right

For the longer I am in Congress, the more I am persuaded of the truth of what President Johnson once said: "My problem is not so much doing what is right as knowing what is right." And, as a doer, I would suggest to you that my own problem in knowing what is right, substantively, to put into an education bill, may offer some useful lessons about the relationships, generally, between (to impose an arbitrary distinction) the thinkers and the decision makers.

Let me then cite you some examples from my own experiences with education that may help make clear what I am trying to say about how public policy makers, concerned to do what is right, encounter the problem of knowing the right thing to do.

Let me interject at the outset that I view this relationship as twofold: first, there is a question of the development of the substance of policy; second, of the development of linkages, of communications, between the thinkers and the legislators. I shall return to this point later.

National Commission

Let me begin my illustrations by referring to the National Commission on the Financing of Postsecondary Education. This Commission was born of the frustration several of us on the higher education subcommittee in the House, working in 1971 and 1972 on a higher education bill, felt in not being able to obtain from the university community in this country thoughtful, reasoned analyses to enable us to deal intelligently with the issues, especially the question of the appropriate basis on which to channel general, unearmarked aid to institutions.

We were, to be blunt about it, mightily distressed at the sad state of our knowledge here and at the apparent failure of the American university community to pay serious intellectual attention to the economics of higher education. I cite one instance. You will all recall the several reports of recent years contending that many of our colleges and universities were in deep financial distress. But when our committee attempted to find an intellectually respectable definition of "financial distress," or even "financial need," our inquiries fell on stony ground.

And as a consequence of this lack of systematic thought by the higher education community about higher education, four of us in Congress had to develop our own resources of information and analysis and, with some help from the Brookings Institution and the reports of the Carnegie Commission, wrote the bill ourselves. On potentially the most important legislation to help colleges and universities since the Land Grant Act, the colleges and universities contributed almost nothing.

You will understand, first, why several of us insisted on establishing the National Commission on the Financing of Postsecondary Education—to begin the serious work we found so lacking when we needed it; and, second, why those of us from Congress who sat on the Commission—and I was one—insisted that it not attempt to draw up a laundry list of bills Congress should pass to help postsecondary education.

Rather, we set ourselves a more formidable but, in my view, more constructive task, that of developing what we called an analytical framework, an intellectual construct, within which, hopefully, all those who make decisions about postsecondary education—congressmen, senators, governors, state legislators, administrators—can more rationally, if you will, decide.

We do not claim perfection for our efforts; we do claim that we set out on a road that needs to be travelled. For surely it is anomalous that there is so little first-class intellectual effort directed in this country to research and analysis of those institutions of our society that incarnate and advance intellectual effort.

As a politician, I would predict trouble for the future federal support of higher education in the continued absence of more systematic effort by the scholarly community to such questions, especially the development of an economics of postsecondary education.

National Institute of Education

In view of what I have already said, you will not be surprised that I responded with such enthusiasm in 1970 to President Nixon's message to Congress on educational reform for the creation of a National Institute of Education as a vehicle for supporting research and development in education in the United States. In March 1970, as leader of a bipartisan group of twenty members of the House, I introduced the bill authorizing the new Institute. My Select Education Subcommittee then conducted extensive hearings on the bill, visited centers of educational research in this country and abroad, and in short went through a protracted process of education not only to inform ourselves about the role of research in education, but to signal to our colleagues in Congress, to the administration, to educators and others, that we regarded the new Institute as a development of the highest importance.

Now, as you all know, the NIE has run into some troubles in its first years of existence and I shall take just a moment to recall them to you because I believe they are symptomatic of some underlying reasons we as a nation have such trouble applying analysis to our gravest matters.

Why should the $162 million recommended by an anti-education administration for fiscal year 1974 have been reduced to $75 million by a Congress that has consistently voted more money for education than the President wants? This is dramatic evidence indeed of the low status of research, at least in education. Why the cuts? For one thing, most members of Congress are not really clear about what research in education is. Whatever it is, they are not sure it makes any difference in improving teaching and learning. Moreover, the lack of short-run payoff is all the more grating to congressmen and senators faced with administration budgets that slash deeply or eliminate federal funds for ongoing education programs.

For the purpose of our discussion today, however, what is most disturbing is that apparently few people outside Congress understand the need for increased investment in disciplined analysis of education. For, rather than seeing NIE as an opportunity to develop a serious national commitment to systematic research to improve education, too many in education, not seeing some personal short-run benefit from the Institute, have stood by or even opposed it. Thus, the American Federation of Teachers, motivated by its opposition to voucher experiments supported by NIE, urges its budget to be cut. And thus, the Council of Chief State School Officers demands that $30 million of the Institute's scarce funds be allocated to them for disseminating proven products—as if NIE were solely concerned with elementary and secondary schools and no other facet of education.

Rather than support the development of a first-class Institute committed to research and demonstration of quality, these groups act more like some county highway commissioners complaining that there is not enough pork in the barrel for them. My point here, of course, is that given the need for the best thinking we can get about how to improve teaching and learning in this country, we are not getting much assistance from those who should be helping.

Elementary and Secondary Education

Let me give you some other instances of areas in education where legislators need knowledge we have not found easy to get. As you all know, Title I of the Elementary and Secondary Education Act authorizes funds to local districts with concentrations of poor families for the purpose of improving the education of children in those districts. The present law, and both the House and Senate versions now in conference, operate on the assumption of a high correlation between economic deprivation and educational disadvantage. But this assumption has been under attack in the House Committee, and the principal reason for the lengthy delay in extending this legislation has not been busing but a fight over the Title I formula for distributing the money among the states. And of course the formula poses such issues as the definition of poverty and the kinds of correlations between economic status and educational achievement. It has not been easy for the Committee to find compelling evidence on either side of the proposition that economic deprivation leads to educational failure. And we had great difficulty in assembling information to show the impact of alternative methods of distributing Title I funds. Reliable evidence and thoughtful analysis were not easy to come by.

That is why I offered an amendment to the Elementary and Secondary Education bill, agreed to yesterday by the conference, to require NIE to conduct comprehensive studies of the operation of Title I and other compensatory education programs and report their findings to Congress.

I hope, as with the postsecondary education financing study, we do not receive simply static recommendations but that the NIE effort will produce some analytical models that can help us think about a range of opportunities in the future for helping children with various kinds of disadvantages to reach various educational goals.

Services for Children

I cite another area where there are substantial gaps between what we know and what we do. Yesterday Senator Walter Mondale of Minnesota and I announced our intention to introduce next week a Family and Child Services Bill, with particular attention to the needs of preschool children. You and I know that highly respected child development experts disagree deeply on the proper scope and purpose of early childhood intervention. And yet we also know that millions of American children do not eat well or receive adequate health care, let alone have effective intellectual stimulation. I hope that when Senator Mondale and I begin hearings on our bill next month, we shall learn of new knowledge about early childhood development, knowledge beyond what we heard in testimony a few years ago on the bill the President vetoed. For we want to legislate on more than our best intentions; we want the best evidence we can get for what is right for the lives of children.

As a final example of how education legislators need more substantive knowledge on the subjects with which they deal, I shall mention another area in which I am working, the education of handicapped children. The pattern of an increasing number of court decisions holding that handicapped children have a constitutional right to an education, coupled with the high cost of educating such children, caused Senator Harrison Williams of New Jersey and me to introduce a bill that would provide federal grants to the states to reimburse local school districts for up to 75 percent of the excess cost of educating these children.

Yet, you will not be surprised to learn, we have run into a very serious problem, a knowledge problem, in trying to define the costs of educating handicapped children. We have found it nearly impossible to get reliable judgments on the costs of necessary educational services for children with various handicaps. Without such basic data, how can we write a sensible formula for sharing the "excess costs"? And without knowing the needs of children with different handicaps, how can we be sure we are setting aside the right amount of money?

These are not idle questions. Next Monday, in the Elementary and Secondary Education Act Conference, I must deal with a provision in the Senate bill, offered by Senator Charles Mathias of Maryland, that would simply hand over to the states an amount of money, equal to $15 for every school-age child, to be used solely for handicapped children. I naturally share the Senator's concern but you will understand, in view of what I have just told you, why I do not view the proposal as a reasoned approach to meeting an urgent need.

Communication

Now I said earlier that the relationship between knowing the right thing to do and doing it was twofold, involving both the substance of policy and the communication of that substance between the thinkers and the legislators. So far I have been telling you of examples where I, as a member of Congress, working on education legislation, have needed knowledge of the substance of policy. Let me now say something of the process of the communication of that knowledge between thinker and decision maker.

The first point I should make is that decision makers also think. Indeed, if you have been paying much attention to what I have been saying, you will have detected an underlying tone of grievance that the thinkers are not thinking enough and that, by default, we politicians have to do a lot of their work for them. But I believe, to speak very practically, that the relationship between professional intellectuals and professional politicians must not be a one-way street, with the congressman waiting for the memorandum from Harvard telling him what he ought to do. There must be built into the process, if it is to be fruitful, a give-and-take that will enable the professional scholar to get a purchase on the way the politician perceives and defines his problem.

I find an echo of what I am saying in this observation of Harold Howe.

> We increasingly find ourselves in a ridiculous situation. The techniques, disciplines, and methods employed by planners and policy analysts have become so complicated and so specialized that the people who must use their product—the political leaders and administrators in the case of public problems (or university presidents in the case of institutional planning)—are no longer able to understand and participate in the processes that are supposed to assist with their decisions.
>
> Somehow we have to find accommodation and communication between those on the one hand who bear responsibility for action and those on the other who try to illuminate the implications of the various options action must consider.

What to do about this question of linkages? I need hardly reiterate that I am speaking to you about the problem of communication not with respect to the executive branch but from the viewpoint of a legislator. A phrase I have found useful in describing what I believe we in Congress need is "operative access to relevant intelligence." We need, first, access, to be able to get at what we require; and second, we need to be able to do so with reasonable facility—operative access. Third, we don't want to know everything about the subject, only what is relevant for our purposes. And fourth, we need access to "intelligence," not simply information. We are already overwhelmed by reports, surveys, paper. We need to be able to get the best thinking as well as the best reference sources.

My own view is that developing a capability for "operative access to relevant intelligence" is far more important to the future role of Congress in the American political system than are many of the reforms of Congress more commonly discussed. What I am saying about congressional access to intelligence is more than a matter of theory.

If, as I believe, there will be substantial Democratic margins in both the House and Senate in 1974 and 1976, it will be imperative, not only for partisan reasons for the Democrats but in the national interest, that the Democratic leadership of Congress make a far greater effort than, I fear, we have so far done to get the best thinking in the country on the crucial problems we face, particularly in the field of domestic policy.

Better Linkages

Let me return to the question of how we can develop better networks between the policy research community and the political community in the field of education. I offer only a few suggestions; I have more. I was impressed recently, for example, at a conference in Marco Island, Florida, not solely by the quality of the discussions but by the fact that key persons in HEW, Congress, the education associations, the several higher education commissions and some state legislators were for the first time brought together to talk about their common concern, postsecondary education. I believe such sessions should be replicated across the country, perhaps at the regional level, every couple of years, with a view not only toward understanding each other's perspectives but also to develop a common semantics with which to carry on the conversation. I also believe we need far more conscious efforts to establish bridges between and among the various communities.

Last Monday I sat in a session of the Advisory Board of the Institute for Educational Leadership in Washington, and the IEL definition of its objective is a succinct summary of what I am arguing we need more of: ". . . to act as switchboard, network builder, broker and catalyst, tying together a number of groups and individuals with relevant expertise and resources so that policy decisions are more broadly based and better informed by the contributions of knowledge and values of a range of actors in the system."

Each of you will have his or her suggestions on how to bring together the worlds of knowledge and action to improve education in this country. As I have said, I have some more myself. But let me offer a final comment.

Some years ago, in preparing an essay on "The Intellectual in Politics," I was struck by Richard Hofstader's separation of "intelligence" from "intellect." Hofstader called the first "an excellence of mind that is employed within a fairly narrow, immediate and predictable range; it is a manipulative, adjustive, unfailingly practical quality. . . . Intelligence works within the framework of limited but clearly staged goals." "Intellect," on the other hand, "is a critical, creative, and contemplative side of mind. Whereas intelligence seeks to grasp, manipulate, reorder, adjust, intellect examines, ponders, wonders, theorizes, criticizes, imagines. Intelligence will see the immediate meaning in a situation and evaluate it. Intellect evaluates evaluations, and looks for the meanings of situations as a whole. . . ."

If we accept the distinction we must, I believe, conclude that we need in the work of rethinking education for the coming decades men and women of both sorts, in both the worlds of thought and action. We have, indeed, men and women of both sorts from both worlds here at Southampton this weekend; persons who are not, in David Riesman's phrase "threatened by complexity" but challenged and stimulated by it: persons interested in rethinking policy as well as explaining it, interested not only in making present policies work but in asking whether they are right.

As a politician speaking to such a group of persons, I like to think there is justification for what I have tried to say in the words of Woodrow Wilson in his address to the American Political Science Association in 1910: ". . . the man who has the time, the discrimination and the sagacity, to collect and comprehend the principal facts and the man who must act upon them must draw near to one another and feel that they are engaged in a common enterprise . . ."

Appendix C
Participants

Martin Green
Tufts University

Lillian Hellman
Playwright

Nat Hentoff
The Village Voice

Elizabeth Janeway
Author

Joseph Katz
The Wright Institute

Christopher Lasch
University of Rochester

Salvador E. Luria
Massachusetts Institute of
Technology

Jonathan Messerli
Fordham University

Howard Moore
Attorney-at-law

Paul A. Olson
University of Nebraska

Claiborne Pell
United States Senate

Albert Quie
House of Representatives

Michael Rossman
Author

Nevitt Sanford
Director, The Wright Institute

Seymour B. Sarason
Yale University

Donald A. Shoen
Massachusetts Institute of
Technology

Theodore Sizer
Headmaster, Andover Phillips
Academy

Page Smith
University of California,
Santa Cruz

Studs Terkel
Author

John Wideman
University of Wyoming

Other Participants

Victor G. Alicea
Chancellor, Universidad Boricua

Jack Allen
George Peabody College

Marilyn Baldwin
Dartmouth College

Ernest Bartell
President's Office,
Stonehill College

Benjamin Bernstein
High school principal, Worcester

Laura Bornholdt
Lilly Foundation

Lydia Bronte
Rockefeller Foundation

Albert W. Brown
President, Brockport State College

Albert Bush-Brown
Chancellor, Long Island University

Rene Cardenas
Bilingual Children's Television

Elaine D. Carter
Columbia University

William Thomas Carter
U.S. Office of Education

Burton E. Cohen
Printer

Deborah Cohen
Printer

Saul B. Cohen
Clark University

John J. Connor, Jr.
Superintendent, Worcester Public
Schools

Emmett J. Conrad, M.D.
Dallas Independent School
District

Fairman C. Cowan
General Counsel, Norton
Company

Alonzo Crim
Superintendent, Atlanta Public
Schools

Harold W. Cruse
University of Michigan

David D. Darland
National Education Association

David S. Dennison
Mayor's Office, Newark

Jefferson Max Dixon
Appalachian State University

W. Patrick Dolan
Educational Systems & Designs

Anne W. Dosher
Consultant

Joseph Duggan
Wilton Learning Community

Mildred Estes
Dallas School community

Nolan Estes
Superintendent, Dallas Public
Schools

Ralph Fasanella
Artist

Frederick Fisher
National Training & Development
Service

Thomas W. Fletcher
National Training & Development
Service

David H. Florio
Northwestern University

Richard B. Ford
Clark University

Rod Gander
Senior Editor, Newsweek

A. Bruce Gaarder
U.S. Office of Education

Richard P. Gousha
Indiana University

James W. Hall
President, Empire State College

J. Archie Hargraves
President, Shaw University

Sarah Haskins
Dallas Independent School
District

James Hayes
American Management
Association

William R. Hazard
Northwestern University

Joel F. Henning
American Bar Association

Vivian C. Jackson
New Careers Training
Laboratory

James B. Jones
Texas Southern University

Nancy E. Judy
Dallas Independent School
District

Clara R. Kanode
U.S. Office of Education

Bernard Kaplan
Clark University

Charles D. Kelso
Indiana Law School

Samuel R. Keys
Kansas State University

R. W. Lid
California State University,
Northridge

Milton Luger
New York State
Division for Youth

George E. McDonough
Seattle Pacific College Library

James H. McElroy
Commission for Educational
Change

John Macrae, III
E.P. Dutton Company

John Maher
Delancey Street Foundation

Peter Marcuse
University of California,
Los Angeles

Harry A. Marmion
President, Southampton College

Ted Marsten
Cummins Engine Company

Jacquelyn A. Mattfeld
Brown University

Robert Medrano
Dallas Independent School
District

John Merrow
Institute for Educational
Leadership

Leonard Michaels
University of California, Berkeley

M. Hayes Mizell
American Friends Service
Committee

Gilbert D. Moore
State University of New York,
Albany

Mary E. Murphy
Framingham State College

Samuel Nash
Special Projects & Planning,
New Haven School

Malcolm M. Provus (deceased)
University of Virginia

Melissa L. Richter
University of Massachusetts

Charles P. Ruch
Virginia Commonwealth
University

Phillip E. Runkel
Superintendent, Grand Rapids
Schools

James M. Scott
County Supervisor, Virginia

Harvey Scribner
University of Massachusetts

David Seeley
Public Education Association,
New York

Betty Showell
University of Chicago

John Silber
President, Boston University

Mimi H. Silbert
Delancey Street Foundation

William L. Smith
Director, Teacher Corps

Richard Spooner
Principal,
Southampton High School

James Steffenson
Teacher Corps,
U.S. Office of Education

Henry W. Taft
President, Outward Bound,
Greenwich

John M. Thompson
Indiana University

John W. Tippeconnic, Jr.
Vice President,
Navajo Community College

Richard Todd
Associate Editor,
Atlantic Monthly

Charles Trueheart
Greensboro Daily News

Emmett Wallace
Educational Systems & Designs

Rainie Wapner
Clark University

Wilcomb E. Washburn
Smithsonian Institution

Grace E. Watson
U.S. Office of Education

William Watts
Potomac Associates Inc.

Richard E. Welch
Welch Scientific Company

June A. Willenz
Director, American
Veterans Committee

June P. Wilson
Reader's Digest

Kenneth Wilson
Reader's Digest

Harold C. Wisor
Assistant Commissioner for Pennsylvania
Higher Education

William Woessner
Superintendent, Southampton Schools

Wallace Wohlking
Cornell University

Francis J. Wuest
Change in Liberal Education

Joseph Young
Educational consultant

Appendix D
Background: A Report on TTT Projects

Kirkpatrick Sale

The year is 1971. The classroom is conventional, familiar—ubiquitous pale green walls, tall windows screened against unintentional home runs or intentional target practice, blackboard bearing the hallowed frieze of Palmerized ABCs, bulletin board decorated with children's artwork and a few posters for National Reading Week—for most Americans, homeground. But taking the place of customary rituals are some unusual activities: in one corner a young teacher uses the telephone company's Yellow Pages to give lessons in looking up alphabetized words; off in another space a well-known poet listens to a child's just-finished poem; in another corner a student teacher probes with her group the mysteries of cuisenaire rods. Behind all the activity in this room in a public school in Harlem is a purposefulness—purposefulness made possible and furthered by a unique federal program in teacher education with the unlikely title of "Training the Trainers of Teachers."

Like many other federally-funded programs in education, TTT (as it was known) has come and gone, but during those years of its existence, from 1969 to 1974, the scene above was replicated in many ways across the country at various sites. In each instance the ingredients were a new mix of people, a willingness to experiment,

This report was originally prepared for, has been edited by, and incorporates material from, the Evaluation Research Center of Charlottesville, Virginia.

and an approach to teacher education that broadened the concept of who should be involved in the training of teachers and also in the training of those who train teachers. For instance:

—A professor from City College's Department of Anthropology visited a third grade class at PS 192 in Harlem and led a discussion about the nuclear family and the extended family, linking up this knowledge of familial patterns to the children's circumstances at home.

—At Clark University (Worcester, Mass.) TTT participants established, next to the local North High School, an Adjunct School, where professors came to teach along with undergraduates and one course was given in the history of playing cards and card games—a new way to teach sociology and history.

—At the Cannon Ball School on an Indian reservation in North Dakota, TTT people added more Indian teachers, drew in community members, and emphasized Indian culture—as for example with a new course in Indian cooking which taught not only characteristic elements of the culture but also, through measurements, mathematics.

—At Michigan State the TTT experiment of involving university professors in actual classroom experience resulted in the formal requirement that all language arts and English methods teachers in the education school go back to teach a course in a local public school at least once every three years.

—At San Francisco State a Mathematics System Laboratory established under TTT provided a day-long laboratory in the local high school where interested students and teachers could study sophisticated computer methods and the new mathematical tools under the direction of a full-time TTT-hired specialist.

In sum, TTT participants during these years were experimenting with the open classroom, with team teaching, with the use of paraprofessionals in the classroom—with everything new in theory and methods and equipment. But the effect of TTT went beyond the immediate classroom, though it did have a direct and sometimes dramatic impact on those schools associated with the program at various sites. TTT's real target was elsewhere, as the program's principal architect and overseer, Donald N. Bigelow, has remarked:

"The basic strategy of the TTT program was to involve the public schools, schools of education, and liberal arts faculties in the joint venture of creating new ways of training those who train teachers." It was partly this three-way partnership and partly the emphasis on changing not merely teachers, but those who train the teachers (i.e., the focus on the graduate school), which made TTT such a unique educational venture.

If the TTT program was revolutionary in the way it conceived of those who should be involved in thinking about, planning, and participating in the training of teachers and those who train teachers, it was traditional in that one of its goals was institutional change. According to Bigelow, TTT was designed to achieve institutional change by providing, with the help of federal money, the means for institutions of higher learning to initiate alternative and innovative plans of teacher training. "It was hoped that by providing higher education with the opportunity, in cooperation with the public schools, to try out new ways of performing the traditional institutional task of training public school teachers, the new ways would be assimilated into the institution and help to change the existing structure." It's well to keep in mind this double thrust of the TTT program, for each aspect was in TTT's short life to produce its own characteristic problems.

In retrospect the TTT program seems very much to have been a product of the late 1960s and the feeling of those days that participation is in and of itself a value. TTT challenged not merely the liberal arts faculty to participate in the training of teachers alongside the school of education faculty, it further invited the public schools to join with the university in preparing school personnel. And beyond this— as the program got underway—there was to be the involvement of the community and the development of the principle of parity. TTT was the first program in the Office of Education to adopt the concept of parity and to try to live by it: it attempted with no slight temerity to link *all* individuals and groups concerned with the education of youth—the English professor and the educational psychologist, undergraduate and graduate student, classroom and supervising teacher, school principal, district superintendent, neighborhood leaders, and parents.

TTT's funding was modest as such federal programs go ($12 million to start, perhaps $40 million in all), its support unenthusiastic and shaky, and its duration brief, only four years. But it touched no fewer than sixty-one institutions of higher education, several hundred primary and secondary schools, and some 42,000 people; geographically, socially, economically, its reach was wide. The program was ambitious, idealistic, bold but also, on occasion, brash, and its permanent value as a force for change is not easily assessed.

The TTT program had various sources. Most directly, it was an outgrowth of the training programs managed by Bigelow, a USOE bureaucrat who in late 1964 was given the job of heading the task force to implement Title XI, an amendment to the National Defense Education Act of 1953. From this springboard Bigelow was to oversee during the next four years the creation of literally hundreds of NDEA Institutes, while his own Division of Educational Personnel Development grew to be the largest division within the Office of Education.

The Title XI Institutes were designed to bring elementary and secondary teachers up to date in their subjects. The NDEA Institute model was a simple one. Teachers and other educators were given stipends and brought back to university campuses, usually for six weeks during the summer, to study and work with university faculty in the various disciplines. In the various speeches Bigelow made during these years he coaxed, cajoled, incited, insulted, and tried to shame liberal arts faculties into what he saw as their responsibility:

If the university continues to make and mold teachers as if they did not have to teach in real schools, if it continues to act as if the state government which pays its way and which also pays the school's way were not the same government to both groups, . . . if the university continues to act as if it does not owe the rest of the state-supported educational enterprise a dime, then we are of all bureaucrats most miserable; our project will fail, and its nation will be the poorer.

Bigelow was never fully to succeed in his goal. The liberal arts faculties' commitment was slight—a summer program—and in addition it quickly became clear that many university people did not have the least idea of how their disciplines were taught in the lower grades, and had not thought about what knowledge should be transmitted. Seemingly these were issues of pedagogy—but they were also issues involving the training of teacher trainers. Here, at least in part, the TTT program had its inception; Bigelow did begin to make inroads with various university people who also wanted to reform the graduate schools and were to join him in later programs, including TTT.

Meanwhile, there had been several program advances within Bigelow's Division in the Bureau of Elementary and Secondary Education, which was dominated by the billion dollar Title I compensatory education program. These included, under Title V of the Higher Education Act of 1965, the development of the Experienced Teacher Fellowship Program, which brought teachers back to the university in groups of fifteen or twenty for a full academic year and forced the universities to make a more meaningful commitment to teacher education. At about the same time the Office of Education supported eight Institutes for college teachers ("TT Institutes," as they were known), a maneuver which brought Bigelow a step closer to the concept of TTT. Soon thereafter, he began the Tri-University Project (NYU, Washington, and Nebraska were the universities involved), which took its original impetus from the need to do something about the training of the trainers of elementary teachers and the goal of involving graduate departments in the process of teaching teachers. Each project site included a fellowship program for elementary teachers, so that a "double practicum" situation existed: college professors, on leave from their institutions and in residence for a year, learned about the classroom and the elementary teachers they taught, while the teachers learned about advances in knowledge and new learning theories from the professors. When the TTT program came along, the Tri-University Project was incorporated into it.

One additional Bigelow program contributed to the formulation of TTT—the $1.1 million NDEA National Institute for Advanced Study in Teaching Disadvantaged Youth. The final report of this project, *Teachers for the Real World* (written principally by B. Othanel Smith), was to be a seedbed of ideas for TTT. And the program brought Bigelow into contact with a group of forceful and diverse educators who, like him, were bent on educational change; many of them were to play a role in TTT. The Institute also put Bigelow in direct relationship with the American Association of Colleges of Teacher Education (the ultimate grant recipient) and with the representatives of the schools of education who were to play a necessary role in TTT. It goes without saying that by this time if Bigelow had aroused strong feelings and sometimes antagonism among liberal arts faculties, he had done so among those in professional education as well.

The TTT program was the first U.S. Office of Education program funded under the Education Professions Development Act of 1967. The Act cleared a final hurdle for Bigelow, for under existing legislation he could not use funds to support university personnel. (In the case of the Tri-University Project this proscription was circumvented by an exchange of funds with the Bureau of Research.) If the program had not been so far advanced in planning by the time the newly formed Bureau of Educational Personnel Development became operational in 1968, it might never have been funded, for not only was there a shift in power within the Office of Education, but emphasis was to shift from the university to the public school in most programs administered in the Office of Education.

In the fall of 1967 Bigelow had begun a dissemination program which concluded with regional Institutes at four major universities, each of which invited representatives from other colleges and universities, together with public school people from their areas, to attend and, later, to submit proposals for the TTT program. (In all, sixty-five "proposal teams" attended the Institutes.) At the same time, Bigelow created a National Advisory Council of leading educators who were to review the proposals and select the most promising sites for the inauguration of the program.

So far the notion as it had developed—a university-oriented program—seemed unlikely to cause controversy. But a last step (and the one destined to cause TTT more problems than anyone anticipated) was added, unexpectedly, at a conference of the National Advisory Council in Tucson in May 1968, just as the project was about to be launched. This council had originally been composed of liberal arts people and later of public school people as well. Subsequently, in its expanded form, it included a good number of individuals who believed strongly in minority rights. Meeting shortly after the assassination of Martin Luther King, and during turbulent times on the campuses and in the cities, the group rejected the proposals at hand as timid and exclusionary. It voiced the need to broaden TTT to include more than just professional educators, to reach out to the members of the communities affected by the education systems, and particularly to involve members of the Third World and ghetto communities whose need was greatest and whose contribution—the notion was—could be most valuable. As the Committee put it, "places submitting TTT proposals [should] give clear evidence that they have given parity to the communities—black, brown, American Indian or whatever—which the program must serve within the context of overriding national needs, both in the present planning of programs and . . . in their execution." The days of TTT as essentially a university-oriented program, in sum, were over; more importantly, the strategy to attack the graduate school front was vitiated. Bigelow accepted the notion of parity as it emerged at Tucson, and several months later the Committee's "Parity Position Paper" became an official position for many of the programs administered by the Office of Education.

Finally, in 1969, after an unusual amount of advance participation in planning before the guidelines were fixed, TTT was started. Funds came from the Education Professions Development Act of 1967, which was administered by the Division of Program Resources in the new Bureau of Educational Personnel Development (BEPD), a division headed by Bigelow but reduced in size from his old one after TTT's first year. During that year, however, the academic year 1969-70, fifty-eight projects were approved on the basis of proposals resubmitted in accordance with the guidelines laid down at Tucson; twenty-four of these were given one-year, tentative, "operational" grants under which a university would set up pilot projects or initiate the planning of them, and thirty-four were put into immediate operation and scheduled for multi-year financing (of these thirty-four all but five existed the entire life of the program). The total budget was $11.8 million, not much by federal standards, but for a program that was created without the outside blessing of legislative or presidential approval (granted to such programs as the Peace Corps, the Teacher Corps, or Head Start), it was enough to provide between $100,000 and $700,000 per site, more than enough to get a new idea bruited about on a national level. And indeed, TTT did become well known.

But everything did not go according to plan. By the end of the first year it was clear that TTT had serious trouble with Washington headquarters. Its problems were multiple: normal first-year difficulties, too high an administrative turnover (three directors under Bigelow in the first year), the associate commissioner of the new Bureau antipathetic to college-oriented programs and to TTT in particular, a dozen other programs in BEPD scrambling for money and staff, and finally the Nixon administration's attempt at a so-called "renewal" strategy as part of its New Federalism—one effect of which was to raise congressional ire and open up criticisms both of the Office of Education and in particular of BEPD.

Instead of growing, then, TTT was cut back to forty-three projects for the second year, although the budget itself was increased by nearly $2 million, permitting Bigelow to start other programs as spin-offs of TTT. But all of this was minute by federal standards and an indication that lean times were coming. Further, Bigelow was gradually isolated from his own program, the latest TTT director transferred and eventually replaced by an acting director.

It was no surprise, then, that as TTT was being reviewed for its third year, the axe fell: in May 1972 it was decided that the program would be phased out and that funding would be provided for only one more year. In 1971-72 the number of projects was cut to thirty-three and the budget cut by $4 million to a total of $10.3 million. In its last year, TTT included only twenty-nine projects, though the budget was allowed to expand to $13.2 million to help pay for the previous "extra" funds, to provide for final evaluation, and ideally to help make possible the institutionalization of the salvageable elements of the program.

TTT deserves considerable credit for such aspects of the experiment which were indeed institutionalized and which seem to have had lasting value and effect. It's easier, though, to say what sorts of things went wrong. The utopian ideal of interaction between schools and universities was, depressingly often, unworkable. A university professor might come in unconsciously "wearing his title," managing by his patronizing stance to alienate students, classroom teachers, and administrators. Other academicians could choose to regard TTT grants as merely "soft" money and the program as a free ride, simply going through the motions of an effort unlikely to advance their professional careers. Or in ghetto areas (especially where little, if any attempt was made to involve community people) interested faculty members might never be able to break down walls between white professors and predominantly black students. Also, pre-existing public school faculty or administrative rivalries could exacerbate suspicion of outsiders and easily minimize interest in any program likely to complicate internal squabbles.

But good things happened too. No fewer than twenty-one of the projects succeeded in involving liberal arts professors in one way or another in the TTT program, through consultation on school of education curricula, work with public school officials, or firsthand experience in the classrooms. And in many cases bridges were built which have survived the formal ending of TTT:

—At North Dakota, a New School was established which drew its faculty from all segments of the university community—humanities, social sciences, natural sciences, education—and a new curriculum was designed with these diverse perspectives contributing. The New School was succeeded in 1973 by an even more ambitious Center for Teaching and Learning which formally brought together the College of Liberal Arts, the College of Education, and the New School itself into what is regarded as the focal point for teacher education in that state.

—At Hunter College TTT funding allowed thirty faculty members from ten different departments to take time off to plan a whole new teaching curriculum joining education and liberal arts perspectives; this approach proved so successful that an interdisciplinary committee has now been established to oversee teacher training and periodically revise the education curriculum, and the School of Education has gained a new and gratifying respectability within the College.

—At Clark University TTT helped to add to the liberal arts faculty five new positions designated for academics who have a special interest in secondary education or teacher training, and who will speak for that interest in departmental affairs year after year.

Significant links between university and school classroom were forged too. Dr. Vivian Windley of CUNY described the making of one such link:

Nine liberal arts professors from seven departments are involved for the first time in the in-service training of teachers: an anthropologist, sociologist, geographer, political scientist, historian, a speech and theatre professor, and two English professors. Each of these consultants works one day per week in the project schools. They are beginning to recognize and appreciate the role they play in the training of teachers and student teachers. They are quick to admit that they simply cannot perform their role well without reference to children. They see the experience as an invaluable one in making their course offerings more relevant for elementary school pupils.

This particular element of the TTT program seemed too daring to some institutions and they were unwilling to embrace it, but at those fourteen sites where it was tried the experience was for the most part a valuable one:

—At Clark University seventeen professors worked directly in the grade schools and high schools of Worcester, a psychology professor overseeing a new psychology course in one high school, a group from the education and history faculties setting up sociology courses at another.

—At the University of Illinois two English professors signed up for a full year of teaching sophomore English to "low ability" high school students and brought along a number of TTT undergraduates as well.

—At Temple TTT graduate students taught in the Philadelphia schools along with the university professors, both trying out their teaching ideas and techniques.

There can be little doubt that the professors-in-the-schools experiment was, for the individuals themselves, personally valuable.

Those Hunter College faculty members from the education department and the liberal arts faculty who are working in the schools are themselves being changed while they are changing the instructional programs of the few schools involved. Specifically, the elementary science education team (a professor of science education, a physics department professor, and the school science coordinator) was developing what seemed to be a more relevant science program and more relevant science teaching experiences. If one wishes to call this a "clinical experience," it was clinical for the instructors, students, and teachers.

This is high praise indeed, and assurance that people who worked in TTT programs like this one are the better for it; it's sad, then, to trip over that phrase, "the few schools involved."

The TTT educators were to see quickly other forms of innovation besides the interaction of university faculty and public schools. Given money, people and enthusiasm, ideas abounded. At least twenty-three TTT projects sponsored formal changes of one kind or another in their school-district classrooms, and sometimes a single project was responsible for everything from new learning laboratories to "open classroom" techniques. Creative dramatics, computerized instruction, simulation games, nondirected teaching, team teaching— all these were tried at one or another site. And still intact are most elements of the team teaching instituted under TTT auspices at NYU, Syracuse, and Texas Southern; the individualized science instruction adopted at Appalachian State and Buffalo; and the intensive learning laboratories installed in classrooms by projects at CUNY, Clark, Harvard, Michigan State, California State University at Northridge, and Temple.

The most sweeping of these innovations was the alternative school; one of the most ambitious, run by the Harvard TTT, can serve as an example. Called the Pilot School, this institution was part of the Cambridge school system but operated separately; four of the eleven teachers were supplied by the public school system, the seven others were Harvard doctoral students on TTT fellowships. Innovations included a modular schedule (dividing the school day into twenty-four fluid parts instead of the usual one-hour periods), heterogeneous classes with members of all three grades in each room, experimental courses (an Environmental Program in conjunction with the Cape Cod National Seashore Administration), and parental participation in classroom work, in staff hiring, and in curriculum planning.

But probably TTT's most influential classroom change was its emphasis on, and broadening of, the concept of student teaching. The practice itself was not new, of course, but new and imaginative uses of it were invented, as at Michigan State, where "student teaching clusters," groups of eight or nine undergraduates, were assigned to a single school for a term, observed various classes, took a hand at teaching those they felt most comfortable with, joined with the regular teachers in team-teaching projects, and worked with their colleagues in another class of a different age to present a single science or social studies unit. Temple University expanded this plan, holding demonstration classes and seminars as well. At Hunter student teachers began field experience in the freshman year, and at NYU student teaching in the sciences completely replaced, under TTT, traditional "methods" courses.

It doesn't seem too much to say that TTT, though many of its innovative notions remain mere notions, did influence a good number of universities to expand their student teaching programs and requirements. Sanction by several state governments also followed: Texas, Washington, and Rhode Island have formally adopted certain of the TTT principles and now emphasize such elements as on-site training for undergraduate students, periodic re-education of education school professors, and cooperation between school systems and universities. While other states seemed likely to follow this lead in requiring practicum work and a careful evaluation of it (the so-called Performance-Based Evaluation Certificate) for official teaching licenses, this notion soon became subverted by its expansion into what was called "Competency Based Teacher Education," losing thereby both the initial purpose and the advantage of certification efforts. Furthermore, this all-encompassing "program" permitted professional education to withdraw from reform under the guise of "accountability," while keeping to the status quo and the continued isolation of teacher education from the rest of the academic, if not the real, world. Teacher training from another TTT perspective—bringing the classroom teacher back to school—isn't being neglected either: the schools around Southeastern State in Oklahoma are continuing to send superior teachers to the University's Experienced Teacher Fellowship Program, where they can earn master's degrees under professional supervision. Similar in-service programs are—or are being—institutionalized at Buffalo (SUNY), Pittsburgh, Harvard, Appalachian State, Miami, Michigan State, Nebraska, San Jose, and the University of Washington.

But hardest of all is to know what to make of TTT's pursuit of parity. As Bigelow saw it, parity meant "mostly the involvement of the *community* people, because of course they were the ones not normally involved, especially not in Federal programs. . . ." But interpretations differed—genuine interaction here, tokenism there, wooing ghetto parents in one system, recruiting minority students in another. And it's impossible to discover how this policy affected the student in the classroom.

In those TTT projects which used a community "resource person" (there were twenty such projects) the effort was usually claimed successful. At the University of Pittsburgh representatives of the inner city (as members of the TTT teaching team) visited high school classes and served as informal tutors, organized and ran university seminars to acquaint future teachers with the realities of the ghettos, and participated in overall evaluations of TTT programs and personnel. At San Jose State 114 volunteers, mostly people without university educations, were trained as teacher aides and worked as paraprofessionals in the San Jose school system; fourteen of them went on to college to increase their training or earn teaching certificates.

And here and there "community concern" was institutionalized. Under TTT guidance Fordham installed a new Division of Urban Education in its School of Education and Michigan State created a four-year system for students interested in field teaching and community involvement. At the University of Wisconsin "Teaching Public Issues" and "Learning in the Community," two of the new courses developed under TTT, are now a regular part of the undergraduate curriculum. The Los Angeles schools around California State University at Northridge found funds to help continue the University's TTT-developed Learning Center and Bilingual-Bicultural Teacher Training Program, and now enroll more than seventy teachers every term.

Recruitment of minority students has worked well at Southeastern State in Oklahoma, CUNY, and Appalachian State, and at several places (Hunter and Southeastern State are notable) positive results have been reported where nonacademic representatives have been placed on TTT committees to oversee projects. But all too often (as at CCNY) community participants were phased out after the first year, leaving many with their original conviction that all this was just another ripoff. Rare indeed was the school where it was assumed that a local mother and a university president would have an equal influence on decision making; the notion was rather that giving a voice on the parity board to a parent who had previously had none at all represented equality; but "equal voice" in these instances usually meant something closer to "let them come along and have their say...." Frustration and resentment were unavoidable.

Academic, racial, cultural, and economic gaps were harder to bridge, then, than TTT's planners might have liked to think. Years of being ignored or manipulated were not easily shrugged off, and those whom the advocates of parity sought to reach could hardly be blamed for a certain suspiciousness of attitude. Yet while not always workable, and by the worst interpretation only a piece of political prudence, the concept embodies a principle adaptable to other federal programs and may well become an increasingly important element in future national projects. This element of TTT was carried over into Project Open, for instance, another Office of Education program but one emphasizing almost exclusively broad community involvement, continual interaction among educational groups, and the spreading of innovative ideas through "networking."

Some real accomplishments, then, and some unquestionable failures and mistakes. And now the voice of sober responsibility asks: What did we do wrong? How to go about it next time? No fully confident reply sounds, but *some* of the answers are easy ones. What happened to TTT was, as John Merrow has noted in his dissertation on "The Use and Abuse of Discretionary Authority in the USOE," partly the result of a struggle between its originator and others within the Office of Education—the traditional struggle "for money, personnel, and office space; in short, for power." Bigelow lost. Also, in the eyes of some, TTT was rushed to birth prematurely to capture federal money which had become available before plans for the program were really complete, in spite of all the planning that had gone on. To its program manager, on the other hand, TTT as it came into being had an open-endedness about it which was character- istic of the way his mind worked on educational issues: "We deliber- ately employed the strategy of not spelling out some things to those who applied for and received funds. . . . We were not out to create unnecessary ambiguities or complexities where they did not exist, but we had become aware that, given the opportunity, many people who apply for federal funds will follow whatever guidelines are pro- vided and will not think things through, or, perhaps more important, work things out for themselves."

To some this open-endedness represented a failure to establish clear-cut goals for the program, with the seeming result that money was spread around more on the basis of hope than certainty. This aspect of TTT was in keeping with Bigelow's general mode of opera- tion, for he tended to back people, not projects, and to believe that if you got good people involved in innovative schemes they would come up with positive new ideas and education would inevitably be enriched. Such an approach might have worked, too, had there been money enough and time, but the Nixon administration and other powers within the Office of Education wanted tangible and im- mediate results—results not consonant with Bigelow's hands-off policy and his belief in project directors. As one friendly critic put it:

There appears to be the general feeling that the project directors are highly competent people (many quite famous in their fields) and it would be presumptuous on the part of staff to attempt to function as consultants or monitors. There is an essential sense of confidence in the directors and a feeling that information gained from them is valid.

While this assumption is hard to fault (let Michelangelo paint what he wants) it sometimes led to a failure of direction in the program. There was a Washington staff and a National Advisory Committee, but the former suffered from rapid turnover and the latter from a lack of information and power. Most of the time cross-project communication was ineffective although, through a system known as "clustering," every attempt was made to help the national as well as the project leaders know what others were doing. Finally, although there were three different sets of evaluations, until close to the end of the program there was no sophisticated or systematic evaluation process.

And the parity concept—introduced after the initial proposals had all been written—was disruptive and unfortunately abrasive all around, even while it was a laudable notion fully consistent with the nation's avowed democratic values. Many educators involved in writing TTT proposals felt betrayed by Bigelow when he accepted parity, though the Tucson meeting had in fact ended in a compromise between the radical and conservative members of the National Advisory Committee, which can be seen in the Committee's agreement that the first wave proposals should not be turned down summarily but that the writers of the proposals should be helped toward involvement of the community in their plans. The guidelines for the second wave of funding were to embody the full position taken in the Parity Paper, but a new wave of funding was never to be, and TTT essentially remained in subsequent years those projects funded the first year.

At the roots of some of TTT's problems were contradictions produced by parity; the attempt was to involve the decision makers in education in the training of teachers—those who had the power to change the system—but this conception of TTT was at odds with the counterthrust of democratization through parity. The decision makers tended to be people at the top of the hierarchy in education or society at large. For them to want to change or to become agents for change meant, in many instances, that they had to be willing to alter their own positions and power alignments—and this they were frequently reluctant to do. And of course TTT maintained that the program should include on the one hand the most reform-minded and innovative segments of the powerful, elite universities, and on the other the tradition-bound and conventional poor minorities of America. But frequently the most reform-minded were young assistant professors (powerless to change their institutions), while the community tended to be suspicious of all professionals, those who seemingly had already disenfranchised them from the schools.

Finally, TTT too frequently found that its allies were among those who should often have been, theoretically at least, its adversaries. While a lot of the initial planning included people from the liberal arts, in the end most of the project directors came from education schools and most of the individual project designs were moulded to suit the professional educators. Money was given to education schools to administer as they saw fit. In a sense TTT was frequently co-opted. It wanted to change the training of teachers but it too often ended up by putting that job in the hands of people who had been training the teachers all along and—according to TTT— had been doing a pretty poor job of it.

But to speak in more constructive tones, TTT projects seemed most successful (1) where the project's goals coincided with or reinforced local priorities and interests; (2) where projects used preexisting institutional mechanisms and the culture of the surrounding community and did not try to force new methods and standards; (3) where project goals and methods were flexible, allowing continual modification through trial and error, creating constructive tensions; (4) where there was not only a steady amount of money permitting long-range planning but enough so that the project could fit in with existing reward systems of the university; and (5) where the project leadership coincided with institutional and administrative leadership (usually the case not at the large and prestigious institutions, where TTT was just one more federal project, but at lesser-known schools where it was a visible national program with a relatively high status). And just as some of TTT's failures can't at this point be explained or understood, some of its successes can only be accounted for as some fortuituous combination of talent, vision, and energy.

The strength of the TTT program ultimately was to lie in the individual projects and what they achieved. Within the projects themselves, on a day-to-day basis, there is no doubt that the central emphasis was always on training teachers; but over the years the larger sphere of attention moved from, first, the community, to the liberal arts, to the university. And as the program ended, the university had indeed assimilated some of the features of the TTT program.

Maybe this doesn't seem like much to have achieved from such an investment of money, time, and thought. But some significant changes came about across the land as a result of TTT, and even if all its formal innovations were to be cleared away, one might claim that for a little while some people of good will worked together in pursuit of what they thought were worthy goals and changed themselves, some in small ways, some more profoundly, in the process.

Acknowledgments

Acknowledgments

Many people have been involved in the making of this book. Four contributors deserve special recognition—Benjamin DeMott, R. W. Lid, Peter Brooks, and Marian Simpson. Without them there would have been no book. They helped me to shape what became a more modest and, I think, a more meaningful account of the Southampton Summer Sequences than I had originally conceived. In the process they helped to select the material we have used from an abundance of essays, reports, position papers, letters, and full transcripts of the meetings. I particularly wish to thank Eugene E. Slaughter, whose friendship and counsel I have enjoyed for many years. Without him there would have been no Southampton.*

To say that many people have been involved in the making of this book is also to acknowledge the role of the people in the federal programs which led to Southampton—programs which I describe in the preface. These people are best represented by the four men to whom I have dedicated *Schoolworlds '76*: my deputies, successively,

---

*Dr. Slaughter's involvement with TTT, Project Open, and the Southampton Summer Sequences is carefully delineated in his final report, *The Experiment That Worked* (Durant, Okla.: The Southeastern Foundation, 1976), which describes a project that he directed after Southampton, during the academic year 1974-75. See pp. iii-v, 117-39.

307

between July 1965 and January 1974. They stand for that small band of people to whom I am most indebted and whose work lies behind, rather than between, the covers of the book.

Project Open and Southampton were two formal attempts to learn something about federal intervention in American education from the experiences of the 1960s. Originally, Southampton was seen as the beginning of a national "network," an unofficial, largely self-generating means of maintaining a dialogue about national educational policy, which began with the passage of the National Defense Education Act of 1958. The extent to which Southampton fell short of our intentions may be offset in part by the lessons learned there. This book deals with some of those lessons, among which is the concept of networking, as I call the process of sharing resources across institutional boundaries. This still seems to be an idea worth developing if one concludes, as I do, that the 1960s revealed a continuing need for help from the federal government to support people in their own—not the government's—small-scale, independent efforts to improve the way people are educated. A network of people attuned to national needs but focused on local or regional matters may still be one way to educational reform that deserves a more thorough trial.

My hope is that *Schoolworlds* '76 will be read as a manifesto calling for continued national leadership, the kind which will always be recognized by "its accurate sense of the crisis, its outrageous and unheard-of assertion of responsibility, and its ability to elicit assent in those it would lead."

Donald N. Bigelow